The Invisible Source of Authority

THE BEGINNING AND THE BEYOND OF POLITICS

Series editors: James R. Stoner and David Walsh

The series is in continuity with the grand tradition of political philosophy that was revitalized by the scholars who, after the Second World War, taught us to return to the past as a means of understanding the present. We are convinced that legal and constitutional issues cannot be addressed without acknowledging the metaphysical dimensions that underpin them. Questions of order arise within a cosmos that invites us to wonder about its beginning and its end, while drawing out the consequences for the way we order our lives together. God and man, world and society are the abiding partners within the community of being in which we find ourselves. Without limiting authors to any particular framework we welcome all who wish to investigate politics in the widest possible horizon.

THE
INVISIBLE SOURCE
of AUTHORITY

God in a Secular Age

DAVID WALSH

University of Notre Dame Press
Notre Dame, Indiana

Copyright © 2025 by the University of Notre Dame

Notre Dame, Indiana 46556

www.undpress.nd.edu

All Rights Reserved

Published in the United States of America

Library of Congress Control Number: 2025934547

ISBN: 978-0-268-20956-8 (Hardback)
ISBN: 978-0-268-20957-5 (Paperback)
ISBN: 978-0-268-20967-4 (WebPDF)
ISBN: 978-0-268-20958-2 (Epub3)

GPSR Compliance Inquiries:
Lightning Source France, 1 Av. Johannes Gutenberg, 78310 Maurepas, France
compliance@lightningsource.fr | Phone: +33 1 30 49 23 42

To My Enigma Variations:

J. McC.

J. O'C.

C. O'R.

B. P.

CONTENTS

	Preface	ix
ONE	How Can We Forget What We Must Remember?	1
TWO	The Spiritual Escapes Us	29
THREE	Symbols Hide What They Say	51
FOUR	Atheism Is Impossible in Practice	73
FIVE	God beyond Being	97
SIX	The Invisible Source of Authority	123
	Notes	151
	Index	171

PREFACE

At first glance writing a book seems like a solitary affair. You are alone in your study with nothing but your books and notes to keep you company. But then it dawns that it is through those very materials that others, innumerable others, accompany you along the way. The voices in your head are other voices who make it possible for you to think. It is in relation to them that we test the worth of our thoughts and find the courage to seize upon ideas we might otherwise have hesitated to grasp. Confidence in the enterprise builds because we have been joined by others who assure us of a truth that even in disagreement is shared, for it can only be shared on the basis of truth. Does it survive the test of joint attention? That was the feature of thought that so impressed Aristotle that he regarded it as the centerpiece of the life of philosophy. Peer review is only a pale imitation of the vibrancy of intellectual comity that is at the heart of all science and all knowledge. Truth is never alone. Only the one who conceals is alone with what he dare not let others know. Violence, we have learned, hides itself behind lies. Love gives itself away with an abandon that shares and creates a common world with others. The present small volume is one such small effort to reach a shared self-understanding. Problems of disorder as we discern them are only the beginning of a dialogue that heads toward a deeper account of ourselves. How should we characterize the age in which we live? Consciousness of the challenges, moral and political, that arise in a world without God, as we think of our secular age, define much of the conversation we have with one another. But is that the way to think about the time in which we find ourselves?

We must resist the temptation to contemplate our moment in history as if we were sociologists from Mars. There is no viewpoint on it that does not include the viewers themselves. We are within the secular moment and can only discern it from within. That, however, means we bear responsibility for it. We are the ones called upon to respond. Rather than take a video of the disaster, we must put our cell phones down and lend a hand. We are engaged with the scene before we even arrive. It is in that way that the parameters of the reality in which we find ourselves are disclosed. We hear the voice of God only when we have prepared ourselves to follow his command. Pronouncement of judgment is not our prerogative for we are in every instant under judgment ourselves. That is the meaning of the term "crisis" that has long been used to bemoan the present age. Yet the luxury of detachment is unavailable to those who must take up the task of reshaping the age in which they live. No one, Eric Voegelin reminded us in an underappreciated remark, is required to yield to the disorder of an era. Thinking is the first step in that movement of resistance by which we enlarge the limits of possibility that confront us. If the present work has any merit, it is offered as an aid to those who wish to live beyond the boundaries of a world that has for so long failed to satisfy the longings of the human heart. Even if nothing is changed in the world around us, we ourselves have been changed by opening a perspective that unalterably shifts the horizon conventionally imposed on us. Christendom may not be on the point of returning, but we can resume the enlargement of vision from which it has always arisen. We have overturned the boundaries of the secular age by no longer taking its self-imposed limits as dispositive. This suggestion is intended, not as a quixotic withdrawal, but as a dwelling within the invitation that reaches us from a world no longer satisfied with what it takes itself to be. We find within invisibility the God who prevails, precisely in invisibility. The challenge we gradually discover is that we are confronted, not with a unique historical moment, but with a historical continuity that reaches all the way back to the rupture of transcendence that marks the only genuine turning point of history.

The bonds of friendship are thus immeasurable as we look back within the historical record available to us and forward toward a future we cannot yet perceive while it is dimly before us. It is therefore with particular warmth that we must regard our closest collaborators as the friends of the journey of whom we are most intensely aware. It is the duty and the privilege of an author to include such specific acknowledgments.

Without diminishing the affection for the many American friends in both the academic and nonacademic worlds, I would like to single out, for particular mention, the Irish friends who were the first circle of discovery with whom my thinking began. Joe McCarroll and Brendan Purcell were from the beginning partners in a meditation that for each of us was a voyage of discovery. James O'Connor has been a friend pure and simple, which is more than enough. Cyril O'Regan is the Irish friend who bridged the transition to America that deepened the bond between us. I have been blessed to have old friends who remained steadfast on the long journey but doubly blessed to have made new ones along the way, especially in the fraternity of the Eric Voegelin Society, founded by my first American friend, Ellis Sandoz, of blessed memory. To all of them this small volume of reflection is dedicated in friendship and love. As always, I would be remiss if I did not mention with appreciation the indomitable director of the University of Notre Dame Press, Steve Wrinn, and his staff, especially Megan Levine, and also my copy editor, Sheila Berg, who by believing in an author make it possible for him to believe in himself.

CHAPTER ONE

How Can We Forget What We Must Remember?

"Men have forgotten God, that is why all this has happened." So declared Aleksandr Solzhenitsyn as he quoted a Russian proverb to account for the desolation of the twentieth century.[1] The clarity of that judgment seemed compelling to one who contemplated the horrors through which the age had passed. Destruction on a mass scale had shaken the self-confidence of modernity in a way that was not likely to be regained. Wariness of even greater disaster had barely stayed the hand of governments from the doomsday weapons they now possessed in abundance. A nuclear standoff maintained an armed peace, while a Cold War intermittently flared within carefully demarcated zones of contention. Yet it was under the shelter of that uneasy peace that the destructive appeal of ideologies of global transformation silently crumbled. In 1989 collapse of the last great ideology, Communism, seemed to usher in a new era with its peace dividend and the apparent triumph of liberal democracy. Institutional management of conflict seemed to have dawned. Yet under the surface, we now know, forces were gathering for new irruptions of violence in a history whose end had not in any sense arrived. Even without the militantly atheistic ideologies there would be many who stepped forward to claim the mandate of history as their authorization to remake the world. God might no longer be forgotten, even if his voice was peculiarly muffled in the brutality of those who now spoke in his name.

A resurgent Islam, spectacularly evident in the events of 9/11 and its jihadist offshoots, was only the first to awaken us from our secularist slumbers. But that could easily be set aside as arising from a source far outside the mainstream of our thinking. We could focus on binding Islam within the web of neutrality while remaining unaware that it was just such an entrapment that Islam opposed the most. A secularized Islam would cease to be Islamic. The violent shaking off of that envelopment should not have come as a surprise to any who pondered the millennial tenacity of this quintessentially historical religion. But it did, and the West was ill equipped to grasp what it had missed. Pierre Manent was among the few to perceive the limitations of the self-understanding of secular society as it grappled with the nonassimilation France was uniquely positioned to experience. Yet even he did not trace the deepest roots of the problem that would require a more radical overhaul of the very meaning of the secular. The shortcoming is of a piece with the wider failure of the West to grasp the nature of the ideological foes it had simultaneously nurtured and confronted throughout the twentieth century. Even today it has not been able to comprehend the source of the vehemence it encountered because it was unable to see that it arose, not from political rivalry, but from a spiritual intensity long receded from a world that revolved around more mundane preoccupations. Secular messiahs were strangely incomprehensible to people utterly without any echo of the messianic. It was hardly surprising, therefore, that we were equally unprepared to recognize the remnants of that totalitarian past in the ramshackle ideologies of the twenty-first century. We could not see that the revanchist dream of empire would always clothe itself in the trappings of a spiritual mission.

Ideological Style without Ideology

Even without the cover provided by the militant ideologies of transformation, as in Russia and China today, the habit of justifying the abuse of power would still continue. Imperial ambition has of course rarely stepped forth in all its nakedness. Both the practitioners and the victims must hold a more palatable rationale for the violence entailed, as it was in the age of colonial empires with their mission of extending the benefits of civilization. The difference was that the latter were still anchored in the residue of classical and Christian morality that did not always bend to the convenience of those who ruled.[2] Inflexible demands of justice and truth could not so readily be set aside for the shifting dictates of the moment. But it remained different for those who had just exited the all-purpose rationale of a great ideological system. They had not yet found their way back to the unvarying judgment of an eternal perspective. Having suppressed the voice of conscience, it was difficult to hear again the voice of God. The lie that sustained totalitarian power had become a habit that was difficult to break.[3] But what then would provide the cover that the perpetration of evil would still need in the absence of an ideological system? Even ordinary criminals cannot sustain their criminality without invoking something high minded, whether defense of the family or the tribe or race. On the larger scale, political leaders would have to cobble fragments of ideology in order to replace the coherence that had fallen apart. It was enough that there remained the will to rationalize wrongdoing that enabled them and their supporters to stay in power. The one thing that could not be admitted was that they served only their own interests and never the common good. If nothing else, the age of ideology has heightened our awareness of the need for power to clothe itself in the trappings of higher purpose even, and especially, as the claims become increasingly threadbare. The ubiquity of justifications has been one of the indisputable additions that totalitarianism has contributed to the classical analysis of the tyrant as defined by self-interest. Violence must conceal itself with lies.

This is why in a secular age the contest between good and evil endures, for good is most needed by those who would commit evil. It turns out that we do not live in an era of sheer relativism. "Everything is permitted" may be displayed in our actions, but we cannot admit it in what we tell ourselves. Others may be nihilistic, but we must hold fast to high-minded principles, even if we no longer believe in them. Indeed the imperative of moralistic stridency increases the further we depart from moral restraints. Ideological patterns remain, even when the ideologies have waned or exhausted their appeal. The pattern is at its clearest when it comes to drawing the contrast with opponents. Even more important than the righteousness of the elect is the disdain of the reprobate. Deplorables allow the radiant to shine.[4] The increasing virulence of domestic politics mirrors the conflicts we see on the world scene, and the source appears to be the same. It is not so much that we find ourselves in irreconcilable disagreement as that we have chosen the ideological style that allows us to vent maximum vituperation. Clashes in our imaginations have spilled over into conflicts in the streets. Indulging the politics of absolutism, absolutists now find it difficult to accommodate diverse viewpoints and interests. Liberal polities teeter on the brink of illiberal politics. Cancel culture and smash-mouth rhetoric veer toward the violence that would rather silence opponents than find common ground with them. Once again we are hard pressed to explain the passionate intensity, especially in the absence of any great ideological division, and we are forced to concede that it is self-chosen for no other reason than the gratuitous satisfaction itself. Without impassioned ideologies there remains a desire to wrap our prejudices in their all-purpose rationales. Even the liberal democracies are in worse shape by becoming susceptible to a style of ideological confrontation that will brook no compromise. Their condition too is ripe for populist demagogues to exploit.

But we must not overestimate the strength of either kleptocratic or demagogic regimes. Unlike their great ideological predecessors, the roots of justification in grievance, resentment, and illegality remain precariously shallow. Rationalizations easily dissolve, and the support flows quickly away once the mendacity is exposed. We are not returning to the great ideological systems that concealed wrongdoing on a mass scale from all but the most penetrating citizens.[5] It is simply that politics has not renounced the need for fig leaves that would absolve wrongdoers of responsibility for evil or furnish bystanders with an excuse for doing nothing about it. In other words we are back at an acknowledgment of the imperfection of political life that Augustine identified as its permanent condition. A nonutopian state no longer promises any secular prospect of perfection or transformation. Instead, threadbare rationalizations offer little more than their inability to suppress awareness of the evil they seek to conceal. Yet in invoking the hypocrisy that is the compliment vice pays to virtue, they bear witness to the measure that shines undeniably above it. It is especially in the fabricated rags of ideology that the precariousness of their hold on truth becomes apparent. No matter what the coercive apparatus is, it can no longer operate in the full light of day. Criminality is exposed when nothing very exalted conceals it. A band of thieves, as Augustine observed, cannot function without justice between them.[6] What then is their fate when they have failed to even keep up its appearance?

The unraveling is already underway, whether it is in an autocratic disregard for the rule of law or the populist contempt for it. They know the fragility of what they have assembled to serve the convenience of the moment. Desperate to leave an imprint on history, they lack the endurance that would make them worthy of historical memory. A readiness to sacrifice others remains a far cry from the self-sacrifice of patriots. Instead, there is a grasping at greatness without greatness of spirit. Cheap grace of self-aggrandizement hardly approaches even the hollow greatness of the ideological predecessors. In the end hastily stitched excuses for aggression rest less on residual appeals to nation and tradition than on disdain for the imputed weakness of the rest of the world. At the same time that world seems peculiarly roiled by a fractiousness that itself barely conceals its own loss of faith in the experiment in self-government. The faults of liberal democracy do not define it but are in effect open invitations to join the collaborative enterprise of incremental remediation. When opposing sides castigate one another as bitter enemies to be utterly crushed, intolerance of disagreement endangers the liberties the rule of law was intended to preserve. Partisans of the extremes have yet to be resisted by the conviction that we must remain friends even while we hold opposing viewpoints. The vital center from which the project of constitutional self-government arose is in danger of slipping away. We are at a historical inflection, similar to the moment in 1939 when T. S. Eliot spoke for "the many persons who, like myself, were deeply shaken by the events of September 1938, in a way from which one does not recover; perhaps to whom that month brought a profounder realization of a general plight."[7] The absence of all-encompassing ideologies may be the one decisive difference, for we are no longer dealing with the certainty of revolutionary apocalypse.

Without a messianic foe it may be difficult to call forth a comparable willingness for sacrifice. Both China and Russia, to take the largest examples, have rebuilt themselves on the bourgeois social model they claim to despise yet their citizens have not been prepared to reject. Prosperity is not the route to historical greatness. It is thus at an ideologically reduced level that the issues of the past return in Cold War 2.0. Can authoritarian regimes, rooted in thinly disguised appeals of power, prevail against a free world wrapped in the illusion of choosing the challenges it will confront rather than those that have chosen it? Deeper than the division between expansionary and contracting regimes, there remains the quest for a spiritual depth that unites them. On the surface, it would appear that the manufactured rationales of autocrats remain weaker than the self-absorptions of liberal democracies. A pandemic readiness to sacrifice freedom for the sake of life hardly compared to the heroic readiness to risk life for the sake of freedom. Once again it is the dissidents of the authoritarian societies that bear most convincing witness to the transcendent order within which life is lived. At the same time they are an invaluable reminder that we are not divided at all. None of us can evade the question they openly ask about what finally matters in human life. Revanchist totalitarians will not simply modulate into ethical regimes even when their ideological fig leaves have fallen away. The habit of unlimited power remained harder to break than our own wish fulfillment had considered. Now we have no alternative but to find again the wellsprings of conviction we had neglected or thought we would no longer need.

"What Men Live By," is the title of a story by Tolstoy that the patients in Solzhenitsyn's *Cancer Ward* discussed, as it remains the question that all who consider their own end must contemplate. The present work is conceived as a small contribution to a task that is at once personal and universal. It begins from the starting point from which political theory today must set out. That is, meaning cannot be found ready-made but must emerge from the search itself. This is so palpably the condition of our world that it scarcely needs recalling, yet, for all its familiarity, only those who confront it have gathered it fully into consciousness. The foregoing sketch of our contemporary moment is offered as a startling reminder of what is at stake in the meditation on which we embark. In a sense we have all been thrust into the position of that extraordinary line of dissidents who, without preparation, were compelled to meditate on the ultimate questions by which they are to live or die. Even those who thought they possessed some measure of conviction concerning the spiritual order in which we live would be challenged to find a deeper, more personal appropriation under the immediate shock of imprisonment. But what about our larger modern world that has for centuries proceeded on a path that denied there was anything more than the material comforts and amusements with which we fritter away our lives? Is there a higher purpose to which we are called? Can we avoid forever the question of God? The question lingers at the edge of consciousness, often with an insistence we are loath to admit. Now we begin to see that freedom is already an opening toward responsibility whose parameters we are beginning to discern anew.

If any further prompting is needed to note the urgency of this question, we have only to consider the growing abdication of self-government and self-responsibility. A taste for confrontation and violence is increasing along the lines of populist and personality cults. At the same time, we witness alarming tendencies to stretch freedom of choice and expression beyond all boundaries. Constraints of biology, economics, and politics are routinely dismissed as outmoded obstacles, to be swept aside as irrelevant to our vaunted liberation from all limitations. Principles of liberty can be elevated into ideological absolutes that will brook no check on their exercise. Just as alarming has been the rise of an intransigence that refuses to take account of the plurality of perspectives and interests that remain in every society. When the monopoly of truth is confidently held by one side, then there seems no need to take account of other viewpoints or to find a modus vivendi for living with one another. "Benedict options" and dreams of "integralism" are touted as a way back to the lost utopias of an age of imagined social cohesion. Impatience with limits and indulgence of nostalgia seem of a piece with diminished responsibility for sustaining social harmony. The mood is not too far from the makeshift ideologies we observe on the world scene, tatters that scarcely provide cover for ambitions they cannot admit openly to selves or others. In the absence of truly grandiose systems the will for small-scale excuses for extensions of power remains. Believing in nothing, we are now ready to believe in anything. This is what explains the pugnacious character of politics in both its domestic and international enactments. Of course, there are always real material and security interests that cannot easily be reconciled. But the irrationality that is the distinct mark of an ideological mind-set is a readiness to sacrifice more than the disagreements are worth, and usually only for the exquisite satisfaction of crushing the opposing side. It is only when the victors are as defeated as the victims that clashes burn themselves out. That point may be reached far sooner in an aged of diminished if residual ideological appeal than it was in one where large segments of the population had more fully internalized the revolutionary expectations. It took seventy years for Communism to be defeated; it will be far less for plutocrats and autocrats to fall of their own accord.

God When There Is No God

The return of law and its foundations, however, will not be secure until we begin to deal with the unfinished remains of the ideological mania that engulfed the twentieth century. Now we see that the ideological collapse did not evacuate a residual taste for unchecked power. It is notable that regression to an ideological mean occurred most virulently in those locales that had never truly renounced their totalitarian past. Repentance and self-limitation may have been called for but rarely undertaken, with the exceptions of Germany and Japan, which spent three-quarters of a century in deep submission to a pacifism they are now beginning to exit. What has yet to occur is the shift of modern self-understanding more broadly toward a similar admission of its role in countenancing the unlimited exercise of power. What after all can restrain human beings who recognize no higher authority before which they must bend their wills and their knees? Was it not the embrace of a wholly secular civilization, beginning with the Enlightenment, that led to the great convulsion of totalitarianism and still retains a lingering hold in our own chaotic imagination? The roadblocks against unlimited power could only take the form of such fragile defenses as the profession of human rights that must not be violated and the dignity of the person that must not be abrogated. But that too remained an incomplete project.[8] Even the steady growth of national and international tribunals has, despite continuing progress, not quite articulated the moral principles implicit in the judicial authority they seek to assert. To do so would be to answer Churchill's quip about the Nuremberg trials, as representing the justice of the victors. Real legitimacy would derive from acknowledgment of their validity by the vanquished, as it occurs in the more familiar domestic jurisdiction of courts of criminal and civil law. Ordinary criminals rarely dispute the entitlement of the court to pass judgment on them. International tribunals, by contrast, rest on nothing more than the self-binding commitments of the states that compose them. As such they can set themselves free from agreements they themselves have made. Resting on the air of their own affirmations, it is evident something more is required to ground their order.

It was thus no accident that one of the first great theorists of international law in the modern period, Hugo Grotius (1583–1645), confronted the question that threatened to overturn its establishment before it had even begun. Would the basis in natural law he had adduced hold if we suppose what should not be supposed, that there is no God? Right at the beginning of the modern world he had cast doubt on its capacity to survive. Is a rule of law independent of divine authorization possible? The question itself already evinces a destabilizing effect as it arises from an anxiety that cannot readily be assuaged. Nothing in the intervening period has succeeded in quieting the uncertainty hidden within its depths. Where is God?, we continue to ask when he is nowhere clearly present within a world that has erected itself on his absence. How can we even regard humanity as of value, Nietzsche asked, when nothing exalted clearly shines through us?[9] Can there be crimes against humanity when human beings have become nothing more than the sum of their parts to be manipulated at will? Does the element of free choice constitute the decisive difference in what can be permitted? These are the deep-seated concerns that trouble our secular confidence even if we rarely admit them. Indeed, that avoidance and immersion in the ongoing business of life is one of those protective mechanisms most frequently adapted and adopted. On the rare occasions when we admit what we would not normally care to admit, the results have not been promising. Most often we depart with a polite exchange of views that neither change nor advance the positions of the participants. We are compelled to acknowledge that we lack the intellectual means of grappling with the question that most deeply troubles our world. Yet it is to this the present reflections are addressed.

The only justification for inviting the reader to one more attempt at resolving the irresolvable is that we set out from a certain faith that the question of a secular world can be answered because, in practice, it has. Having endured the great trial of the past century, from the shattering of confidence in the Great War, the arduous defeat of the totalitarian menace in the Second World War, and the endurance of the long Cold War, a civilization of slender spiritual resources seems to have met the challenges history had thrown in its path. Only an inclination to lapse into forgetfulness of the moral vigor it had regained allowed it to slip back into the old absorption with immanence. Nowhere was this more precipitous than in the euphoria that attended the collapse of the Berlin wall. A holiday from history had been declared that, even after the punctuation of Islamic terrorism, never seemed to call forth the firmness of resolve that would have been needed to redeem the pledges made. The recently bungled departure from Afghanistan is only the latest in a line of failures to live up to commitments. Now the rise of powers that are determined to revisit the unfinished business of the Cold War compels us to also return to the question of the reserves of spirit on which we may need to draw in the uncertain struggles before us. Past success is no guarantee of future performance, and every generation must find its own path of spiritual enlargement. But we see from the witness of history that the question of whether secular civilization possesses the resources to survive, the question it has agonized over more than once, can be answered in the affirmative. The challenge is to understand the depth that is concealed within its self-denomination as secular or worldly. What is it for which men will die when they have lost all reference to a measure beyond this world? Perhaps now is the moment to ponder at a more fundamental level what our modernity has really been about. Now that there is no longer a holiday from history, we must also admit that there is no respite from the demand to think clearly about where we stand within it.

A beginning can be made in distinguishing between the character of the illusions we presume to have outgrown in our secular self-understanding. The project of drawing heaven down to earth that was the core of the militant ideologies has certainly been exhausted by the sheer weight of contrary evidence. Utopia remains where it has always been in its designation by More as "no place." But what of the "illusion" of heaven itself that has so often been blamed as its source? Is that too doomed to disappear and if it must, to be replaced by what? One more false substitute already deemed an impossibility within a secular world? If there is no heaven on earth, then nothing earthly can furnish a replacement for what is not there. This life may turn out, as St. Augustine taught us, to be nothing more than a long trial of temptation, imperfection, and defeat.[10] But he could see that clearly only in light of a glimpse of a higher life that saves us from searching vainly for what we know is missing in this one. It is not that we need one illusion to defeat or check another one but that we sense that they are aspects of the one illusion, that is, that heaven can be gained on earth. It is the imagination that heaven is a mere extension of the pleasures enjoyed in life that is the source of the problem. So long as we hold onto the realization that heaven endures only in heaven, then it can no longer be a source of illusion for understanding our mundane condition. What is deathless cannot die; that is preeminently the case of the world of spirit. Far, therefore, from dispelling the illusion of an afterlife, we may begin to see that a secular society is premised on it. Such is the perhaps surprising burden of the present reflection. Not only is the sacred built into the notion of the secular, as I will explain, but it opens upon it in ways that imperceptibly work to overturn its self-understanding as merely secular. Even further, the dynamic suggests that the sacred fulfills its destiny most fully by holding the profane at a distance, while the profane is free to furnish the finite satisfactions of which it is capable when it no longer has to support the impossible burden modernity has placed upon it.

The very rationality we regard as the hallmark of the scientific and technological world we inhabit turns out to depend crucially on preservation of its distance from the dreams of unattainable perfection that continually threaten to overwhelm it. This is an aspect on which my work has touched before as I contemplated the singular contribution Christian revelation has made to the life of reason.[11] In this respect it was the full differentiation of divine transcendence through Christ that definitively displaced all other mediators between man and God. It became apparent that the only adequate representation of a transcendent God is the Son who is also God, the fullness of divine reality. No other intermediaries could reveal the God who is beyond all but God himself. Nor were any needed once the Word of God, emanating from before the beginning, had entered history in the particularity of a man, Jesus Christ. The distance between man and God was simultaneously established and abolished in the entry of transcendent Being into time. What could not be reached by means of human effort had been freely offered as a divine gift. This was what enabled the church fathers to look on the world for the first time as a *world*, for they beheld it from the vantage point of those who participate in a perspective beyond it.[12] Augustine could inaugurate a realistic account of politics uncontaminated by reverberations of a golden age in the past or the future that could remove the clash of power and ambition as its permanent condition. The appeal to nature that even in Aristotle retained echoes of the myth from which it had emerged could now be definitively viewed in wholly naturalistic terms. The possibility of a realm of nature turns on the de-divinization of the cosmos. What we today take as the distinctive mark of a secular order is unthinkable without the divine order from which it has separated.

Reason may have been discovered by the Greeks, but the enlargement to its unsurpassable limits is the fruit of the Christian revelation. What made it possible for them to contemplate a world without God, to behold the flight of the last gods without the nostalgia that still perfumed the Greco-Roman world, is that they knew the God who was now more present than ever before. No longer tied to manifestations in particular times and places, God had become available to every person in the inwardness that each had at the same time discovered even without articulating it.[13] Every soul could reach out in prayer to the God who already bent toward them in the inwardness of the call of Jesus. Each could hear the voice that also joined them together in the community of the church. Sacred and secular had become correlative in a bond that unites them in a mutuality that, even when its genealogy is overlooked, ensured that it could never finally be forgotten. It is to the probing of that interrelationship that we are now directed. We could not think of living in a secular world without remembering that it is the world from which God is absent. But in that instant we remember God who now must be present in a very different way. Even when he is forgotten, God cannot be forgotten in a world that knows itself as the absence of God. The paradox of a secular age, nowhere more transparent than in the laments about the invisibility of God, is that it is a thought that overturns itself. We have no sooner begun to think of our separation from God than we realize that we have returned to him. The secular cannot be thought without the sacred, without separation from the sacred. Yet the dialectic is more than a conceptual and linguistic interdependence. It is a differentiation that emanates from the axial age breakthrough to the transcendence of God in the revelatory outbursts, echoed in the world religions, as we call them, that simultaneously reveal our universal humanity.[14] That pivot of history, which is clearly not an event in history for it is the event that constitutes history, remains the inexhaustible source of our reflection on the meaning of the whole in which we find ourselves. Our contemporary moment, marked by a heightened awareness of being alone, cannot be taken as the last word. It is also far from being the first word on how we arrived at what concerns us.

To be alone we must first have a memory of a togetherness we have lost. *The Invisible Source of Authority* is an attempt to remind us of this. One cannot be without the other. By thinking that mediation to its root, we begin to perceive the impossibility of a secular age that already begins to intuit what it had thought it had surpassed or forgotten. But beyond the psychological instability of suppression, since memory can only be dismissed by the constant vigilance against recall, there lies the deeper possibility of an encounter with the One whose very absence was itself the only mode by which that event could take place. We are not too far away from the dynamic of the axial age in which men and women first heard the voice of the God who could be neither seen nor heard. The only difference is that now we see that necessity more clearly. In order to know God as he is in himself, all intermediaries but God must be removed. Neither the burning bush nor the Platonic cave could be anything more than the contingent circumstance that it was, for all that really mattered vastly exceeded what it was incapable of pointing toward. Only the transcendent can reveal itself as transcendent. Nothing immanent can disclose it. Nor can human beings catch a glimpse unless they are given it as a gift they now recognize as beyond their capacity. The divine condescension is integral to the self-revelation that is ultimately a sharing in the divine being. Christ is the culminating instance beyond which there can be no other, but that does not mean that there is not a profound premonition of Christ wherever the encounter with the Beyond occurs.[15] To the question then as to how the mystery of transcendence is to be known today we may begin to think of the self-assigned parameters of a secular age as peculiarly appropriate, for they compel us to look for him nowhere but within himself. Only in a secular society is God properly revered as God.

The acuteness of God's absence becomes as it were an invitation to know him in the inexpressible depth of who he is. However much this may run contrary to the prevailing narrative, I believe that the latter points inexorably toward a realization that is continually on the edge of its horizon. By thinking of the God who is absent we draw constantly closer to him. The turning point arrives when we see that he has withdrawn precisely to leave an opening by which he may approach us as we approach him.[16] Rather than the rush of a mighty wind or the flash of a thunderclap, there is the dusty stranger met along the roadway who left behind an unpromising ragtag band of disciples. Those who would hear would have to listen to the still small voice heard nowhere but within. Worshipping in spirit and in truth, they have left the world of visible and material for a God whose transcendence is only disclosed in inwardness. Those whose hearts burn as he opened the Scriptures, including the sacred writings of all religions, are eventually the ones who recognize him in the only way he can be recognized: in the breaking of the bread. The veil of externality has been torn away as it becomes clear that divinity cannot be contained within an idol but only in the icon through which it shines. That piercing of the veil by which the transcendent is glimpsed is both a gift from what is beyond nature and a demarcation of the limit of nature. Where the Greeks still held onto the reverberations of the divine within nature, with a richness that was often overlooked in the later transmission of their thought, now nature was denuded of divine presence to become the realm of brute materiality. The separation, however, did not constitute a severance, for the mystery of the correlation prevailed. God could not be known apart from the world and the world could not be known apart from God.

The mutual implication of transcendence and immanence that forms the pivot of our secular self-understanding is redolent of a mystery barely comprehended, that is, not only that the secular implies the sacred as its other, but that the distance between them is bridged in that affirmation. What has been deemed mere bread and wine is transformed to become something other than it is without losing the reality that is its own. Matter does not cease to be matter when it becomes the bearer of spirit that can and cannot be contained in it. Mystery prevails again within a cosmos that, without becoming a vehicle for divinity, is yet an opening on the Beyond that is more secure than any manifestation of presence could claim. Just as ink on paper is only that, it becomes an event of surpassing significance when it is a declaration of love. Spirit does not inhabit the material reality in which it lives but continually gives itself by virtue of a means that is in no way altered by that service.[17] It is only in the special case where the self-giving is so intimate and so complete that the bond acquires an inseparability that will no longer permit a reversal. The real presence is a singular case of becoming present in a way from which departure is impossible. But even in that limiting case, where spirit has submitted itself wholly to the risk of desecration to which all embodiment is subject, it does not abolish the line of distinction that has emerged. We may say that it is only out of an excess of love that spirit gives itself in material form. Indeed it could not bridge the gulf with such love if the opening between the inaccessible and the incapable had not occurred so definitively. The condescension that makes impossible communion possible is the highest fruit of what a secular order contains. While we may be accustomed to thinking of the life of reason as realized most fully through the departure of the last gods, we forget the most momentous consequence, that is, that it would not have occurred without the descent of the God who is beyond and who does so by giving himself, most of all in the person of his Son, his other self.

Touch of Transcendence

The insight that a world without God may be the world where God as God is most readily found has struck many of the most farsighted sufferers of the unfolding contemporary immanence. When nothing points to God, then God can approach us through himself. The very bereftness of our experience opens us to the touch of the One who mysteriously speaks to us.[18] Elements of this perspective had already begun to emerge, not coincidentally, in the first wave of revolt against God as it broke in the nineteenth century. Kierkegaard was certainly familiar with the dynamic of irony along which it unfolded. But it was Nietzsche, whose proclamation of the death of God marked a watershed, who named the troubling intimation in pronouncing his demise. He identified the nihilism that followed as "uncanny" (*unheimlich*): "Nihilism stands at the door: whence comes this uncanniest of all guests?"[19] His arresting perception, widely echoed, might be taken as the hallmark of a secular age that senses its own shortfall without being able to express it and, therefore, without being able to know itself as secular. My reflections will pursue the logic of that intuition, although their purpose is to yield far more than the inconclusive musings in which the more sociological observations of our contemporaries terminate. They are well-intentioned efforts to understand a phenomenon whose roots are spiritually deeper than either the observers or the subjects are willing to acknowledge. We live in a world where human beings have increasingly secured their own finite fulfillment. A sociological approach that measures human beings in the immanent terminology of that world is especially unsuited to grasping the heart of the issue. Rising or falling numbers have nothing to do with truth, as both Socrates and Kierkegaard remind us.[20] Only a dwelling within can explore the interior of a reality that cannot be accessed from outside of it. This was why Nietzsche was not content to rest with mere observation or prediction and came achingly close to the Zarathustra who was recognized by the retired pope as "the most pious of those who do not believe in God."[21]

That intuition would lead, even if only unconsciously, toward the deepest realization of the meaning of God's absence in the harrowing century that followed. A long line of patient bearers of loss dwelled with such steadfastness that they reached the God who had also shared it by their side. They were the ones who grasped that extreme loss is also the path of extreme gain. All is returned a hundredfold and running over. Even the deprivations of torture and death could not dislodge the certainty they reached on the other side of abandonment. The vanishing trail of these astronauts of the spirit can scarcely be traced in the biographies and testaments they left behind. We do not comprehend how they could soar so far above the catastrophe that fell upon them, crushing so many of their companions yet providing them with an incomparable opening toward transcendence. How could they look back and say, as Solzhenitsyn did, "Thank you, prison, for being in my life," or confess with Victor Frankl, "Suffering had become a task on which we did not want to turn our backs"?[22] Nor is this a line of spiritual witnesses that has by any means reached an end or left a complete list. Liu Xiaobo's ringing declaration, "No enemies, no hatred," as well as the aptly named film about Franz Jägerstätter, *A Hidden Life*, are among the more recent reminders.[23] When I wrote *After Ideology* I tried to unpack the extraordinary significance of those who lived the truth that demolished the lie. I now think that we should add to that characterization the illumination of a secular age as more than it appears to be. Beyond the overthrow of ideology, there is liberation from the framework of immanence that was its precondition. All of those who responded to the call of transcendence saw that they had begun to reverse the drift of history in which they found themselves. They had overturned the secular paradigm as the measure of relevance.

Among the most visionary explorers of that transformation was the great Lutheran martyr Dietrich Bonhoeffer.[24] He was perhaps the one who grasped the theological implications in their starkest form. The encounter with God in the moment of the complete absence of God was not only a supreme consolation, but a model of the deepest truth carried by an age that no longer knows or cares about him. It is when God is absent that he is most present, not only in the divine condescension that stretches toward the heart of every person, but as a revelation of the way he can most surely be approached. Perhaps the bereftness of a secular age, its unshakable sense of the uncanny, intimates a new paradigm of the spirit that includes the divine indwelling in loss. The present essay, intended less as an examination of texts and events, is a test of the aptness of that vision. Without dwelling in detail on these figures, I am concerned with the depth of logic of their thought. This is needed because scholarship, too easily absorbed with the details of its own laudable probing, often lacks the indispensable distance that would allow the magnitude of what is being probed to shine through. Not wishing to rehearse what has been well cataloged by historians and social scientists, I am more concerned with their paradigmatic significance. Having learned from Thomas Kuhn about the obstacles that stand in the way of a paradigm shift, the present work aims at the perspective of actors within a prevailing paradigm whose limits and limitations are becoming cumulatively apparent. Enough has happened for us to suggest that the time for talk about a new paradigm has passed and that the time to enter upon the perspective of those who have lived it has arrived. Political theory is among the disciplines uniquely suited to the task since without a professional allegiance to the stance of observation, it can step into the historical struggle to share at least in part the practical responsibility of its participants. That is the linchpin on which my meditation turns.

Nothing is viewed from the outside, as if we were observers from another planet. The historical reality with which we are engaged remains the one in which we find ourselves. It is our destiny that is at stake as we struggle to make sense of its ramifications. The advantage of the approach is that the narrative has not been fixed in advance by a reigning construction, for it is one we too must take a hand in shaping. As a consequence, what a secular age means is susceptible to enlargement within the dynamic of our own responsive unfolding within it. This was something I came to appreciate in the contentiousness of liberal political societies that are a constant invitation to go beyond the often-unpromising prospects with which they began. They are polities that seem to pull themselves together only in the struggles that confront them. It is only then that their character is disclosed through what I named "the growth of the liberal soul," a dynamic that comes as much of a surprise to the bitterly divided partisans as to those who would despair of any commonality between them. Human existence is never a fait accompli but a process whose forward movement enacts and reveals what it is about, without ever reaching a resting place that can declare its consummation. Our horizon in the end is not confined to history at all but to the perspective of eternity from which history becomes visible to us. That component of the paradigm shift was explored in the growing awareness of the impossibility of thinking of ourselves in objective terms. What we know most deeply we know through the luminosity that unfolds from within reality where thinking and being are one. This was reprised in *The Modern Philosophical Revolution* and distilled into the notion of the person who stands within the light that emanates from beyond being in *The Politics of the Person as the Politics of Being*. Of course, it goes without saying that these animadversions on the author's odyssey, liberally sprinkled with missteps and misjudgments, are only offered by way of an indication of the scope of the paradigm shift *The Invisible Source of Authority* intimates within a secular age. They are adduced only to forestall the understandable objection that our historical moment is more properly viewed as one in which God and man have parted company more than ever.

It is to strain against the impression of the issue as somehow settled that the present text is offered. Instead we are invited to contemplate it as an open question, even an invitation to an opening that might yield a far different account from the one that has hitherto dominated our world. If we are to enlarge our horizons we cannot simply talk about them in the conventions of scholarship, but enter into them in the only way that can move them forward, that is, with the whole of our existence. We are guided in this by those who staked their all on the answer to the question of God or of Being. They knew it, not as a topic of casual conversation, but as the indispensable opening from which all else springs. Philosophy can thus return from a subject matter to a way of life, as its best practitioners have always known. What this means is that there is no Archimedean point from which an inquiry might be launched, for our narrative has already begun even before we have stepped into the scene. We are immersed in the meditation and must begin to find our way as Pascal did when in the *Pensées* (S94/L60) he asked about the foundation of justice. It was a question that would scarcely have arisen except for his premonition of a shaking of the foundations so familiar to us but only dimly glimpsed by the early moderns who first grappled with it. Historic changes in science, religion, and politics were already dissolving an older sense of who we are and our place in the universe. Are we alone in the vastness of it all? The question, Pascal knew, could not be answered for it was premised on a capacity to stand outside it. Whatever we know, we must know from within.

This was what set him on the course of the *pensées* distilled into the aphorisms that allowed him a glimpse of what cannot be fully contemplated. It was a style of reflection adopted by many of his successors who also came to see that the principles by which they lived could not be accessed without presupposing them. Once the question of the foundation of order is asked, the questioner is already bound by its authoritative force. We too stand under the judgment that is synonymous with the term *crisis*. If we wish to interrogate justice we can do so only under the imperative of justice itself. Morality cannot be scrutinized from the outside, as if we possessed a mastery that allowed us to fix the scope of its validity. It is rather that we discover the reach of its hold as we submit ever more patiently to the authority of its requirements. Obligation is prior to our arrival at the event, for we could scarcely be obligated if its source derived from a discretionary acceptance or rejection. To perceive the depth of pre-obligation we must resist the illusion of mastery that the paradigm of objectivity, so characteristic of the modern worldview, has given us. It takes considerable effort to recognize that objectivity too is rooted in an orientation within being that, without being subjective, is nevertheless authoritative for us. Truth too is an order to which we submit for we cannot invent truth without the claim that we have been truthful. What matters most is, therefore, not immediately visible as we embark on a course of action by which the inexorable contours of what is right begin to imprint our own existence.[25] At the beginning they are only dimly intuited, and that sideways glance is, Pascal understood, best conveyed in the form of an aphorism.

The virtue of the medium is that it carries the source of truth within it. Without appealing to external evidence, it reveals its authority within the formulation itself. The title of the present reflection is drawn from one of Pascal's (1623–62) most piercing observations of the way in which his meditation unwinds into the disclosure of what is present invisibly from the beginning. Quoting his equally penetrating contemporary, Montaigne, Pascal remarks on the futility of the quest to find a foundation of justice beyond it. There is no going behind it for "whoever tries to reduce it to first principles destroys it."[26] He saw that Montaigne's elevation of custom to unquestionable primacy was, far from an appeal to the merely given, a deeper acknowledgment of metaphysical primacy that could not be superseded. Custom is, in the formulation of Montaigne, the *fondemment mystique de l'autorité*, the mystical source of authority. It derives, not from its mere existence, but from its inscrutability. To examine anything, we must do so in light of what remains beyond examination, the unscathed. At the time when Descartes was planting the seeds of doubt ever deeper and, simultaneously, discovering that there was a limit beyond which his exhortations could not go, Montaigne and Pascal had glimpsed a faith that lies on the far side of doubt. A secret or invisible source of authority remained as the boundary of life itself. It was what could not be surpassed. They were not quite at the insight of Kant that doubt presupposes itself, and certainly had not arrived at the other side of nihilism that Nietzsche broached. But the pattern had become clear. Even in the age of mastery, the horizon of mastery could not be transcended. The framing moral obligations remained impenetrable and irreducible, for mastery too would have to submit to the eternal verities that enshrouded it. Truth and goodness could not be abrogated without losing all that made thinking and acting possible.

To say that this was custom, as Montaigne had suggested, was clearly not sufficient, for it did not explain what made the hold of custom possible. Instead custom functioned as a place holder, as it did for David Hume and others, for an authoritative source no longer transparent. The divine had retreated into invisibility and reigned all the more impregnably in that mysterious transcendence. It is a transition that may be taken as emblematic of the presence of God in a secular age whose reality may be all the more palpable for all his invisibility. Montaigne and Pascal speak of it as a source of certainty beyond the vagaries that afflict all mundane pronouncements of truth. Uncertainty is itself glimpsed in light of a certainty that is barely known. It is in that scarcely accessible intimation that the source of its hold lies. Invisibility is itself the way that God has become visible. This reading of course departs from the more conventional account of Montaigne and Pascal as skeptics who are tinged with fideism. But that is to treat the searching intensity of their thought as a probing without direction, when the reality is that it is driven by an awareness of that for which they search. Skeptics do not doubt; they see ahead. They keep their eyes on the fullness of what has surpassed all earthly defeat. Bearing witness to the indefeasibility of what is true and good, they open a window on another world that may no longer have an evocative presence in this one.

As martyr-witnesses of a secular age they have overturned it before it has even begun. In this task they are preceded by one whose prescience has often been taken as marking the opening salvo in the determination to do without God or to pronounce his demise. Hugo Grotius penned his meditation in the context of a preface to that great flowering of natural law that appeared to provide a sufficient foundation to *On the Law of War and Peace* (1625). International law was, as it is still today, the one instance in which in the absence of law, human and divine, modern men are thrown back on their own resources to work out the rules of order by which they may accommodate one another and minimize the conflicts between them. Grotius was sufficiently steeped in the great medieval architecture of law to know that natural law, resting on eternal law and confirmed in divine law, could not remain fully accessible through reason alone. This was why he could suggest that even between belligerents who lacked a common theological framework, natural law could become the basis for peace. The rise of natural law thus converged with the expansion of a world from which God was becoming increasingly absent. Even before there was a secular age its emergence in practice was clearly on the horizon. It was this prospect that prompted Grotius, a humanist of great theological attunement, to contemplate the abyss that opened when men could manage their affairs without God. Through the daring glance he cast ahead, Grotius became unwittingly the prophet of an age from which he instinctively shrank back.[27] He allowed himself to venture what he immediately retracted, that is, the appalling thought that there is no God. I will have much more to say about this notorious passage in a thinker who did all that he could to resist the implications embedded in his own project. Here I mention it only to call attention to the way he confronted the enormity he himself had admitted. This is all the more necessary since the few lines of his passing remark have acquired a notoriety that has overtaken the larger impact of his labors that move in a contrary direction. Contemplating the invisibility of God, Grotius was really the first to point out the invisible source of his authority. He had glimpsed the God of a secular age as its defining paradigm.

This is why the present essay, without being an extended examination of Grotius, continually circles around the ellipsis he appends to the magisterial opening of his guide for order in the modern world. *De Juri Belli ac Pacis* ushered in four centuries of reflection on natural law, or its equivalents, as the self-sufficient basis for the fabric of law within and between nations. In many ways the secret to the success of that project, transacted over the tumultuous centuries that followed, may be found in the moral daring of Grotius's remark at the dawn of the age. Would natural law hold if we suppose what should never be supposed—that there is no God? Much has been made of the self-reversal that seemed to indicate a doubt deeper than the author intended. On closer examination, however, Grotius glimpses a dynamic of hiddenness and disclosure that is inseparable from the revelation of a God beyond all visibility. Unlike the fool who said in his heart, "There is no God" (Psalm 14), this was no embrace of a liberty without constraints. It was a profession of faith in natural law that, even in the absence of God, would become a path that leads us back to God. Rather than an undermining of natural law, the remark can equally be read as an affirmation that restores it to its source. Instead of seeing God as the guarantor of natural law, he may more properly be viewed as its consummation. If there is law, then there is God. Even if the immediacy of God's presence is no longer available, we already intuit the way toward him. To the extent that law is already a mode of transcendence, by which we set ourselves aside for the sake of obligations held as greater, we are on a way that culminates in the divine presence. It is only from the end point that the invitation, the gift of possibility, can be seen as invisibly present from the very beginning.

The fascinating implications of a passing remark turn out to contain the spiritual dynamic from which a secular world unfolds. "Even if there is no God" is the path by which an age without God comes to know itself as such and, in that instant, revolves again toward the God it finds it never left. The pattern may be compared to the Platonic myth of the ages in which the god shepherds souls until, once released from his care, they discover their participation in the guiding divine Nous within them. In the context of the *Statesman* that mythic history was, however, only a visual narrative. The dialogue itself pointed to a path it did not undertake but that, for that reason, lies at the very heart of the inner change it exhorts. What is intimated cannot be talked about, as in our own laments about the decline of faith in a secular age, for they are conditioned on the countermovement by which the flight of the gods heralds a return. The key moment is the realization that return is different from the prior dispensation. Now God must be found within and after absence. In many respects that was Plato's project, just as it was that of Grotius whose daring matched the search in the *Republic* for justice in the soul, apart from all calculation of consequences in this life or the next. Only those who entrusted themselves to the order of right, dimly intuited, would reach the point at which the Good or God discloses itself as the foundation of the whole. Grotius's seemingly casual remark turns out to hold within it the possibility of justice within a world evacuated of all higher authority. It is the very absence of God that is the invitation to find him beyond all temporal mediations and, therefore, to know him as he is in himself—that is, in his transcendence.

The growth of the soul, previously invoked in my study of liberal democracy, contains a parallel application to the question of God in a secular age. "Anatheism" and the "post-secular" are ad hoc conjectures about the impossibility of excluding God even when he has been excluded.[28] Such formulas include or reverse what they seem to assert. They carry within them a dynamic of self-overturning that may be sensed without being explained. It is to dispel the ensuing confusion in the self-understanding of a secular age that the present reflections are offered. It is one thing to suggest that a secular world cannot be atheistic and quite another to say why that is so. In order to reach a fuller insight, it is necessary to focus not only on the logic of reversal from which the secular mind lives, but on the far deeper understanding of what sustains it. That was what Grotius invited as he contemplated the growth of the soul by which, even without God, the imperative of natural law restores us to God. By forgoing God, he sensed the disclosure of God even more fully. Sacrifice of all assurance is the path of God himself, from the crucified One to the mystics of the dark night of the soul. But where then is the faith that sustains this movement? The answer is nowhere in the tangible aspects of existence but in the unfolding by which the soul eventually touches on that which is beyond all being. The adventure of transcendence, which historically began in the "axial age," has reached an apogee in the secular outlook that knows itself optimally within the exodus from itself. "My soul was visited in that hour," Alyosha Karamazov declares, for about transcendence nothing more can be said.[29] Now we begin to see why so much emphasis must be placed on the movement that underpins a secular world. What is beyond the boundary cannot be known; it can only be glimpsed as marking its limit. But that is sufficient, for the encounter itself opens the transfiguration of all earthly perspectives. In that glimpse the secular worldview not only reaches its limit, but exceeds it, as the innermost secret of its being. A secular world is not only impossible in principle, but is already a transcendence of its own expectations.

It is because our thinking has failed to keep pace with the promise of transcendence that we have failed to grasp the deepest intimation of our secular age. The paradigm shift may have been a long time building, but, as with any series of anticipations, it is punctuated by the prophetic glimpses that foresee it. Retrospectively we can identify the farsighted observers. In the process of differentiation that constitutes the drama of history all is present from the beginning, even if compactly discerned. The only advantage possessed by those who come later is the availability of more aptly fashioned modes of understanding. They can behold what is more fitting even though the fitting might also have been glimpsed by those who came before. In this respect the emergence of a secular age may be regarded, not as a falling away from God, but as a fuller disclosure of what had previously not been manifest. How otherwise can the transcendence of God be displayed than in a renunciation of all mundane entanglements? Perhaps this withdrawal is the very means he employs, perhaps the only ones, by which he can disclose who he is. But in that realization we see that absence has become a fullness glimpsed at the boundary of a world whose every aspect is a hymn of praise for One who would not crush the broken reed or quench the flickering wick. The divine condescension could not be more perfectly expressed than in the complete abnegation of presence. Everything worldly becomes a sacramental means for the disclosure of the One who cannot disclose himself. The finite ceases to be finite when it is the vehicle by which the infinite is poured out. Such an overhaul may challenge the capacity even of the believers, solidly planted in their respective communities within history, to embrace. But it is not beyond the capacity of a world that has already set out to show that natural law holds, even if there is no God. That world already knows the invisible source of authority that is present nowhere but within the faith that sustains its moral and political practice.

Transcending the Secular Age

Now the question is whether it is possible to articulate that openness to the transcendent that is at the heart of the secular paradigm. Can invisibility be understood as the distinctive mark of God's revelation in a secular age? It was the early modern thinkers who first voiced unease with the notion of living in a world from which God has disappeared. By the nineteenth century the ebbing of faith, epitomized by Matthew Arnold's "On Dover Beach," came to be viewed as a full-blown catastrophe looming over modernity as a whole. All of the world religions would have to grapple with it sooner or later in varying ways as they shrank from, or struggled with, a world now shorn of transcendent reference. The inclination from the start of this outburst of hand-wringing was to assume the crisis could be approached from the outside and therefore could be measured and remedied by instruments of worldly success. Loss of faith was viewed as a historical phenomenon, and depicted in the language of social science reports about the rise of the "nones" who disclaim any confessional allegiance. Application of a sociological perspective reached a high point in the most famous study of the past twenty years, Charles Taylor's *Secular Age* (2007). His well-intentioned project, of understanding the character of a secular world from within its own parameters, slipped into an increasingly external mode that could never find its way back to the deeper affirmation of faith to which it aspired. Having taken the event of faith as a phenomenon, it could never become an event within the mind of Taylor himself. This is what accounts for the strangely inconclusive character of the treatment of which even his most admiring readers complain. It is, however, a demonstration of the challenge facing any attempt to think through the meaning of the secular without conforming to the methodological limits of that worldview. Somewhat greater success is enjoyed by the more philosophically attuned approach of Robert Bellah, Shmuel Eisenstadt, and, most recently, Hans Joas. Theirs is informed by an awareness of desacralization as not simply a moment of secular modernity, but a correlate to the differentiation of divine transcendence that marks the axial age. Joas, in particular, makes considerable headway in *The Power of the Sacred: An Alternative to the Narrative of Disenchantment*.[30] In many respects he goes further than Taylor in recognizing that secular society is constituted by its own heightening of a sense of the sacred, as the rights and dignity of the person are elevated into a center of reverence.[31] But as the subtitle of his book indicates, sensitivity to an increase of sacrality is still couched within the sociological framework of Max Weber. Enchantment / disenchantment is not how people living in a secular order experience their lives but instead reflects an external vantage point assumed by observers of the phenomenon. Detachment cannot quite access the interiority from which luminosity prevails, despite the opaqueness of an uncomprehending world surrounding them. The observers are not included within the growth or loss of meaning of the events they examine.

A secular science detailing the character of the secular regime is scarcely even in touch with the condition of its own possibility, that is, that the breakthrough to the transcendent has made possible the differentiation of a world that is secular and open to the rise of secular sciences about itself. Thus thinking about a world without God turns out to be more elusive than anticipated. It cannot be clarified by simply emphasizing the transcendence of God as Karl Barth and his many successors among the radical neo-orthodox theologians have sought to do. The result may yield a useful corrective to the overconfidence of secular disciplines that discourse about the God who, by definition, lies beyond their horizon. While the neo-orthodox judgment may be correct, it does not account for its own condition of possibility as one rendered by scholars who also reside within the same secular horizon.[32] A similar limitation applies to the more long-standing efforts to think about the natural as if it could be separated from the supernatural. Henri de Lubac built his great reflection on *le surnaturel* from his dissatisfaction with the scholastic treatment of the issue, as have such notable successors as David Bentley Hart. Without in any way diminishing the value of those estimable reflections, we are inclined to feel that there is yet a failure to push the meditation far enough. Not only do the natural and the supernatural mutually imply one another, but our ability to perceive the difference is itself the axis within which we live and move and have our being. The Platonic notion of the Between, as introduced by Voegelin, and extensively mined by William Desmond and others, is a useful alternative way of grasping the polarity within which existence unfolds, without itself including the poles.[33] It is, however, doubtful that the structure of the Between can become transparent without a more concrete unfolding of the path that arrives at that conception. It is thus to show rather than to talk about the arrival at such a practical unfolding that the present meditation is undertaken. This is why it follows the path of political reflection.

What distinguishes it from the exemplary efforts listed above is that it begins, not with a general formulation of the problem, but with the concrete challenges of order within which we live. In that respect it is similar to the more concretely political focus of two French thinkers, Jean-Luc Marion and Pierre Manent, who in their respective ways have sought to think through the meaning of secularization.[34] France was the first modern state to attempt to codify the concept under the rubric "laicity," a source of confusion that both Marion and Manent skillfully expose. While it is evident that the notion of a lay separation presupposes a sacred realm from which it is distinguished, it is not clear that these thinkers follow out the implications of their analysis for the secular world as a whole. Certainly, they are aware of the instability of the notion of a secular realm and make good use of that insight in exposing the groundlessness of authority that is its public face. A confrontation with resurgent Islam that denies the separation of social reality from divine authority offers a formidable challenge to secular self-understanding. Manent fully recognizes this, but his own strictly political alternative hardly constitutes a sufficient response to it. Even the building up of community through joint action does not yet arrive at a conclusion adequately transparent. In contrast, Marion's preference for a Catholic witness to a transcendence beyond power, a sacrificial openness that furnishes the possibility of meeting, remains too remote from the event that constitutes community. Dwelling too much on the shortcomings of the secular paradigm, they each fail, in different ways, to find their way through to its positive affirmation. A secular order is not simply reducible to the incoherence it displays, but already carries the seeds of a deeper spiritual truth within it. *The Invisible Source of Authority* sets its sight on the opening toward the transcendent that remains implicit within the self-limitation of a secular age.

Even if lament at the absence of God is a first word, it cannot be the final one. The prophets who developed the mode of lamentation did so, not for the sake of condemnation, but in order to recall their listeners to the God they had forgotten. Critique must stir up the consciousness of truth from which it derives. Diagnosis cannot be separated from therapy. It is the obverse of what a secular age seems to be that is the principal goal of this meditation. Without discounting the critical emphasis of the historical narrative adduced above, it seeks to press the direction further than its exponents have generally been prepared to go. Why would the secular age be a topic of concern if not for the sense of a need to transcend it? The age in which the absence of God is heightened is also the age that draws ever closer toward what it is missing. What it most needs is a way of comprehending the sense of the uncanny that afflicts and pervades it. It needs a way of understanding how the absent God is even more intensely present by virtue of that absence. A speculative grasp of necessity, even in the hands of a thinker as fearless as Dietrich Bonhoeffer, does not necessarily carry the meditation all the way. For that conclusion to be reached there must be a deeper receptivity to a revelation of what has already been revealed. To the extent that life is in advance of reflection on it, the attunement to the right order of existence takes precedence over all formulations theological and philosophical. That is why the present inquiry takes its bearings, not from any general statements of principle, but from the imperatives that become clarified in the experience of living them. Rather than dismiss the remark of a practical statesman like Grotius as incoherent or deficient, we take it as abounding with riches not yet visible on the surface of its formulation. What do men live by when there is no God? The question can only be answered by living it out, and in that unfolding the horizon of transcendence is immeasurably enlarged. In the always unanticipated opening beyond the mundane we are given a glimpse of the God whose absence makes the world without him both possible and impossible.

Over the course of the chapters that follow, *The Invisible Source of Authority* eschews extended analysis of texts and the attendant scholarly debates. It takes its cue from the early modern figures who saw that the meditative glimpse could grasp more in passing than even the most extended discourses could hope to comprehend. Without adopting an aphoristic style, it nevertheless begins to approach it in the form of meditations that concede what scholarly convention tends to overlook. The question of the meaning of the secular age cannot exclude the thinker who raises it or the scholar who grapples with it. Canons of scholarly objectivity retain all of their validity, but they do not exhaust the imperative from which they are derived. Only those who have pledged a personal allegiance to truth can invoke the authoritativeness toward which scholarship aspires. But that implies a more than scholarly commitment. Perhaps without realizing, we have begun to pledge our very selves in the task. Scholarship about the individuals and texts touched on remains indispensable, but the existential disposition from which it is derived holds a priority. That cannot be examined or verified but only glimpsed in passing. A meditative unfolding of what is already present, as it is in an aphorism, holds the best hope of disclosing how a secular age should think about itself. Without ceasing to be secular, it must heighten its awareness of the presuppositions from which its scholarship lives. Only by way of a meditation can it discern clearly that the intellectual disciplines available are insufficient for its self-understanding. That is the turning point in which the present essay reaches the transparency at which it aims. To think about God is to stand within the truth that is synonymous with the viewpoint of God.

CHAPTER TWO

The Spiritual Escapes Us

Things are not what they seem. Even if it is only in unguarded moments, we sense the uncanniness of the moment through which we are gliding. Everything is passing and nothing lasts, it all seems to say. Sometimes we are overwhelmed by the burden of the realization that nothing remains or matters. "Everything is permitted" echo the great nihilists of our age. Yet we cannot fully accept that desolate conclusion. Somehow somewhere the incalculable endures, and we can endure too if only we hold onto it. We must not let emptiness pervade and define our existence. It is not true that we are a mere clump of atoms bound to a temporary identity that spins for a few brief years on a planet in empty space. We are not over and done with in the instant we are alive. No, there is more to us, we cry out, than all that can be said about us. Beyond the description of our occupation or social role, beyond what an obituary or a biography may catalog, there is me. I am, over and above it all, as what cannot be quantified or counted. There is that one irreducible shaft of infinity within a world crushingly finite. At the very least, I am the moment that has been able to contemplate it and in that, at last, have transcended its limits. But is that enough to say that I have a soul? How can we find a way back to the hope that seemed to sustain our ancestors that something far greater awaits? Is faith possible in a world without faith?

Ghosts Haunting Matter

Perhaps the very sense that we matter more than we do is the greatest illusion of all. We have learned to be skeptical about the self-importance human beings desperately attach to themselves. Is it credible that we alone are significant in the vast universe? That we are the goal of evolution and not merely a way station on its journey? How can it be that with me reality comes to a halt so astonishingly that it surpasses everything else? Am I the one without whom the whole cannot go on? Only the little circle of family and friendship seems to suggest as much. They mourn our passing in a way the rest of the world can only formally register. We are not missed by the companies for which we work, although they pay polite lip service to our irreplaceability. It will not delay them in securing our replacements. The same is true for the businesses that will find other customers and the governments that will find other taxpayers. Everything about that great public world seems to shout our inconsequentiality. They may count individuals. They may even count on individuals. But as individuals we definitely do not count. How then can we hang onto that first precious assurance of our parents that we are alone all that matters in the universe? Everything else attests to our expendability. We are cogs that play a part in great collaborative enterprises but, like any ball bearing, unmissed when we are worn out and replaced by another. There is nothing of transcending importance about you, it all screams. Of course, you are free to carry the illusion that you are the indispensable one even while you play your anonymous part. Mass marketing and mass culture approach you only in the homogeneous vista of big data. Their task is made all the easier if you fail to see the extent of their indifference to you personally. We forget that Facebook does not know your face, nor does the phone company remember your number. As a result we seem to inhabit two universes simultaneously. To those who love us, we are everything; to the rest, we are insignificant nothings. Small wonder we have difficulty navigating between these different worlds. The artificial glamour of celebrity can strike us as more real than the daily grind of our own lives.

Yet only rarely do we fall for the fake. We still want to live our own lives, knowing they are nowhere near as glittering as the manufactured alternative. Truth remains in that much smaller world of those who know us personally, as persons. There we find affirmed what we cannot discover anywhere else. You are the center of the universe, each glance and smile seems to say. Right now you are all that matters. It is as if the cosmic vastness has condensed into the instant in which we meet as persons, that is, inwardly. For that brief moment, space and time melt away as we inhabit a space and a time outside of them. We are not creatures of this material world but spiritual beings whose origin and goal are unmistakably different. We move like ghosts through an earthly realm that cannot have any permanent hold on us. Each meeting with another, each moment of intimacy shared in inwardness is a definitive revelation. We are not what we appear to be, nor are we what we often casually take ourselves and others to be. Nothing external or quantifiable can contain us. The customers have left the building, the online traffic has departed, because they were never really there. It was an illusion that we were present in any of it. More than all that is done is the doer, who has eluded the mask before the face. We know what it means to be a person. We are invisible, while visibility is all we present to the world that appears to contain us. Uncanniness seems to be our most pervasive feature.

We are homeless in a world where nothing seems to affirm who we most deeply are. There can be no doubt about our transcendence of all that is finite because we live so thoroughly within it. Nothing contains who we are since we escape every container. This is so intimate a part of our self-awareness that it is virtually identical with it. Philosophers and neuroscientists may puzzle about the "problem" of consciousness, but we, who are conscious, know it with certainty. What could be less problematic than the transcendence of beings who can contemplate their own transcendence? The so-called problem of mind arises only when we ask how conscious beings can inhabit a physical brain. Meanwhile there is not the slightest difficulty in thinking itself. Consciousness is its own activity, absolutely irreducible to what it is conscious of. Otherwise we would be incapable of consciousness. Nothing explains it since it is the possibility of all explanation. If there was a problem in consciousness as such, then of course there would be no possibility of addressing its "problem." The puzzle of its relationship to the brain is quite different from the relationship of consciousness to itself. In the latter area all that matters is that we are conscious and not unconscious. Otherwise we are merely talking about the relationship of two very different dimensions. It all becomes an irresolvable puzzle only when we refuse to admit that they are distinct realities and insist that they must be reducible to one.[1] Mind must somehow be matter. But this odd perspective only arises because we cannot conceive of what it means to be a spirit, despite the fact that we are spiritual through and through. Indeed it is essential that we remain completely immaterial if we are to tackle the consciousness problem at all. Uncanniness has given way to disorientation.

The spiritual escapes us even when we are engaged in the most spiritual activities. It is not only conceptually that we fall into confusion, for something similar afflicts us as we enter upon the great events of our lives. Getting married, for example, can be a very expensive affair. It's so costly that there's a whole wedding industry devoted to maximizing expenditure on the event. Everyone gets paid, except the two people on whom it depends most completely. The bride and groom cannot pay one another, or be paid by anyone else, because to do so would undermine the meaning of the vows they exchange. One cannot get married unless one receives and gives freely. Commercialization may touch many aspects of the celebration, but it cannot contaminate its core. The most important element cannot be bought. It must be freely given by persons who have definitively departed the economy of exchange. Their reciprocity exceeds all reciprocity, for it is unconditional. In giving and receiving their very selves, they attest to their inescapably spiritual reality. Without inner self-giving no quantity of exterior gifts can accomplish the result. One is only wed if one has freely surrendered oneself and received the other in the same moment. If there is a defect in the marriage contract it is not traceable to any material lack but lies in the innermost core. The spirit is everything. It contains the whole reality, including the partners who bestow themselves on one another. We invest it with as much material opulence as we can afford because we are incapable of signaling transcendence of materiality in any other way. It is what the economists call "efficient waste."

But that is just another way of conceding that the language of materiality fails when it seeks to encompass the spiritual. It is as if we cannot look directly at what concerns us most centrally. We can only distract ourselves with busy talk and tasks that make up such an occasion and yet fail to say what is most crucial about it. At best we catch a sideways glimpse of what is uttermost. In passing through the material, we intimate the immaterial. Perhaps the only trace of the spiritual is the air of solemnity in which the events are enacted. That most indefinable element, spirit, has imparted itself to the visible actions and transactions. Yet it is only visible to those who are touched by the same spirit. Spirit knows spirit, and that is the only way it can be known. Everything else has proclaimed its unreality. This is why even people who are nonreligious, often avowedly atheistic and secular, seek to endow the major turning points of their lives with sacramental significance. Births, marriages, and deaths, they declare, are about more than their mundane components. Here, if nowhere else, transcendence has erupted. Jürgen Habermas recounts his attendance at a church funeral service for an atheist, which he regards as an appropriate reflection of our historical moment.[2] Even a secular age cannot entirely dispense with the spirituality that must accompany us into that other realm. The discrepancy between our intimations and our conceptualizations could hardly be greater. Yet it does not mount to a conflict because it has been publicly conceded. In admitting that we are in contradiction with ourselves, perhaps we have even begun to overcome it. This is the signal importance of the concession of a secular intellectual, like Habermas, that we have now entered upon a "post-secular age."[3] The era of the secular is over as we have come to acknowledge its incapacity to account for who we are. The spiritual still eludes us, but we have begun to take note of its absence.

This is in marked contrast to an earlier phase of modernity that insisted on the obsolescence of spirit. Of course, even then such an assertion could not be maintained without providing a substitute spirituality for what had been so totally rejected. The irony of militantly atheistic regimes that insist on mummifying their founder in a mausoleum and deifying their leaders within a new pantheon, as well as the mass hysteria of mourning accompanying their departure, was never lost on careful observers.[4] The quasi-religious character of the spectacles of Fascism, Nazism, and Communism has given rise to the well known category of political religions. It is just that the irony was never permitted to penetrate the regimes themselves. The atheistic exterior could not be touched by the perverse spirituality within them. They could not see that the goal toward which they struggled by means of violence and terror could not be achieved in that coercive way. Ideological movements of spiritual negation attested to the enduring hold of the spirit upon them. Even when they sought to shake the awareness most decisively, it returned to haunt them even more thoroughly. As a result, doggedly atheistic regimes gave powerful evidence of the transcendent fervor that still animates political societies. Theocracies do not always believe in God. What they do show, however, is that the spirit can only be eradicated spiritually. That is, it cannot be eradicated. We may be inclined to think that the spiritual escapes us, but they attest to its inexorability. That which cannot be killed discloses its durability.[5] If the attempt to remove it assumes a spiritual form, even if that form is derivative, the life by which it lives is real. Perverse spirituality remains a spirituality, and it is this that explains the formidable power of ideological movements.

Spirituality endures most powerfully when it aims at its own elimination. Perhaps this is what the elusiveness of spirit really signals. As that which is *not*, spirit prevails within a world constructed on what is. In the reign of being, spirit transcends being. Now we begin to understand why spirit has survived within our materially self-defined world. Not only does it escape material incorporation, but it is precisely its uncontainability that is its central feature. Spirit does not elude us; it is the process of elusion. It has been said that spirit is only the trace of what is not, or the trace of itself, or simply the trace. But that metaphor too readily suggests that it is no more, although, as a trace, it is not what has performed the tracing. The accent of reality falls on what remains rather than what has evanesced, and it is that surpassing quality that is decisive. Spirit is not the minimal level of reality but its maximum. Compared to it, the trace as material remainder has only a diminished existence. Spirit is not that which is least in being but that which contains being and is therefore uncontainable. It is reality in the most eminent sense. Considerable effort is required to hold onto the notion that mind is the fullest reality and not what mind apprehends in front of it. Too often the effort is defeated by the well-intentioned models drawn from materiality itself. Then spirit is assimilated to a higher, more refined matter, just what a spirit, a breath, is supposed to be. The shock is to discover that it is more primordial still. Before anything *is* there is the transcendence that grasps it. Spirit does not have being at all. It is before all being. This is its transcendence. The advantage of a secular age is that it has so thoroughly discredited all compromised spiritualities. It will have no transcendent substitute, or it will have the real thing. This is the deep longing we sense in our contemporaries. Religion may have faded, but its spiritual thirst remains. A secular spirituality is one purged of all false spirits. Having dismissed all metaphors, it can only hold out for the truth. That is the astonishing realization that the transcendence of spirit is most at home in a world that can find no room for it. It can only exist as transcendence.

Uncanniness has reached its limit and overcome itself. Spirit is at home in the secular and finds the secular as its home. The interesting consequence is that the secular is then at home with itself. It is no longer "post-secular," a term that implies the confusion from which all *post-* suffixes arise. Now the secular can understand itself as secular. That is, as it has always been, as what has been withdrawn from service to the sacred.[6] It is secularized. Without the sacred the secular has no point of reference by which to apprehend itself. This is why it has so often succumbed to the pressure to reoccupy the space vacated by the disappearance of the sacred.[7] From a truly secular perspective, the sacred cannot disappear. The quasi-religiosity of the ideological movements, especially the militancy of their rejection of God, had always assumed the form of what they opposed. But now they need no longer embrace the agonistic pose. This may be what Habermas's "post-secular" moniker intimates at the deepest level. Now all that remains are the vestiges of the great conflict between science and religion still reverberating in our "new atheists." They have yet to discover the truth of Marx's observation that within a secular age "atheism has become impossible in practice."[8] Marx may not have grasped the full implications of his declaration, but he too had an uncanny ability to evoke the uncanny. The anti-theism on which his own conviction rested could not be sustained if it should attain its fulfillment. Such surmises flickered at the edges of his thought without being fully confronted. For us the situation is quite different. We live in a time, not when the secularizing tendencies have reached their apogee, but when they have glimpsed their exhaustion. We can see more clearly that there never really was a secular world, that it depended on a world of faith it could not abandon without also losing what defined it.

Spirit Prevails through Loss, Most of All

We are at the stage when the secular points decisively to what it cannot contain. We are post-secular in the sense of having left the secular world behind. The only problem is how to understand that other dimension that seems to be present solely by way of absence. Spirit, I have said, is that which has transcended. How then can it be manifest? Most importantly, how can it be manifest in a way that avoids the millennial distortion by which it is assimilated once again to the form of the present?[9] Can spirit be known as spirit and not as a refined materiality? Ironically, the prospects for a breakthrough are better in a secular age than almost any other because the spiritual is so clearly what surpasses. The evidence is abundantly on display if we consider the secular world, not as failing to fulfill our spiritual longings, but as calling attention to its own incapacity. Money cannot buy happiness. But was that ever its purpose? Happiness is not on sale anywhere, and it cannot be ordered online. The best we get is stuff we may temporarily confuse with happiness itself. Clever advertisers continually hint that their products deliver more, but they cannot be accused of breach of contract for what they carefully avoid including in it. They can deliver a new TV, but neither they nor we mistake it for happiness. Not even the largest retailers have a division that supplies happiness, no matter how much their gadgets and trinkets may imply it. Happiness is not a product. It cannot be purchased even from the most assiduous seller. In the words of a commercial society, we get what we pay for, and neither seller nor buyer has expended sufficiently to gain what is priceless. Both are stuck within the bounds of an economy confined to the continuous exchange of things. What cannot be exchanged is rightly excluded from it. Under the rules of the economy everything can be bought, except what must be given. The gift shines splendidly and unattainably beyond it.

It is not just happiness that cannot be bought, but everything that is really of value. All that cannot be priced is withheld from the realm of price. No regulatory enforcement is required. The law of supply and demand is defeated by the abundance that overwhelms it. Generosity is not subject to any law, because it consists in going beyond all that may be required.[10] It is not that the spiritual kingdom is not at home in a material world but that it at every turn exceeds its boundaries. Survival of the fittest means nothing when one gives one's life for another.[11] It is an enduring testament to the loss of the fittest or at least of those who are prepared to lose the most. This is not to judge the mundane realm by higher standards than ordinarily prevail within it. Competition is not just an option to be pursued, but may define our responsibility, if we are managing a business or a sports team. We cannot simply let the other side win. But it is to acknowledge that winning isn't everything. Only losing is everything, and the greatest defeat is the greatest victory. The struggle for survival, for the tangible reward of material gains, for money or power, is not unworthy. It is simply not the most worthy. We know this not from profit and loss statements but from nonaudited truth. The only scale of measurement is the immeasurable. We can live in a world of economic rationality because we know that we do not live in such a world. To measure things in economic terms, we must already stand outside of them. Not everything can be bought and sold, least of all the buyers and sellers themselves and all that is most indispensable to them. Everything else can be dispensed with, can be exchanged and commodified, but not what lies beyond them. The condition of the possibility of a market is that it is transcended by what cannot be marketed. The spirituality of the market may be a strange expression since it seems so obsessed with the generation of material wealth. What other kind is there, we might be inclined to ask? But in reality we know that markets themselves could not exist without the integrity that underpins them. That is their real wealth.[12]

We do of course give a customary nod to honesty and trust as virtues that are essential to the proper functioning of markets. Business scandals are followed by predictable demands for more ethics in business. Tighter regulation may even be proposed as the only way of policing markets that will not police themselves. Overlooked in the headlong rush to judgment is the realization that integrity and honesty are not extraneous factors to be imposed on unruly markets but the very meaning of markets as such. As cooperative enterprises between human beings they do not simply depend on the level of virtue we bring to them. They are exercises in virtue themselves. We do not become honest and then decide to sell automobiles or soda. Rather honesty is one of the consequences of a process of open exchange between buyer and seller. Sharp dealers not only fail to survive, but they fail to make money, except in the short run. Purveyors of Ponzi schemes make a quick profit, but they cannot hold onto it. They are punished more swiftly and surely in the subsequent collapse than any court order could inflict. Recent financial crises are not the result of greed; they are the result of greed insufficiently aware of the conditions for its own satisfaction. The titans of Wall Street lost billions because they failed to recognize the most elementary principle of human cooperation. One must think of how one's actions will affect others. The most successful company is the one that puts the interests of its customers ahead of its own. Adam Smith's famous depiction of private profit as the force that constitutes markets only describes the transaction from the outside.[13] While actually engaged in exchange, the parties must accommodate one another before they turn a profit. The invisible hand is a metaphor for what after all is invisible. We see the gain that each walks away with, but we miss the mutuality they have thereby created. Smith was most impressed by the amazing coordination, surpassing the capacity for the most minute planning, that the market disclosed. But is not the inner coordination of sentiment its most impressive outcome? Certainly, suppliers and consumers have learned to combine their interests, but this means that they have really coordinated their sympathies. They know they need one another.[14]

Markets are spiritual communities all the way down. We behold great quantities of merchandise plying across the oceans, but we know that nothing would move out there without a prior movement within. Every container signals a mutual containment of minds. And beyond the specific transaction each of them represents is the far broader and deeper relationship that is ongoing. No one wants to be a seller once but to return again. Sometimes buyers and sellers even become friends in the course of that steady contact with one another, but this is only a recognition of a readiness for friendship that is there from the start. We cannot easily go to war with countries with whom we trade, nor can we treat them with impoliteness. Prejudice and discrimination have no place, not because merchants are saints, but because they are in contact with people. But is this only the appearance of virtue and not the real thing? Is there a point at which participants in the market are prepared to subordinate and even sacrifice their self-interest for the common good? Would anyone die for the phone company?[15] Hardly, if it was only the phone company for which one died. But if it was something more for which the phone company stood, then it would be different. Normally the market does not call upon us to make such an ultimate sacrifice, only that we yield preference to the other over ourselves. Yet it is not impossible for such moments of high drama to arise. They occur when responsibility for the common good has become imperative. By remaining true to our word, refusing to sell bonds we know to be worthless, we will be wiped out financially.[16] Obviously not everyone takes the higher road on that day, but those who do demonstrate an inescapable truth. The rectitude of markets derives from the rectitude of those who keep their word. Without it the market evaporates. Just as we saw at the time when global financial exchanges virtually seized up, the disappearance of trust is the disappearance of markets.[17] On that occasion it was the residue of trust remaining in governments that sustained them. Ordinarily markets rely on the great reservoir of goodness in their ordinary participants. Each must be ready to lose rather than undermine it.

Ethics is not an extrinsic aspect but the real capital on which markets depend. Punishment to wrongdoers may be swift in regard to individual malefactors, but that would not be possible without the innumerable honest participants who place the good of the whole ahead of their own short-term gains. Not only is virtue a prerequisite for markets; it is their reality. Without it they simply would not exist. This is why virtue cannot simply be seen as an incidental or extraneous feature. We might say that over and above what markets produce, that vast panoply of goods and services they generate, is the community of virtue that they constitute and that constitutes them.[18] This does not mean that every participant in the market is virtuous and that there are no cabals of criminality. It is simply to assert that markets would not function in the absence of that modicum of virtue that sustains them. Aristotle thought that economics is outside of politics, the part of household management that secures the means of household subsistence. What he did not consider is the extent to which the economy too is a moral reality and therefore properly culminates in the self-understanding that constitutes political community. The latter is principally a moral community since it exists for the sake of the good life. But that is also what characterizes the economic community bound together as a market. It only has the appearance of a coordination of private interests, but, as Hegel noted, that would not be possible unless it were first a moral community as well.[19] The truth of the market is not private profit or economic growth but the common sense of right by which it is constituted. It is like the political community, only without the full self-disclosure of its character. That is both its weakness and its strength, for it pays less attention to its sustaining virtues but also remains less vulnerable to their subversion.

Work Liberates Spirit

In the end the economy escapes the logic of economics. Instrumental rationality does not define our world, for it must be continually overturned. Almost everything we do must be regarded as an end-in-itself, otherwise it will fail to serve its purpose. Making hamburgers may be a task that can be broken down to a mechanical process, but to do it well still requires doing it more than mechanically. Of course, that is much more the case with really good cooking. The purpose, whether it is pleasing a customer, earning a tip, or winning a prize, must be forgotten. A good cook serves nothing other than the food itself. The cook's task is to bring out its inner perfection, to make it the best it can be. Being paid or winning approval is incidental to that process. Persons put themselves into the task in such a way that they proclaim there is more to what they do than what they do.[20] The spirit they bring to the work shows that the activity has been spiritualized. They have gone beyond what is required in order to accomplish what is required. It is not just monks who have made work a prayer. That is what all genuine work demands. Rather than a subordination of oneself in the service of matter, one has demonstrated an unmistakable transcendence of what merely is. The dialectic of master and slave, as Hegel explained, overturns the Greek disdain for all menial labor.[21] We may be compelled by the necessity of our nature to undertake the effort of work, but we cannot complete it without transforming it into free labor. All work thus escapes economic necessity in its fundamental character.

For that reason payment must occur outside of the service performed.[22] Everyone who works knows that this is its secret. Initial reluctance must be overcome by persevering in the task up to that point where we find ourselves carried forward by its momentum. Work has become pleasant. The satisfaction to be derived from the most menial task proclaims our liberation.[23]

We do not live in the humdrum routine but have, at least briefly, floated above it. This is even more the case when the tasks in which we are engaged are spiritual in their nature. Nothing worth doing can be done well if we simply go through the motions. The violin cannot be played simply by hitting the notes. It must be made to sing, to soar into the realm where music is released. Singing does not remind us of the spiritual. It is spiritual and can only be engaged in to the extent we have departed from the physical. This is one of the reasons that sports play such a big role in our lives. Even if we don't play baseball, we catch just a little of the exhilaration of the crack of the bat that sends the ball over the fences. It is not just the ball that has rocketed into the ether. We are there too. To call this an aesthetic experience is only half right because it goes beyond mere sensations. Ball and bat have become the means of an ascent beyond what can be seen and sensed. Materiality has been spiritualized. To play the game well is to understand that it is all about the moment in which we leave this world behind. Sport is not a substitute for religion. It is a form of religion because it is a form of ascent.[24] The pain, the expenditure, the struggle and all that is endured make sense as just what is demanded as the cost of spirit. Of course, we know that it is a business, but neither the players nor the fans can permit themselves to think about that when they are at the game. So long as they are playing it, they have left all tawdry considerations behind. The romance of the game is not a mere by-product. It is what the game is about and what the business must serve if it is really to stay in business. Like music, also often termed an industry, it cannot be about the money. Money cannot make music, nor can contracts supply home runs. Only spirit can deliver on the promise of spirit. Making money is a necessary requisite, but it can never be confused with the point of it all.

Yet we routinely slip back into the materialistic pattern of thinking that suggests that all we do is for the sake of being paid. The benefits of science are often extolled as the reason for supporting it, although there would be no benefits without the willingness to pursue knowledge that has no benefits. The Hubble and Webb telescopes and the Large Hadron Collider are massive investments in service to the strictly nonutilitarian.

Alfred Nobel's famous prizes are a reward for those who do not care about rewards. They have dedicated their lives to knowing what we can about the world in which we live, for they are our contemporary ascetics of the spirit. The idea of giving cash to someone who has already demonstrated it is of no significance to them is one of the great ironies of the prizes. Awards honor the awarder rather than the awardee. Besides, what honor can be bestowed on those who have utterly transcended them? A scientist who wished only to gain the plaudits of his fellow scientists would not be a very good one. One who thought that the plaudits of nonscientists were of any value would be risible. Only a world that knows very little about the nature of science would offer such baubles to those who already possess the true treasure. Science does not exist for the sake of anticipated benefits. Strictly speaking, science is only for the sake of science. Even its applications, which can produce a better battery or a better vaccine, require that we set aside every other consideration but whether it will actually work. We surmount our interest in benefits to ask about their truth. It is not that we do not have material incentives, or do not harbor a wish for social approval, but that we are prepared to set them aside for the sake of apprehending the way things really are.

Spirit as the Reality of Freedom

The idea that scientists themselves might just be material beings, that their thoughts are merely brain waves, is surely not one of the "brain waves" of science. If they have transcended the hold of incentives, how can they be defined by electrochemical forces? Thinking, we all know, must be free, otherwise it is not thinking. We are spiritual beings who find spirit itself inconceivable. Only occasionally is that self-forgetfulness shattered and we catch a glimpse of the higher reality we inhabit. Drifting somnolently between pleasure and pain, comfortable in our dreaming and scheming, we are abruptly awakened by the shock of a moral imperative. Now we have no choice. We must reach out to the person who calls to us. Whether it is a child, a spouse, or a neighbor in need, a weight of cosmic consequence has been placed upon me. I am the responsible one, the one who cannot shift responsibility to any other. This is not a moment indifferently passing by like all the others. This one is different. It is not even a moment, for all of time has suddenly condensed into that knot when the entire fate of reality is being decided. What happens now will last forever.[25] I cannot disavow it by saying it was another time and another place and, besides, I was another person. No, now everything has suddenly contracted into the now. We are at the still point of the turning world, the moment of decision that decides everything. Am I to choose good or evil? Who I am to be is being decided. I hold my whole existence in my hands and not only mine, but the option between good and evil as a whole. On my choice hangs the irrevocable preference that pervades it all. I am in the role of Adam and Eve. Original sin begins with me or is defeated by me. Immanuel Kant said that in choosing an action we also choose the principle implicit in it. I make universal law, he suggested. But he did not think about the awesome responsibility of such a lawgiver. If I give the law, then somehow I am outside of it. I too am eternal. Intuitively we sense the enormity of our moral decisions. We decide on behalf of ourselves and the whole world and forget that now we have become the point from which moral judgment pervades the cosmos.[26]

We know about the judgment of God because we sense we are already located within it. Through our moral freedom we legislate for the universe as a whole. There is no such thing as my private action, whether good or bad, that affects only me personally. John Stuart Mill's famous harm principle, that there is a fundamental difference between actions that affect me and actions that affect others, does not quite hold.[27] Intuitively we know that what we do affects all others even though we may not be able to trace the links. It adds to or detracts from the sum total of good in the universe. I bear a surpassing responsibility. That is what is decisive. But like Mill, we cannot quite find a way of articulating it other than to insist that no one else is entitled to interfere with my liberty, except to prevent a comparable denial of the liberty of others. We know it without being able to explain it. Lacking the language of spirit, we can only say that liberty marks the boundary of our being. It is what must not be breached for to do so would be to negate what is most true about us, that is, that we are what cannot be compelled because to do so would be to deny who we are. Without saying "spirit," we insist on the primordial freedom of spirit. As that which contains its own existence, as the being that decides what it is going to be, and therefore is before it becomes, there can be no interference with the freedom from which it unfolds itself. I cannot be if I cannot be free, was Mill's deepest conviction, but he could not articulate it without justifying its utility in the advance of progress.[28] Yet without spirit, freedom could not arise from itself. It could not therefore be free, just as progress would have to be something other than progress in freedom. But Mill's contradictions are not just his. What makes them of interest is that they are ours too.

We forget that only a spirit could be interested in its freedom. The closest we get to an account is when we approach it obliquely at the point where we are tempted to abandon our freedom. Make us contented slaves, we are inclined to blurt. Let government or someone else take care of us as the strain has become too much to support. What saves us from that abyss is the whiff of self-contempt that unmistakably arises within us. We know that to turn our back on liberty would be the deepest betrayal of who we are. We are not made to be wards without the wit to take care of themselves. The idea that we could belong to anyone else, no matter how benevolent, simply appalls us. It would be to sink below the human level, to become an unthinking beast. As beings who are limitlessly self-aware, we must remain our own masters. There is nothing that comes before us, to whose control we must submit. If we accept the divine guidance we do so as free beings, that is, as beings who must consent to such obedience. Human beings can only submit freely, otherwise they submit in the way that stones submit to gravity. We certainly do not want to receive others, whether in marriage or in citizenship, except by means of their free self-donation. Any other contract is not a contract. Neither in heaven nor on earth is there anything that can bind us but ourselves. From the perspective of heaven and earth that is the only kind of binding worth having.

Nothing else in creation is capable of binding itself in that way. This does not of course mean that we are free to bind ourselves to anything we wish. We are not free to throw away our freedom as if it had no value, for it is already constituted by the pull of what makes freedom of value. We could not be free without knowing the touch of the higher reality that is the source of our freedom. We are not its source. Our freedom consists in listening to the voice of freedom that comes to us from elsewhere. We are of course free to disregard its call and go our own way. But that does not eradicate the call itself for it continues to reach out to us. Our freedom, it turns out, is the freedom to respond to the obligation freedom imposes on us. We would not be responsible if we were not free. What we thought was ours, that inalienable capacity to determine ourselves, is not really ours. It has already been spoken for before we have even spoken. We are bound to those for whom we are responsible before we have been asked to respond. This is the interchangeability of responsibility and freedom that defines our existence. While nothing compels us, we are, for that very reason, even more deeply compelled. What could be a more powerful constraint than the one that is most deeply ingrained in us? Nothing in the physical world can match its hold. The fortress within is more impregnable than any granite fastness. The triumph of spirit over matter is what our freedom abundantly proclaims. We are always free to refuse its call, for we are free, but we are not free not to hear, for hearing is identical with freedom itself. In obligation we are free.[29]

Spirit as the Economy of the Selfless

The problem is that we are ill prepared for the "enlargement of the heart" that freedom holds out to us.[30] Accustomed to the mode of a material universe, we become the consummate consumers. Ours is an acquisitive society where success is measured by our capacity to obtain what we want. Freedom, we think, is the instrument that gives us mastery over things. All that limits our freedom must be removed, either through the expenditure of our own efforts or through the collective resources of society as a whole. Money is the most universal means of ensuring the satisfaction of needs and desires. This is the putative purpose of the modern economy whose goal is the generation and accumulation of wealth. We work for a living and then find ourselves living in order to work. Productivity becomes the measure of worth rather than the producers themselves. "Alienation" was the term Marx used to identify that indelible discontent with a scheme in which what is produced takes priority over those who produce it.[31] Human beings have been lost in a process originally developed to serve them. Marx attributed the failure to class divisions, but its real source lies much deeper. Even the capitalists, he conceded, have lost themselves in the profit motive. If anything, they are even more alienated for they scarcely recognize it in themselves. A fundamental inversion occurs when freedom is directed toward the attainment of goals that are only material. Freedom no longer serves freedom itself. We have lost our freedom. How could it be retained when it was placed in the service of mere wants and desires? Rather than master them, we submit to their mastery. No amount of talk about freedom can disguise the fatal misstep in which having took priority over being.

It is the contradiction that lies at the heart of an economy that exalts freedom but compels work. We are free to choose anything we want but only so long as we do not choose to be idle.[32] Working and consuming are the treadmill on which we turn. The contradiction between freedom and necessity cannot be broken so long as we have allowed ourselves to be defined by it. Somehow the path to the world of spirit must be recovered. But that means confronting the realization that even embodied spirits are ultimately defined by transcendence rather than physicality. Just as we cannot be free in part, so we cannot be spiritual in part. At some point we must face the limit of all embodiment. Do we have what it takes to surpass physical existence? This does not mean that we turn our backs on the material world with all of its fascinating possibilities of development. Nor does it mean that we can expect human beings to attain the mastery that would release them into a wholly spiritual state. It is only to admit that it is that challenge that most defines us. We may not live up to it, indeed we may be incapable of meeting it, but we cannot deny its primacy. More than anything else, it is a question of the truth about human beings. Are they cogs in the wheel of material production, efficient consumers of what they efficiently produce? Or are they utterly incapable of absorption within the process from which they have emerged? Is spirit forever forgotten, or do we acknowledge its hold on us? If it is the latter, then we are set inexorably on a path from which we cannot step aside. We may not reach its end, but we remain within its journey. Before any talk of fulfillment there must first be recognition of the goal. For now that may be all that can be achieved. We have become clear about who we are. Spirit is the reality on which we will not turn our backs.

Spirit is indeed the process of the return to spirit. Having wandered away from ourselves, having become alienated, we find our way back by means of what can never be lost. How can we lose what we never had or could only hold by giving it away? The laws of logic, like the laws of physics, no longer apply. There is neither limit nor proportion nor measure to what is immeasurable. Dimly we sense this as we count our entitlements while behind it all is the generosity that dispenses itself freely. Total loss is total gain. That is what we intuited while we struggled to comprehend it. Nothing in our world provides a model for an expenditure without return. Everything has been made to serve a purpose. So what are we to make of that which transcends purpose? Gratuitousness is the opening onto another realm. Sometimes we catch a glimpse of it as we see that beyond the daily round of giving and taking is the gift itself. All possibility arises from what is beyond it, from what is impossible. That is the freedom of the gift in which spirit dwells.[33] Transaction arises from what cannot be transacted. It is simply given. Giver and receiver may not even be disclosed, but giving is. This is the epiphany of what is beyond epiphany because it makes all epiphany possible. What cannot be said and what cannot be given are contained in giving itself. The impossible has transpired. It is the advent of spirit. Materiality contains what it cannot contain because it has become the vehicle of spirit. Loss is gain, and total loss is the occasion of total gain. This is the curious arc on which a secular society turns. Not only does it raise the question of spirit even more loudly, but it provides the occasion for its definitive disclosure. Most of all, spirit arises within a material age. It is ripe for the self-sacrifice that is spirit.

This is the complete outpouring of self for which Marx called. Shattering the economy of the self, we leap into the economy of the selfless. We embrace "the association in which the free development of each is the condition for the free development of all."[34] Communism is the truth of capitalism. This does not mean that communism is the future toward which capitalism is headed, as Marx thought. It is that communism is the innermost longing of a capitalist economy, the point at which it puts the welfare of human beings ahead of the profits and commodities they produce. Marx himself gave voice to that deepest contradiction. A system of cooperation is in conflict with itself so long as it prioritizes what it does over those who do it. Modern work may integrate man and machine, but it cannot afford to identify them. Human beings are not machines. They are spirits, the great "materialist" declares. But having deprived himself of the language of spirit, Marx could not express his own spiritual vision. Religion is merely the ineffectual "cry of the oppressed creature, the soul of a soulless condition."[35] Its aspiration must be reached through a violent revolution that will overthrow the existing order of the world. From the ashes the new spiritual community will arise. Absent is an awareness of its utter impossibility. Not only is there no reason to believe that the new order will be markedly less oppressive than the old, but there is absolutely no way of bringing about a spiritual result by a purely physical means. Spirit can only be awakened by spirit. It cannot be forced to yield itself up, for it has always already done so. Self-giving is the reality of spirit. How can we take what has been given? We can only fail to receive its gift, for it cannot be taken. Marx epitomizes the contradiction of a secular world that refuses to recognize the transcendence toward which it so intensely aspires. The violent seek to bear it away, while the wealthy seek to purchase it.

Either way spirit is not to be had so cheaply. It cannot be gained at any price less than the whole self. Neither the weapons nor the resources of a material civilization are sufficient to obtain it. Spirit surpasses all that might be obtained within this world. In that realization we gain the distinct sense that our everyday perspectives have fallen away. We have been living in an unreal world of making and getting but now awake to the possibility of giving as the way. No revolutionary overthrow has occurred, yet the curtain of the existing order has parted. We see what Marx saw but could not recognize within himself. The spiritual community of those who give themselves is the transparence toward which everything strives. We simply mistook material means for what is immaterial, although we would not even be susceptible to the mistake if we did not already live within transcendence. The vision itself attests to its hold on us. Like Marx, we do not live in a material world. The pull of transcendence is inexorable. What we lack is any means of entering upon it. Every step we take, because it is an imposition by the self, is a step away from it. Virtue assails us with the shock of its truth. Now the overwhelming rightness of the good presses itself upon us in a way that is quite different from the utilitarian purpose it is normally assigned. Virtue, we see, is not just a way of mastering the world, but is the flash in which mastery itself is mastered. "Virtue is its own reward," may be a conventional formulation. But here we have left the calculation of reward far behind. What about the virtue that cares nothing for its own comfort or profit? The virtue that leaves itself out of all consideration? The virtue that sees there can be no other virtue? That is the lightning that flashes across our darkness as if it was all in daylight. We may have been ill prepared for its blinding illumination, but we cannot deny its radiance.

Spirit as the Uncontainable Container

The secular world is the world that has been exposed by what utterly escapes it. Spirit is the truth it cannot contain. Our world depends on a community it can do nothing to bring about. The simulacrum of community may be coerced but not its reality. Like friendship, it is genuine only if it is free. Virtue is in this sense not only what eludes all coercion, but what definitively transcends its capacity. Power is rendered powerless by the powerless.[36] That is the astonishing discovery of a world erected on regimes of incentive and discipline. Our methods are incapable of attaining what we desire, for even if they succeed, they rob the value of what is robbed. Virtue is virtue only if it is attained freely. No one can force you to be friends with them, not just because you cannot be coerced, but because you could not be friends on such terms. The astonishing superiority of spirit manifests itself as that which alone is worth having. To identify it by the familiar term "virtue" seems to miss its most radical impact, for it denotes a complete overturning of the scales of significance within the world. As what makes virtue possible, spirit is the transcendence of all merely finite reckoning. However impressive virtue may be in the fidelity, honesty, generosity, and courage it sustains, it is the condition of its possibility that surpasses all conceptualization. How can we imagine what can scarcely be imagined? That a man would lay down his life for another. Such an individual has given tangible proof that he does not belong to this world. Virtue may be seen, but its source seems to have utterly escaped us. This is the elusiveness of spirit we have struggled for millennia to name without success. How can we put a word on what leaves us speechless?

That is what we nevertheless must put into words or ourselves die in the trying. It is only in hazarding a raid on the inarticulate that we pay due reverence to its hold on us. We are preserved by what we cannot preserve. We simply exist within it. Yet that does not leave us without access to its inexhaustible mystery. The luminosity of spirit includes us within its illumination. At no point does spirit withhold itself from us, for it communicates itself unceasingly. That is what spirit is. Seeking nothing it gives all. That is the source of its originary power and the reason that it escapes us. It is not merely that spirit slips the surly bonds by which a secular age seeks to entrap it, but that spirit is the uncontainable as such. In every moment it has escaped because it has given itself. It is such a different order of reality that it exceeds our capacity to assimilate it to that which merely is. Nothing can furnish a suitable likeness since it has gone beyond all of them. Incapable of attachment to self-preservation, spirit has defeated death. Deathlessness is not some future condition to which it aspires but its reality in the present. Spirit cannot die because it is beyond death. How can it be defined by what it has already given away? Inconceivable and unimaginable, spirit is the transcendence of what can be conceived and imagined. It not only escapes us, but is the movement of escape, as that which gives without return. By owning nothing spirit is owned by nothing. But how then can we catch even this fleeting glimpse of spirit that sets us on the impossible errand of proclaiming it? Surely it is because its reality is not so unfamiliar, as the preceding formulations continually indicate. We know spirit because we are touched by it. We participate in its dynamic.

Spirit can be known only by spirit.[37] That is its secret. It is because we are not so completely immersed in the merely present that we have an intimation of what overleaps all presence. The release of spirit from itself is something we glimpse within ourselves. We may not always live on the spiritual plane, our earthbound attachments may hold us more than we would wish, but we cannot fail to sense the inexorable abandonment that calls us. Death itself stands as the final moment of departure from this world. We may not retain a strong sense of a life after it, or if we do, it may be strikingly similar to the life we have left behind. Yet we live in relation to a boundary of transcendence. Even when we have not transcended it, we know about it. This is what makes our existence different from that of everything else we know. We are aware of death. This is why we can die rather than merely slip out of existence. In knowing death, we participate in the deathless. We take our stand outside of it. But where then is that stand? It can only be in the realm of that which exercises the same capacity to go beyond itself. We live unmistakably within spirit. Its reverberations reach us because we are not so completely cut off from its appeal. We are called to go beyond ourselves, to give ourselves away, to pour out our lives. We wish to preserve ourselves but not if it means losing what makes life worth living. Life for us means living beyond life. That is the touch of immortality that reaches into our most elemental reality. For it to become anything more than a vague intimation, for it to confirm our reality as spirit, it must be embraced with a more vital commitment. We must be prepared to stake our lives on it. Then it becomes the lodestar by which we are defined. We leave the limits of this layered material world behind and launch ourselves on the path of the infinite. Spirit no longer escapes us when we have made it our own. The prodigal self-giving of spirit is no longer so mysterious when we cease to calculate our costs and benefits. When there are only costs the benefits become incalculable. The gift that spirit is has become our own when we have embraced the spirit of the gift.

The difficulty has always been for us space-time travelers to visualize what exceeds all visualization, because it is definitively beyond space and time. How can we be present and yet absent at the same time? The language of spirit with its affinity to spiration, breathing, is a vaporization of the physical, not a departure from it. We cannot so easily dispense with images, even as we struggle with their limits. The long spiritual journey of mankind has wrestled continuously with the problem and has developed various strategies of accommodation. We know that the self and the soul are not things in the same way as my shoes and my hat are. Depictions of the afterlife are premised on the awareness of a distinctly different mode of existence to this life.[38] But all of that nuanced understanding of spirituality as another mode of being could no longer make its way when the constrained viewpoint of science began to dominate. This is a world that is material all the way down. There is no room for spirit when external causality explains everything. Science has gained its astonishing foothold by refusing to entertain any other mode of explanation. Purely physical accounts are all that we have, and we cannot conceive of any other. That self-imposed contraction even blocks the understanding of science itself. How is it possible for there to be in the universe an entity capable of comprehending it? That there is a being so detached that it can be set apart from all that affects it for the sake of reaching the truth? How can there be truth without self-transcendence? Amnesia seems to have reached its limit when we have forgotten what makes thinking possible. Yet it can never become total, for we remember that we have forgotten. Spirit may have escaped us, but it has not vanished. It is still there in the mode of what has escaped. This is why it cannot ultimately escape. The cosmos may not have a place for mind, as Thomas Nagel observed, but that thought is already its return.[39] Our challenge today, a challenge as great as any of those that science confronts, is to find a way of acknowledging the spirituality of science. Hitherto the language of spirit has been tied too unreflectively to what is present. Now it must recognize the extent to which spirit too is an attempt to name what escapes all naming. The language of spirit must partake of the transcendence of spirit.

CHAPTER THREE

Symbols Hide What They Say

To say that spirit is absent from our secular age may seem inaccurate. After all, religion appears to retain a robust vitality. Despite its recurrent dismissal as an illusion without a future, the rumor of its demise often appears to have been exaggerated. Globally religion may even seem to be on the ascendant. At the very least, affirmations of faith have undergone periodic rejuvenations and revivals that demonstrate an impressive durability. Believers will not go gently into the good night of secularism. Even when it assumes the form of fundamentalism, or clothes itself in the garb of militant defensiveness, religion attests to the tenacity of its appeal. Martyrdom we have long known is one of the ways of planting its seed. Even the willingness to confront the challenges of an encroaching secularism, to reaffirm its convictions, is evidence of a spirit that is far from defunct.[1] We live, in other words, not in a secular world, but in a world where secular and religious live side by side. Occasional intemperance may erupt, but the accommodation is generally peaceful. Expressions of mutual respect are not uncommon, as epitomized by the Ratzinger-Habermas exchange, as well as the multiple forms of humanitarian cooperation that draw on the resources of believers and nonbelievers alike. A readiness to put aside our differences, whether between religions or across the secular divide, evinces an impressive convergence where conflict had historically prevailed.[2] All that is missing is the conceptual framework that admits both points of view, for without a genuinely sympathetic understanding, such displays of goodwill are often empty gestures. They mask the chasm that exists between elite opinion that is abidingly secular and an increasingly beleaguered religious majority unable to make its case in the public arena. Believers are not necessarily at war with their age, nor is the latter bent on their eradication. They simply live in a condition of mutual incomprehension.

Religion as Obstacle to Faith

Often there appears to be no common ground. Sacred and secular exclude one another so completely that they only meet when one side or another gains dominance. At occasional stages of this debate various intermediates have been proposed as the meeting place they both share, but that integration has proved elusive. It is not enough to favor the role of reason or nature, for they too must be comprehended within the more overarching horizons of spirit or matter. Is reason spiritual? Is nature material? Can either of them stand apart from that which makes them possible? The standoff has not so much been resolved as transferred to another plane. The tension between the twin poles of our existence, absorption in physical life and inextinguishable transcendence, cannot finally be denied. We live at that juncture and cannot cede final victory to either side. The problem is that the intersection of the timeless with time is present in neither of the antipodes. We do not live in eternity, but, equally, we cannot completely lose ourselves in the temporal. Several observers have termed this peculiar locale the "in-between" or the "between," and that has an attractive ring to it.[3] The only problem is that it conveys an odd sense of unreality, of the place that is nowhere, or of the view from nowhere, that makes it all the more difficult to sustain. It is notable too that the suggestion of the between has so far not gained wider traction. Perhaps it does not ultimately address the challenge it was designed to serve: to explain how a God who is transcendent can be known in the world he has created. It would seem that the symbol of the between is inherently unstable, since it continually points toward what is beyond it. Thus, it is a movement rather than a thing.

What the symbol of the between does do, however, is call our attention to the struggle that has been at the core of all attempts to symbolize order since the dawn of history. In one sense we have always lived in a secular world. The rational coordination of means and ends has been crucial to our survival. However much we relied on the gods, we could not abandon the pragmatic pursuit of self-preservation. Even in a world full of gods we had to operate like practical atheists who cannot count on anyone but ourselves for survival. It was only when we had done everything we could that trust in the gods seemed appropriate. We could not control what lies outside our control. A charging boar prompts defensive action; for a raging storm we must look to higher assistance. The practical operation of reason depends thus on a recognition of limits. It cannot extend beyond the sphere subject to pragmatic action. We could of course attempt to extend it into the sphere of the gods. They might be propitiated by prayers and sacrifices, but that was a very different order of instrumentality from building a life raft. Such appeals to heaven pointed to the inscrutable depth beyond the gods, a mystery so profound that perhaps it could not be reached by our most desperate imprecations. We live thus within the between that reaches from the sphere of rational control to the ineffable mystery surrounding it. All of this is known from the beginning. Without it we would neither survive nor sustain the effort required. However much we are practical atheists, we cannot maintain that as our default outlook. We must trust in the order, the cosmos, we cannot see in order to initiate action within it. The problem is that we lack any symbolic means of articulating the invisible Beyond. Initially it may seem that everything is manifest. Where the visible presences come from is shrouded in a mystery that cannot even be named. In one sense, this is the perfect symbolization of what cannot be symbolized, even if the aptness of it has also eluded us.[4]

Absence of God is a recognition that fully emerges only with the secular age. Yet this age so deeply marked by the disappearance of God may be the one that most perfectly affirms his transcendence. Nothing within time can symbolize that which is beyond time. We may be in the between, but we cannot so easily say what lies outside of it. That is the great task on which the human search for meaning is launched. Neither at home within the world nor capable of reaching beyond it, we live within the uncanny. In the beginning, the age of myth, we live almost without awareness of the issue. The depth from which everything emerges has not yet become apparent because we are so completely absorbed by the visible. At best the depth is itself identified as an earlier stage of visibility. Successive generations of gods prompt the suggestion that the highest is the most remote, without the rupture that transcendence must introduce. Instead the Beyond rests as beyond, although without acknowledgment as such. Transcendence is silently present without the full impact of its encounter. That is the breakthrough that constitutes the turning point of history. All of the "world religions" originate in that break from the visibility of a cosmos full of gods. Then there begins in earnest the struggle to symbolize what cannot be symbolized because it is transcendent. The very term "transcendent" is coined within that realization.[5] But it is not that something unknown is encountered. It is rather the case that what is known is recognized. That is the history of faith and the reason that it forms a genuine continuum. Having lived in the uncanny without bringing it fully to mind, now it bursts upon us as the mystery we cannot comprehend. Where previously we failed to say what we knew, now we fail to know what we say. The task of symbolization exceeds our capacity. From the theophanic turning point on, it is that incapacity that marks the history of our reflection. Our own secular condition is not therefore the least inadequate version.

We may regard the secular age as an authentic acknowledgment of the inability of the symbols of transcendence to say what they intend. God is not present in the religious forms we have inherited.[6] People no longer find God where they sought him. It is not so much that they have lost their faith as that faith has lost them. They know that God cannot be reached in ceremonies or formulas, no more than he can be encountered in churches and places. In other words, they know the God whom they seek. They would not seek him if they did not. It is their knowledge of God that compels them to discard the false divinity that convention presents.[7] Their faith will not allow them to be satisfied until they arrive at God himself. Knowing what they seek, they have already arrived at it. It was this knowledge that first made it possible to search beyond the gods of the myth, the first gods from whom our faith receded. Remember, it was the Christians who were called atheists in the Roman Empire. To those who believed in the tangible gods of the cosmos, those who held out for the God beyond them had to appear as disbelievers. It was in this context that Cicero coined the term "religion," as what binds us back to what we know as the basis for our world.[8] Religion thus names the divinity accessible within this world. It cannot therefore name the God who is beyond it, who affirms the world as simply itself. The problem is that the first breakthrough to divine transcendence also became misidentified as religion. "The fool has said in his heart there is no God," had become the problem.[9] The transcendent God would have to be brought more solidly within the cosmos if the danger represented by fools was to be addressed. That is the strategy that is religion.

What was designed to preserve faith was becoming an obstacle to it. Faith was no longer needed when dogma replaced it. The containment of the transcendent God within the definable parameters of the law, of Being within a being, meant that the original openness was no longer needed. The word of God is identified with a text. Gone was the need to listen to the voice that Moses first heard. How indeed could he hear what could not be heard by anyone else? Now the word of God is distributed to all. The availability of the Bible is one of the things that can block access to God. But how can God be encountered if it is not through God himself? Within the pages of a book we can behold only words. The Word itself escapes us. Not only is this evident in the methods of scriptural exegesis, but it pervades all of our everyday discourse about religion. Its presupposition is that religion is something one can examine. It is objective within the world, and we stand outside of it. That is indeed the genesis of *re-ligio*. Through it we bind ourselves back to what we are in danger of losing, but, in the process, we may lose it even more profoundly. The fool who says in his heart there is no God is perhaps not as far from the kingdom of God as the one who wants to draw divinity into this world. The fatal turn had been to think that faith could be preserved by anything other than faith. Transcendence cannot be manifest by anything within this world. Nothing furnishes a likeness of God. Being cannot be represented by beings. The radical separation from all that *is* can only be held onto by that which has undergone the same separation. Only those who are willing to lose their lives will save them. Security can be neither gained nor retained by any half measures. Whatever the value of boundaries on the unfathomable mystery, they cannot be confused with the mystery itself. Faith that lives solely by faith is alone capable of scaling transcendence.[10]

That is the conviction that still drives the great spiritual opening of the "world religions." But once formed in that epochal breakthrough of transcendence, they proceeded to close over what had made them possible. The transcendent was too fraught to be left within the inwardness that beheld it. Instead, a more worldly presence was shaped to guard its truth. The danger of losing the path of transcendence necessitated incorporation in the immanent. How else could the fragility of the event be retained? Even to retain it in memory required an aide-mémoire apart from it. The bearers of the breakthrough could hardly be sure of the reality of the event that occurred nowhere but within. The mountaintop may have been the location, but what happened could not be located anywhere. Certainly what was most decisive eluded external description. Even to concede that it was an interior emergence is to displace it into a different place. Besides, it was definitely not a merely inner experience. The experience may have been inward, but the event was transcendent. How could one experience an encounter with the transcendent? The command of God was neither an audible thing nor an inaudible echo. It was the indefeasible sway of being. Those who heard it could not disobey it for it is the command whose mandate is irrevocable.[11] But how was one to explain this invincibility? How can you convey the inexorability of its command? When people ask who is it that sent me, what am I to say? That was the concern that struck Moses, and he is given a word, the name YHWH, that becomes the axis around which the whole text revolves. It is the name that cannot be pronounced, that cannot be said, that cannot be named. The strategy is a good one, for it calls attention to the limits of language and thereby says more than can be said.[12] Yet despite the care with which transcendence is invoked, it could not prevent its absorption within the specificity of words and text. God is, after all, named and forever available to be summoned.

To avoid this, a greater self-awareness of the character of the event would be required. Thought would have to think itself if it was to retain its hold on what is beyond thought. That is the promise of Greek philosophy, which begins within a more self-conscious search for the ground of all things. What comes to Moses as a revelation is deliberately sought by the philosophers who thereby preserve a more explicit awareness of the path they follow. Here the accent falls more heavily on the search. When faith is lost in the world full of gods, the path beyond them is consciously pursued. This makes it possible to include the way to transcendence within the encounter with it. Revelation could avoid its termination within the historical setting of its occurrence. It could remain what it was in its irruption. Rather than regard it as an event within history, it could be seen as the event that constitutes history. But a similar fate overtakes philosophy too. Rather than become the practice that maintains the opening to transcendence, it succumbed to the same identification with what was said. Despite the witness of Socrates and the warning of Plato, philosophy became assimilated to what is written down. What could not be written down, the event that gave rise to the text itself and therefore could never be included within it, becomes of lesser importance. The success of philosophy is its failure.[13] It too joins the religious traditions that must struggle perpetually with the presence of what, at most, signals what it does not contain. The great history of what they have accomplished has become the principal obstacle to reaccomplishing it. Nietzsche remarked on this pattern in his essay, "On the Uses and Disadvantages of History for Life," but it is by no means confined to that application.[14] Perhaps it would be better if every person and every generation had to discover anew the truth that transcends all saying. Yet that would truncate history to the life of each individual, and we could no longer benefit from the great collaborative enterprise as it unfolds. Somehow a way must be found of resisting the closure that begins as soon as the rupture of transcendence has occurred. Within this realm of paradox perhaps it should not be too surprising to discover that the worse the problem becomes, the nearer we are to its resolution. Our own extreme of secularization may well be one of those moments when the reversal is close at hand.

Faith as Ever Returning

In the opaqueness of every historical realization the awareness endures that the rupture of transcendence must be carried forward through itself. Besides, the impact generated by its flash of revelation has never entirely been lost. The perception of the great spiritual outbursts as subsequently lapsing into suspended animation is hardly a fully accurate depiction. In reality, the world religions remain vibrant communities that have found ways of resuscitating the spark of openness in each generation. Far from declining to a trickle, they manifest a vibrancy that continually reaches ever wider circles of influence. Congealment of the original outpouring is not a problem they have overlooked. Perpetual renewal is virtually what defines the path of their historical transmission. Religions, like economies, do not exist in a steady state. They know that they cannot remain stationary. Either they grow or decline; they have no other option. They live by this realization for they know they must continually find a way of communicating what cannot be communicated. They do not live in buildings or organizations, nor can they afford to be defined by the externalities of ritual. All that matters is what lies within. It is the spirit out of which everything is done that must remain alive. That is what must be enkindled and dispersed throughout the world. Religions are in the work of transcending all that is merely routine. They know that they must be ready to yield up the trappings of religion if they wish to retain its core. Of course, not every spiritual community manages to rise to the challenge. Denominations and movements often decline, dwindling in numbers as their inspiration recedes. But they remain branches within the great tree of faith, a trunk whose main lines demonstrate remarkable endurance. Their genesis within the axial breakthrough to transcendence has proved powerful enough to carry them beyond the possibility of forgetting. They have repeatedly regenerated themselves.

The exterior they present is not what they are. Behind the facade of convention is the adventure of each soul that discovers for the first time the touch of the inexpressible. Staid formulas and repetitive ceremonies somehow manage to impart the startling novelty of the event. In many ways it may be the absence of innovation that allows the miracle of transcendence to enter the heart. But this is far from an accidental surprise. The touch of God, divine grace, that can be neither commanded nor predicted can nevertheless be awaited. This is the sacramental mystery in which the unremarkable becomes the vehicle for the irruption of the transcendent. Teachers and ministers may not possess the potency of inspiration. Charismatic leadership cannot be counted on. Yet all may instill the waiting in patience that is expectation. Even when our own engagement with transcendence has diminished, even when God is absent, there remains a trace in the waiting for his return. All that is needed to convey transcendence is the openness toward it. Prayer is neither a speaking to nor a hearing of God. It is the inner turning of attention that, when it stretches far enough, is the point at which opening is sufficient to receive him. Over and above all that is said is the mystery of openness itself. It does not have to be explained or defined. It is glimpsed directly. Once you witness a person in prayer you know that an overleaping of the boundaries is taking place. It is an initiation into something greater than can be said or described. We know it because we too are susceptible to the same inexorable undertow. Prayer is what we live within. We do not contain it, for it contains us.

Yet even when we are successful in conveying the irresistible brush of the transcendent, we still face the challenge of translating what has occurred. Therein lies the great problem that ever confronts the world religions. They may have managed to reanimate the faith buried within them, but they cannot easily connect it with the world in which they find themselves. Often they have obtained that reminder at the cost of turning their back on the secular reality around them. But they cannot so easily split their lives. The world cannot simply be ignored, for if ejected by the front door it will make its way in at the back. Moreover, turning away from the world is contrary to the spiritual openness to which they have been called. It is not a private gift to be enjoyed by a privileged few. Rather, the divine call is a sending forth to the ecumene. It is for dissemination, not for separation. To fulfill that responsibility we must be prepared not only to proclaim the good news, but to explain how it is good news, in the language of our world. Rather than hold itself aloof from the secular, the community of faith must be prepared to show that it holds the fulfillment of the age's deepest aspirations. To those who have transcended it the world is not what it appears to be, even to itself. Movement beyond the world opens a longing that cannot be answered from within it. The secret of the visible is the invisibility of the eye that sees it. Every limit proclaims the unlimited as the perspective from which it is apprehended. The highest self-awareness of which a secular age is capable is the admission of its own futility. Man, in the words of Sartre, is "a useless passion."[15] What cannot be grasped is the source of that insight itself. Transcendence eludes it. That is the great opening that the secular world offers to the historic carriers of transcendence and the point at which they can affirm the deepest intimations hidden within it.

It is not enough to oppose the secular world in the name of transcendence. A neo-orthodox resurgence insists that the secular world is incapable of containing it and therefore must stand before its judgment.[16] No doubt there is something bracing about such an uncompromising confession, for it is a far cry from the timid withdrawal that seeks to hold itself apart from the world. Like the confidence that underpinned the great spiritual civilizations of the past, we recognize unwavering transcendence as the bedrock on which a more enduring order can be erected. Neither fearful nor hesitant, truth is proclaimed to a world incapable of absorbing it. But therein lies the greatest difficulty. It may indeed be the case that the dichotomy is inescapable, that the world is by definition incapable of comprehending what lies beyond it, but what has been gained by heightening irreconcilability? Lines that have been drawn are less likely to be dismissed, but have they succeeded in enclosing the needful within them? It is one thing to insist that the world must come to terms with spirit in terms of spirit, it is another to insist that they persevere across an abyss of mutual incomprehension. Stalemate cannot long endure without the opposing perspectives losing the basis for their opposition. They may simply shrink to the emptiness of the confrontation itself that is carried on long after the reason for it has been forgotten. There are no permanent footholds in history. Only the forward motion carries any possibility of constancy. By remaining in place, we run the risk of becoming defined and immobilized by the polarity to which we have committed ourselves rather than by the convictions that first prompted engagement. The movement of transcendence has become that which it is not, a mundane distraction. The freedom of the Christian has been lost in the stridency by which it had been proclaimed.[17]

The Secular Waiting for God

The incompatibility of the transcendent and the immanent cannot be the starting point of the conversation. Instead of asking whether the world can comprehend what comes from beyond it, we must begin with the more immediate question as to whether the world can comprehend itself. This is not simply the rhetorical strategy of beginning where one's audience is, placing oneself in their position, but a far deeper witness to what cannot be identified with any worldly presence. It is the strategy of abandoning all strategy, for what can success mean when it is only measured in terms of complete loss? The only adequate triumph is that which has triumphed over itself. Then truth shines as what is beyond all "truth." Instead of proclaiming the transcendence of all that is finite and material, we insist on the indispensability of the latter if the former is to be known. The radical otherness of God is not so incomprehensible within a secular world, for that world knows what it lacks. The meaning of *secular* at its deepest level is abandonment. An "awareness of what is missing" is not just a newfound openness to the transcendent, but the defining mark of the secular as such. How else could it conceive itself as finite if it did not know what the infinite is?[18] This is why the transcendence of God is not so unfamiliar. The uncanny remains, at some inextinguishable level, canny. The dichotomy between God and the world that has been a staple, enabling both believers and unbelievers to understand themselves, crumbles in the face of a deeper mutuality. God cannot be God without the world, and the world cannot be world without God. This is not simply a matter of definition, but of a far more intimate interdependence. A secular world is impossible, not just because it could not understand itself except in relation to God, but because the world continually presents the trace of God. As that from which God is absent, it proclaims God even more emphatically.

But more crucially, it proclaims God as God. This is not the God depicted in visible manifestation, but the God who cannot be manifest because nothing can depict him. The only adequate representation is that of God himself. This is the meaning of the advent of Christ, who alone can reveal God because he is God. He definitively abolishes the gulf between God and his representation by showing that there is nothing that cannot be a sign of the divinity that is nowhere present in the sign. The voice of God, inchoately sensed by human beings as far back as we can find them and building gradually through the history of revelation, is now unmistakably the voice of a person. The complete absence of God from creation is also his complete presence within it. All that is not-God not only points beyond itself, but carries the divine as its meaning. The trace of God is the language of God's disclosure. How else can the transcendent reveal itself except by means of what is not transcendent? But this means that now there is no longer the spiritual and the material, the finite and the infinite, for they not only imply one another but also mutually interpenetrate. The Incarnation is the turning point of history because it is the axis on which history turns. Retrospectively, all can now be viewed as drawing us toward that culmination, and prospectively, we long for a culmination beyond all mundane existence. Transfiguration is not simply a Christian idea, but is most fully understood within it. Christ is both the promise of transfiguration and its veritable actualization. The eschaton is not in the future.[19] We do not await an event within history but already live within its definitive irruption. This sets the peculiar status of historical existence from this point on. It is existence that can no longer take itself seriously for it is no longer ultimate. The secular world pervaded by the awareness of its own inconsequence grasps the very meaning of secular and slips, albeit imperceptibly, into the viewpoint that transcends it. With Christ the secular and the transcendent are abolished as separate categories and have become thoroughly interrelated. When only God can reveal God, the nondivine has been fully differentiated.

The gulf that separates God and the world has been opened but at the same time bridged through the most complete outpouring of love. In Jesus, God puts himself in place of the world. Alienation is overcome when God substitutes himself for creation. The separation that had seemed so definitive turns out to be only a prelude to a deeper union in love. The chasm that had seemed insuperable has been abolished within the inwardness of God. Love, the transcendent, has accomplished the impossible. What could not even point to divine being suddenly discloses the inner heart of God. There is no gap because God has himself become the bridge. It is still the case that nothing can reveal God but God himself, but everything can become the occasion for that transcendent disclosure. All things can speak to us of God because God can speak to us directly. The divine is not in the voice, no more than he is in the thunder or the lightning. The transcendent transcends all separation. The secular world is not the world from which faith has ebbed in that long rushing roar.[20] It is rather the world in which faith is most of all possible, for now it can rightly grasp God as the transcendent. This is the great epiphany of the secular age. We are no different from those who first encountered Jesus and realized that they could not say whom they encountered. It was only those who were drawn by the Father beyond all who could see what could not be seen. The only difference is that we are further away from the possibility of anything becoming identified with the presence that transcends all presence. Paradoxically, that means that we are closer to the real presence, the Parousia, the Eucharist. For in all of the great monuments of the past, the cathedrals and temples in all their massiveness, we can perceive the failure to capture the spirit from which they arise and toward which they strain. Only what is within can reach what is beyond. That is the mystery of a secular age, one that provides no access to the truth but truth itself. Symbols that say what cannot be said have done their work, and we are the wide-eyed shepherds at the stable.

The sacred prevails but without the trappings of sacrality. Now the transcendent makes itself known on its own terms, as transcendent. Even believers no longer look toward a return of the great spiritual empires of the past; or if they do, it is an anachronistic longing they already know is doomed to futility. Violence may even be inflicted in that last desperate struggle to enforce an orthodoxy that could never be enforced without ceasing to be orthodox.[21] But it is a violence that betrays its own powerlessness. The sacred cannot be compelled, for it exists nowhere within this world. It is what is capable of embracing the whole world and therefore cannot be found within it. We cannot but view with a certain tenderness the poignant efforts to restore it within this world. Of course, all previous civilizations have sought to build the timeless within time. The pyramids of Egypt are among the most impressive of many such investments that made all that is productive serve the transition to what is no longer within life. The afterlife is massively present within this life. Monuments of the useless, they nevertheless failed to convey the life buried within them. Awaiting an afterlife, they could not perceive their arrival at it. Only faith could carry them toward that goal that they already carried within. The true life is not in the future, for it is in eternity, in that which transcends even the believers themselves. They do not live in relation to an illusion, a liberation that recedes indefinitely, for they have given tangible evidence of its actuality within them. Muscle and bone, straw and mud, were the material means, but what really raised the pyramids was the spirit that could nowhere be contained within them. They stand forever as a silent rebuke to the mistaken notion of containing the uncontainable. We honor them because we recognize the same aspiration for permanence within ourselves. Who would not want to enclose the unsurpassable mystery of being within solid affirmation? But we cannot suppress a wry smile at their incorrigible naïveté. The sacredness of place, the point of maximal access to the divine, retains its powerful hold upon us, but we cannot simply submit to the hold of the cosmos once its boundary has been crossed in opening to the transcendent.[22]

Yet we remain within the space-time horizon that, now we know, exists nowhere in space or time. Even in the very earliest symbolizations, the cosmos itself remained the whole that could not be symbolized. The transcendent endures as transcendent even before it has begun to be differentiated. But when it has, the pull of the cosmos reasserts itself to draw us inexorably into the project of symbolizing the transcendent again. What cannot be symbolized must nevertheless be symbolized. This is the paradox within which human existence unfolds historically. We must say what cannot be said and in not saying we say it. The world religions emerging from the axis time when transcendence ruptures cosmological order set about the very varied task of tangibly memorializing the immemorial. These are the great civilizational edifices we regard as the epochal achievements of humanity. Often that glance is permeated with no small residue of nostalgia for what we know we can no longer attain. Their monuments, whether the hanging gardens of Babylon or the ruined perfection of the Parthenon, attest to liberation from all mundane considerations and in this achieve the purpose that lay behind them. Our grandiose creations today, by contrast, rarely leave the calculus of utility behind, or if they do, it is all too fleeting. Great stadiums serve a function that has no end beyond itself, although they are thoroughly embedded in an economic dynamic that is well-nigh relentless. Besides, the liberation from purpose they seek is not transparent for the transcendence that now only faintly echoes within them. We retain only the ruffle of the uncanny we have never been finally able to lose. Our disorientation seems complete. Complete, that is, until we begin to wonder if the confusion might not have been an inescapable consequence of the civilizational project on which the breakthrough of the transcendent launched us. Could it be that the intensification of the transcendent has led to its consummate loss?

Secular Misdirection of Transcendent Longing

The pattern is by now well understood in historical studies of the genesis of our secular age. Ever since Max Weber noted the affinity between the Protestant ethic and the spirit of capitalism, it has been more widely confirmed that movements of religious reform give rise to the kind of disciplined intensity that yield staggering worldly achievements. We recognize in our own smaller-scale missions to the moon and beyond something of that innerworldly transcendence. Once they are accomplished, we are lost without a focus to which our otherworldly longing might now be directed. Even the moon is no longer the moon when it has been reached and now must be incorporated into a mundane scheme of exploitation. Like the capitalist success to which Protestant virtue has led, the achievement erodes the virtue from which it is derived.[23] All that remains is the philanthropic atonement for the transgression of boundaries we no longer know. The disorientation is so pervasive that even scholars of the phenomenon rarely penetrate to the core.[24] We are left with a narrative of unintended consequences, when the demand for spiritual perfection gives rise to the corrupting effects of success. The early monks, who cultivated the wildernesses of Europe to eventually amass astonishing wealth, were not so bedazzled by their worldly achievements. They at least understood it as a fall from their true vocation. It could not be cast as collateral damage of the spirit, compensated by the material abundance it had produced. Only late moderns could be so enthralled to the benefits of progress as not to recognize the loss of spirit behind it.[25] The fall is not incidental but inescapable when discipline has overtaken its finite purpose. Measurement of spiritual success by worldly criteria is the essence of the determination to bring about heaven on earth.

Its seeds are present in the very first efforts to make this world conform with the glory glimpsed beyond it. The impossibility of the task is scarcely noticed. We must live in light of the transcendent even when we cannot adequately do so. What has yet to be acknowledged is that failure is the principal means of success. Initially we are so captivated by the dream of making time an icon of eternity that we forge unthinkingly ahead. Impatience with the limits of finite reality makes us brush aside all the indicators opposing us. The turning point is surely when a single-minded drive is embraced as the indispensable mechanism for the absorption of the timeless within time. We recognize echoes of the titanic striving that mark modernity. Whether it is the modern revolutionary upheavals or the traversal of continents or the construction of vast webs of interconnection, we astonish ourselves by the magnitude of what we have accomplished. It is not that limitless will has not delivered on its promise, for in many ways modernity is powerful testament to what can be accomplished when striving brooks no obstacle. Whatever the limits are, we discover them only by pushing beyond them. The real problem is that all the accomplishments remain penultimate. We are not at the end that drew us, for the closer we approach, the more it recedes.

Success evaporates as it is grasped. That is the tragic flaw that marks our world. Ultimately all is loss in a world that cannot remain and in which all its achievements are stubbornly evanescent. Even memory is not long enough to retain the memorable, for it too is forgotten. Despair before the futility of progress eventually saps the drive that sustained it. This is the crisis of modernity that has touched us more deeply than we have been able to admit. We are thrown back to the question that faced us at the very beginning of the civilizational project. How can that which is transcendent, which structures the meaning of it all, be contained in the ephemeral reality of history? If the eternal cannot be forged within time, how can it nevertheless be remembered?

We are on the brink of a very different mode of symbolization when we acknowledge that representation of the transcendent is impossible. Ignoring impossibility only gave rise to ever more intense demands to accomplish the impossible. Drawing God into the world ended with the identification of them, what we know as secular modernity. His complete presence is simultaneously his complete absence. But the result is not wholly negative. In the failure of worldly presentation, we begin to see the only adequate representation. Secular society in its endless waiting provides a new opening to transcendence as transcendent. No longer tied to the tangible, the transcendent reveals itself as beyond revelation. When its false promise has fallen away, the secular realm can deliver on its true promise. Within its self-limitation is the intimation of what is unlimited. Like the vibrancy of religion that Tocqueville noted in America, its flourishing can be attributed to the renunciation of all hint of official endorsement. Earthly embrace can only corrupt what it seeks to enfold. Spirit must take wing from spirit. All that is incorporated within the regime of power is reduced to the same parameters. It becomes the opposite of itself. This was the great critique of the medieval church that profoundly animated the call for reform within it. A church that fought for its prerogatives no longer remained true to itself.[26] In the same way, the world that sought to incorporate perfection within itself had abolished its own deepest purpose. Not only were the results dissatisfying, but the faith that defined their pursuit had been undermined. The transcendent could be neither realized nor abolished. It would have to remain what it had always been, a sheer nonpresence that made all presence possible. This is why the secular consummation of perfection is not only a crushing failure, but at the same time the first opening to its truth. The secular is the advent of the spiritual, precisely as spiritual, as that which cannot be incorporated or contained in the mundane.

To follow this path, however, the old language of religion and of philosophy must be thoroughly revised. The terminology of soul and self, of the immanent and the transcendent, here and beyond, carried too much of the worldliness they sought to shed. This does not mean that the great breakthroughs to transcendence have lost their historical significance. Even the figurative depictions of such events remain the most precious access we have to the unsaid mystery from which they emanate. But it was a natural and even inevitable consequence of their transmittal that they would be incorporated in the language of what seeks to endure within the world. Heaven would be a higher place and eternity would become a longer period of time, without anyone noticing that we thereby set ourselves up to live in relation to a less appealing universe than the one in which we find ourselves.[27] No one, until Nietzsche, so compellingly pointed out the falsity of the conception. Why live in relation to an illusory reality when we can live in the real one?[28] Ironically, the objection is closer to the truth than the imaginary projections. Heaven and eternity exist nowhere. Like God, they are *not* in the same way as the whole immanent world is. Their being is of a very different order, one from which the mundane analog deflects us significantly. We do not "go" to heaven, no more than "last" in eternity, for we are already there. Before we have departed we know them as the arrival that contains, as well, the departure. Even "beyond" is a spatial metaphor that belies the realization that it is even more deeply "within." The transcendent we eventually realize is neither here nor there but can only be conceived as what provides the possibility of anything being here or there. The transcendent is nowhere but within itself. Containing all, it contains itself or is contained within itself. Metaphysics was perhaps the most inopportune coinage of all. Not only did it originate in an editorial confusion that derived from the placement of Aristotle's most philosophical work, First Philosophy, after the *Physics* (as *Metaphysics*);[29] it had the unfortunate consequence of suggesting that there was such a realm beyond the physical. Even today we suffer from talk about the end or recovery of metaphysics as if it is something else, over and above reality as we know it. In fact, it is the possibility of talking about reality, which, of necessity, cannot be derived from something within reality.

Love Sets Itself Aside as Opening of Secular

Confusion along these lines is fairly pervasive. Eric Voegelin once told a listener that he believed in the afterlife, but "not for too long," as a means of dislodging the nonsense from our thinking about the transcendent. But the situation is even worse when we begin to talk about ourselves. Contact with the transcendent, the God who reveals himself, impresses us as the most central part of who we are. What could be more integral to me than the point at which I gain the deepest apprehension of what is? The notion of the innermost self, the true soul, is immediately seized upon and becomes a fixity not easily dislodged. Of course, when biology and neuroscience actually do get inside our bodies, they discover that there is no such thing.[30] Souls elude us no matter how microscopic the search. Eventually we become reconciled to the nonexistence of what we thought is most inherent to us.[31] Whatever the soul is, it cannot be a thing. But, again, it is in the moment of greatest loss that the axis of recovery turns. The error all along has been to think of the soul as an entity, just like all the other entities in the world. Instead it is that which transcends and contains all. It has no analog in existence for it is that from which existence originates. We realize that this is just what it is to be a person, one who, in the original meaning of the term, holds a mask before the face. The mask is visible, but the holder is not. Soul is of that order. It is what makes everything else possible, all of the actions of our life, but itself is not contained in any of them. Yet we know it. When we encounter one another we do not seek contact with the mask but with the invisible holder.[32] Despite the reign of quantity under which we live, we elude its parameters continually. Even the science that aims at tracking down our innermost core can never reach it, for it too is a process that such transcendence makes possible. We may gain an impressive apprehension of materiality, but that penetration is not itself material. It exists only in the realm of spirit that exists nowhere else but within spirit itself. All the customary language about self, identity, character, soul, and the travails to which we are subject fall away. At best they are metaphors for what has no metaphor.

The closest we come to glimpsing the spiritual world we inhabit is when we are asked to yield ourselves up. Then we realize that we are utterly unlike the familiar physicality around us. Money can be saved by not spending it, but the self can be saved only by giving itself away. Even the language of a true self or a higher self suggests that it is a thing and therefore to be conserved. But that is not so. He who saves his life will lose it, for he who loses his life will save it. The paradox of spirit imposes itself. There is no quantity of soul that must at all costs be retained, for it can only be gained by not counting the cost. The self that pours itself out is the self that is saved. Even the stubborn residue of possession that still attaches to the language of self must be discarded. There is no soul or self other than the soul or self that is expended in limitless self-giving. It is not that we are first selves and then learn to cultivate and increase the virtues of the self. We do not gain character as a result of practicing right action. Good deeds do not win virtue, no more than they gain rewards. What virtue is there beyond the virtue of going beyond virtue? Holding onto virtue is never enough, just as merely meeting the requirements of the law signals a deficiency. And what reward is there greater than the reward of giving one's reward away? Even our moral language has not quite lived up to the unconditional dynamic pulsing within it. Of course, we routinely fail to live up to the requirements of law and morality, but we rarely consider that law and morality are already a falling short. We think we possess mastery within a moral universe that recurrently unmasters us. Therein we catch a glimpse of the true self or soul. Spirit is neither something we hold nor something we gain but the very movement that will not allow us to rest with anything less than the fullness of transcendence. At its deepest we recognize that glimpse, a glimpse beyond what we could ordinarily glimpse, as the true source of the revelation we have received.

The great spiritual texts are written from that perspective even if they do not always unpack it for us. Yet if we return to them, we can discern the awareness of what they could not say. It is the source of the authority they continue to exercise over us even when the means is opaque. Their powerful undertow is evidenced perhaps even more when we no longer approach them literally. How can it be that ancient texts and rituals still draw us into their orbit or compel us to follow along the same lines? Even atheists, it seems, want to pray. And the most secular societies cannot avoid investing the turning points of life, birth and death, with a solemnity that intimates their transcendence. Everything about us insists that we are beyond the sum of our moments. We are endowed with a dignity that is our most precious possession, worth more than life itself. It is for this that political communities struggle so ardently and, when they are successful, enshrine it in affirming the sacredness of every human life. Could it be that the spiritual texts indeed say more than we secularists have been able to say? That they come closer to intuiting the transcendent order in which we continue to live? Neither they nor we, however, manage to pierce the impenetrability of the order by which we are held. It remains invisible to us because we are so completely contained within it. This is why the language of spirit, of a metaphysics that is nowhere present, can do no more than figurate what cannot be figured. It is only in our forlorn secular condition, when all has been reduced to the present, the *saeculum*, that we begin to see that what brings about presence can never be present. The ancient texts may have arisen from depths more profound, but it is left to us to appreciate more fully why their inaccessibility must remain.

This is why the secular age is perhaps most hospitable of all to the divine. By not saying, it guards the possibility of saying more closely. The convergence is best illustrated by the Sermon on the Mount, a text uniquely approved by theists and atheists alike. Its appeal derives neither from the author, Christ, nor from the argument that sustains it but from the way it draws us into its dynamic. We cannot resist its attraction because we are already caught up by it before we even begin. Its boundaries cannot be specified. We simply sense their inexorability. Stripped of all spiritual language, the Sermon evinces the most spiritually perfect momentum, and we begin to realize that it is in that unsayable dynamic that we most fully are. Love is neither a concept nor a capacity nor a goal but the reality within which our lives must unfold. We are called to respond to what is before we have arrived on the scene, and in that unforeseeable prospect, we can either gain or lose everything. Nothing is higher than love for it exceeds every scale of measurement. That is what the Sermon proclaims. Even while it counsels us to be perfect as our heavenly Father is, it nowhere makes either the divine command or the divine nature the source of its mandate. It is rather that the imperative derives wholly from the good itself. Only then do we become like God whose goodness exceeds all limits. There is no resting point, Christ declares, when we have done enough. Everything requires us to go beyond what is enough, because that is what love is. We cannot love in part or for a while or within reason, for then it is not love. The unconditionality of love is the arc stretching over us. It cannot be explained in terms of something other than love because all explanation heads toward it. Not even spirit or transcendence are higher. They have meaning only in relation to love.[33] It cannot even be required by God because it would then not really arise from love. The source of love must lie even higher, beyond God, in love itself. Of course, that is only from our perspective for, as the text reveals, God is love.

We reach toward love, but God is already there. He is the source of love but not by possessing it, as if he could just as easily choose another mode to work his will. It is rather that God is love, without separation or deviation. He cannot not love. When we wonder how this can be, since love must forever be free, we can only find our way by going deeper into the imperative of love. God cannot turn aside from love because he has, out of love, already given himself completely to love. That is why God must be Trinitarian. Love is complete self-giving, and the Sermon, while not explicitly Trinitarian, cannot avoid the implication of that perfect love. The Sermon hovers over that depth while it moves upward from the human level. It is after all a sermon about the good life, not about theology, and so it draws the human toward the divine without entering into the divinity itself. The Trinity is not, in other words, the basis of the movement toward it, except in an ultimate sense. The path toward it remains the mediating one of love itself. For this to be effective it is hardly necessary for us to think about God at all, and that is the pattern of Christ's repetitions, "You have heard it said . . . but I say unto you . . ." Instead the Sermon leads us to God by way of love rather than vice versa. It makes no prior assumptions other than the imperative of love, yet it draws us into such an enlargement of the heart that everything else becomes irrelevant. Whether there is a God and whether we will enjoy an afterlife are considerations that pale in relation to the transcendent significance of love. We do not even need God when we have loved to the limit, that is, beyond all limit. It is love itself that is the transcendence we touch. What we call it is entirely secondary. The Sermon on the Mount, it turns out, is the perfect discourse for atheists. It begins where they are, asking nothing more, and they have more often than not embraced it as the form of religion without God.[34] But more importantly, it has shown that atheism is irrelevant. Even when we reject God we arrive at him nevertheless, so long as we yield to the prompting of love. It is in that consummation that we encounter transcendent reality. The name of love is then of only secondary significance.[35]

The Sermon dispenses entirely with the trappings of theology, just as it does with the apparatus of Christianity. It shows that the meaning of all that spiritual language is to be found in the movement of transcendence in which we are already engaged. Heaven is not in the next life, for it is already in this one when we love completely.[36] Nothing is higher than love. It cannot be understood in terms of something else, for it is the highest. Certainly a turning from love toward another place or time can only result in the loss of love. That, we recognize, has been the core of the atheist critique of faith. It is not so much a rejection of God as a rejection of him as God. But that too is where the Sermon abides. To be faithful to love may entail even the abandonment of God, should it be required of love.[37] We can at least contemplate the possibility, for nothing is higher than love. Not even God, for we arrive at God by way of love. Without love we could not even know him, since God is love. We realize that there is no separation. The divine being is none other than the being of love.

That is the higher reality of which all metaphysics and religion speaks, although it cannot be apprehended until we realize that it is nothing other than love. Love is the highest reality. It does not bring us to anything else beyond itself. What could be higher than love? All other language about paradise and its pleasures is entirely figurative. It does not touch what love already knows. This is why we do not await a disclosure beyond the horizon in which we live. The secular world is not apart from the sacred one. It is simply the same world that has either awakened or failed to awaken to the transcendence buried within it. The value of the secular account is that it refuses to submit to the pictorial version that religion often presents. But this also means that it is closer to the truth that is the secret of religion. That is, there is no transcendence but the movement of transcendence itself. Neither a secular nor a religious substitute can attain it. There is no truth but truth, just as there is no love but love. They can be apprehended only within themselves. This is how God can be reached even if, perhaps especially if, there is no God.[38]

CHAPTER FOUR

Atheism Is Impossible in Practice

Karl Marx understood that atheism depended on theism. This was why he insisted that after the Communist revolution "atheism would become impossible in practice."[1] The question of God would not even be raised. Socialist man would know that he creates himself through his own labor, so a divine creator would become redundant. God would be the first lay-off in a Communist takeover. Human beings would know they possess all the means of bringing about their own happiness and would reorder their social organization toward that goal. The idea of a creator could only inhibit self-creation. Without God there would be no limits to the Promethean drive. All gods, heavenly and earthly, could be dispatched as relics of a past now patently irrelevant. Maturity would replace an earlier immaturity that looked for assistance outside of nature, for now human beings were confident they possessed in abundance the means of tackling the dangers that threaten them. Even the self-created crises, the panics and depressions of capitalism, would be wiped away when collective resources were marshaled to serve the common good. When man had come of age, God is rendered obsolete. Even atheism becomes defunct when theism is irrelevant. The question of God simply disappears. That is the genesis of Marx's famous remark. It put a line beneath all talk of transcendence as the final rebuke to all vestiges of faith.

Rejection of God as Reaffirmation

The only problem is that continuing dismissals of a discredited faith serve only to keep its reality alive. Certainly in the case of Marx, the animus against the spirit belied an inner uncertainty about his own status. As a secular messiah he was in direct competition with the divine messiah, on whom he sensed a far deeper dependence. Could there even be a secular messiah when the messianic had disappeared? The category on which his own project rested seemed precarious when history had overtaken it. He knew too that the revolt against God, to which he had given such ringing declamation, could not so easily dispense with the target of his fulmination. He needed God in order to reject him. The more vociferously he repulsed God, the more seriously he regarded him. Marx was a prophet determined not to be a prophet. Like Nietzsche, he could not proclaim the death of God without professing him. Only what is alive can die, including God. This was why Nietzsche identified nihilism, "God is dead and everything is permitted," with the advent of the uncanny. Denunciation is also annunciation. The death of God is already his resurrection. This is an insight that could not have surprised the Christians who were the first to introduce the theme. Jesus by dying overcame death. His death announces his life. The difference between Marx-Nietzsche and our latter-day atheists, who earnestly exhort us to put aside the unscientific hypothesis of God, is that they lack the self-awareness of the former. Our scientistic atheists have not been able to perceive their own naïveté. How can the deathless die? How can we proclaim the obsolescence of God without transcending the idea of God? Without becoming like God? Even to interest ourselves in the question of God, to the point of dismissing him, is already to take him with a seriousness that must give pause. In renouncing God, we admit that he cannot be renounced.

Atheism, it turns out, is a more difficult position to occupy than it appears. This has always been known, although it has continually been forgotten. God does not exist. He cannot be part of the world that we know as existing since he is before or outside of it, for such terms as "existence" really only apply to the world that exists. Essentially God is nowhere and in no time. This is why he cannot exist. He cannot be found because there is no "there" where he might be. We do not really know him, except by way of the question by which we already know him. That is why the question that Marx and Nietzsche and the new atheist epigones seek to dismiss is so significant. It is the question that most of all cannot be forgotten. The effort to suppress it imprints it all the more deeply within us. We become a-theists, those who believe in order that we may discard what we believe. The intellectual vertigo is difficult to manage, for this is not a question on the periphery of our attention but the one from which the whole possibility of attention springs. Its dismissal unhinges our equilibrium. The one certainty from which we began, that we are not God, has been lost, and we have no alternative but to reoccupy the space that has been left. Or we are sorely tempted by such schemes of self-aggrandizement. The secular messiah attests to the unquenchable need that remains when the divine messiah has departed. We are prepared to insist that we can assume the role of God, even though we are ill equipped for the task. Only an illusion of apotheosis is possible as the final chapter of the narrative we are now inclined to construct. It is an ironic outcome from an impulse that opened with the confidence of having surpassed all illusion. Omniscience is the cruelest illusion of all. It is the fatal conceit of starting with the assumption that everything has become subject to our comprehension. There is nothing we cannot subject to our scrutiny. Even God must yield up his secrets when we have pushed aside the barriers that previously blocked our penetration. Mastery is final and definitive, except for a troubling unease that continues to disturb it. Can the eradication of mystery be the goal of it all, or if it is, can it be sufficient for us? Dystopian echoes may be the aftermath of religion. But do they betoken a deeper failure of the secular illusion?

That is the interior doubt that rumbled within the great secular messiahs, as opposed to the latter-day epigones who lacked the predecessors' sensitivity to the issues involved. They could not see what Marx and Nietzsche knew only too well. That is, there could be no mastery without what could not be mastered, mastery itself. The condition of the possibility of thought is what cannot be thought, because it transcends it. No science can validate itself, and no capacity can endow itself. Everything derives from what it is not, and which cannot be reached within the terms of its existence. Whatever is *is* from what is outside of it. Kant had reintroduced the term "transcendental" for the condition that cannot provide the condition of its own possibility. The term was a happy choice because it pointed toward the transcendent, the unconditioned as such. Such discussions were a staple of the German Idealism in which Marx and Nietzsche were steeped. Unfortunately, they are remote considerations within the Anglophone world within which the scientistic version of "the God question" is currently ventilated. But they are enormously important because they remind us that reflection on God does not occur in the vacuum suggested by the glibness with which the question is posed. Overlooked is the realization that the questioner too not only lives within a certain range of presuppositions, but is incapable of adequately tracing their roots. The divine means, if it means anything, the inaccessible within which we must pursue its meaning. This was well understood by the thinkers who knew that they could not simply discourse about the ground of all, as if one were discussing everyday matters of fact. They could not be, in other words, straightforward atheists. Only Wittgenstein approaches the perspicuity of admitting that the statement that God does or does not exist is meaningless on its face.[2] Marx and Nietzsche thought that one would have to suppress the question. Atheism would have to become impossible in practice by making it the question that simply could not arise.

The palpable instability of their stance was one they were determined to endure. Like every attempt at deliberate forgetting, it had to be constantly recalled in order to avoid remembering it. Psychologically, it was a hard balancing act, but its real costs were evident in the collapse of reason that was its inevitable consequence. Reason had been suppressed, not just in an incidental area of reality, but in relation to the encompassing whole in which we exist. The condition of the possibility of existence is willed to be forgotten. It is not simply a rejection of a particular line of questions but of *the* question from which all others derive. Questioning as such comes under a cloud. All must be carefully navigated to ensure that we do not smuggle in what must be avoided. Science becomes impossible when it must comply with a preconceived account of the world, a world from which the trace of the divine had to be eradicated. The pattern is well known from our experience of ideological regimes that insisted not only on Communist economics but also on a Communist biology, politics, art, and so on. The analysis of cause and effect is deeply disturbed and the rational coordination of means and ends widely distorted.[3] But something similar occurs within the more moderate regime of enlightened rationalism now universally dominant. Science is persistently displaced by scientism. Against all evidence, allegiance to the perspective of reductionistic materialism is the regnant orthodoxy that is virtually immune to objection. A Neo-Darwinian account of evolution is gripped with the kind of desperation that attests a deeper insecurity.[4] Darwin himself was more open to the larger questions than his latter-day successors. One might be inclined to suggest that materialist reductionism functions as a secular religion, although no religion worthy of the name could presume the settlement of all questions. It certainly cannot abolish the most fundamental question of why there is something rather than nothing.

Reason Aware of Its Boundaries

The putative abolition of religion would seem to suggest an impossibility. Atheism has indeed become impossible in practice. This is surely an ironic twist of the observation by which Marx intended to secure the victory of atheism. When the question of God is no longer raised, then atheism becomes a default position that is scarcely even acknowledged. It was a curious turn of phrase by which he sought to suppress his own awareness of the inescapability of the question, especially by deliberately forbidding it. The resulting disorientation has served only to underline the extent to which the life of reason is dependent on an openness to what it cannot fully comprehend.[5] By contrast, insistence on reason's omnicompetence can only serve to damage its functioning within its proper limits. It cannot avoid pronouncing on what it can neither know nor access. The givenness of reality is one such insurmountable boundary. Just as science cannot say what precedes the big bang, since the unavailability of evidence blocks the way, so reason cannot pronounce on the structure or culmination of reality. All of it lies strictly beyond our purview. The canons of science depend on acknowledgment of the limits of their explanatory power. Most of all, we cannot explain the possibility of explanation. Certainly the notion that all might be reducible to the laws of physical causation reveals an astonishing lapse of self-reflection. It beggars imagination to suggest that mind might be physical. To recognize that mind is dependent on the physical is a commonplace, but to insist on its reducibility to the physical is a step without necessity or warrant. The result is the conception of a universe in which science itself, a purely nonphysical event, is impossible.[6] It is for this reason that more fluid secular minds have begun to revise or, more accurately, call for the revision of the ruling worldview. While not becoming theists, Nagel and Habermas, among others, have drawn a line beneath the secular outlook. It is no longer adequate when reason itself is guarded by a mystery it can neither remove nor surmount. Atheism has become impossible in practice.

Yet the vision of an alternative is what continues to elude these more reflective critics of secular hegemony.[7] This is also why, although secularism remains a minority perspective in the world at large, it has elite opinion firmly in its grips. It is difficult to see how it might be pried loose when no intelligible direction has been indicated for it to go. An aspiration is not a goal. What has yet to take place is a deeper realization of the path of secular self-limitation. The critics must not merely express a desideratum in calling for a removal of groundless obstructions, but must undertake a movement outside of them. One cannot declare a "post-secular" age without departing from it. An awareness of what is missing, as Habermas intimates, is possible only because one has in some sense glimpsed it. The secular age is not so much refuted as it refutes itself. Nietzsche understood this process when he observed that every morality, carried far enough, nihilates itself.[8] That is, it reveals its own shortcomings. But what Nietzsche did not fully grasp, and few readers noticed, is that it is precisely this movement that restores morality to itself at a deeper level. Morality continually transcends itself. A similar inexorability is at work in the secular civilization that is the fruit of modernity. Historically it derives from spiritual resources inchoately present within it, but the real surprise is that they eventually bring about the reversal of its prevailing self-understanding. It is not merely Nagel and Habermas who declare the end of the secular age. A secular outlook eventually effects its own overturning. If it is true to the rationality that defines it, a secular worldview must eventually concede the insufficiency of reason as the means of its self-preservation. Kant famously declared that he had put a limit to reason in order to make room for faith. How that notable formulation is to be taken has been far from clear. But one of its sharpest applications may well be in the recognition that it is not just Kant who calls for the self-limitation of reason but reason itself that demands it.[9]

That still does not of course provide us with an indication of how the transcendent may be glimpsed from within a rationally secular perspective. Kant may have begun the line of reflection, but he did not complete it. Even he did not see that the self-limitation of reason portends an absolute limit. In grasping a limit, we have also glimpsed beyond it. The boundary is itself an intimation of what is on the other side. Reason is not as limited as we had taken it to be, for even while conceding the inapplicability of its categories to what is outside of space and time, it has nevertheless been able to grasp that inapplicability. This is the essence of Kant's famous *Critique of Pure Reason* and the signal shortcoming of the work, as his successors tirelessly elaborated. Kant had not grasped the significance of what he had grasped. That may only have provided a rather slender connection to the Beyond, but it was an unmistakable one. Reason had glimpsed what it could not glimpse, that which transcends space and time. Its limitation had never been sheer ignorance but an intimated awareness of what it could never hope to comprehend. The relationship is paradoxical. It claims to know what it does not know. But is that not the structure of Socratic wisdom that coincides with the opening of philosophy itself? Kant's Socratic moment is only deficient in not recognizing the wisdom of that ignorance.[10] Or perhaps we may see this as the fulfillment of the promise of the Socratic understanding, when we see that ignorance is never a fixed state at all. In knowing ignorance, we have ceased to be ignorant. What cannot be grasped can nevertheless be glimpsed, so that nongraspability is never definitive. This is not in any sense a private or subjective event. We do not merely wish for what we cannot know directly. We simply recognize that beyond knowledge is the knowledge of knowledge. The contours of that contextual awareness may not be so clearly demarcated, and we may not be able to summon up its content at will, but we cannot eliminate it, and it occasionally bursts powerfully upon us. We know beyond the bounds of our knowing.

The Flash of Transcendence

There is nothing esoteric about such knowledge. It is what marks our relationships with one another on a continuous basis. The person we know is always more than we can say. This applies as much to the knowledge we have of ourselves. "Mystery" is a common term to apply to this dimension of experience, but it suffers from a notable drawback. It suggests that we do not know at all, while the truth is that we know extremely well. To get to know another person is to somehow know what is hidden within them. It is to know who they are, over and above all that we may say about them. That is, beyond what we know. Such personal knowledge is often undervalued in comparison to the objective factors that can be quantified, as in a credit report. But the truth is that it is the latter that can be manipulated. Who a person is cannot be concealed. The same is the case when it comes to the knowledge we have of knowledge. Far from being merely subjective, it is more valid than so-called objective knowledge because it is the standard of truth. We know when something is true, but we cannot say what truth is. Yet that does not mean that truth is less true than what we judge to be true. We might be inclined to ascribe this deepest knowledge to some inner criterion we carry within, except that it is not really within us at all since we are constrained to form our thoughts in relation to what is beyond them. Like personal knowledge, it is the touchstone of all that is real.[11] It would be more correct to say that we live within it rather than that it lives within us. Spatial metaphors defeat us when we grapple with the transcendent. The subjective and the objective are categories with which we are familiar, precisely because we overlook what makes them possible and is thus neither subjective nor objective.[12] What includes them is the transcendent. It is what makes it possible for us to know both of them and thus stand within what is beyond them.

The question then is, how can we, while a part of the order of things, know the whole? How is it possible for what is within being to step outside of it, at least to the extent of that glance that gives us the most precious awareness of who we are? That has been the central philosophical question. It has been given a variety of answers, but they have all been variants of a basic one. We know being because we are somehow participants in that which is beyond being. Our ability to glimpse being as such attests to this genesis from beyond being. To say we are made in the image of God is a figurative way of depicting it. What it means only gains precision as we begin to see what the transcendent means. While being a part of the whole, we are simultaneously capable of apprehending the whole. We are connected with the One who is the source of all, the transcendent as such. Our movement is a participation in the divine movement, because we are not identical with God. Yet somehow we participate in the same perspective. We are not the source of all, yet we possess some element of that which is. Like God, we do not exist in the strict sense. We are beyond existence or that which merely is. It is this that enables us to grasp what is. Everything about us arises from what cannot be said. The source of saying is prior to it all. The person who holds the mask is not in the mask. Kant approached such thoughts in his notion of the a priori whose status could not be unambiguously clarified. But he came closest in his moral philosophy when he contemplated the dignity of a rational being who could transcend all motivations for the sake of duty. The moral actor who thus held their entire existence in their hands is neither in the action nor in the hands. At that point Kant knew that human dignity approached the divine. Thus, it was in what transcended all earthly particularity that a human being was most real. The critique of pure reason reaches its confirmation in the practice of duty for duty's sake. Nothing could be more real than that which is capable of contemplating all reality while living supremely beyond it.

A reversal of the secular scale of values is inexorably at work as we contemplate the condition of possibility of life in this world. We begin to see that even our discussion of the secular cannot be so neatly placed within it. Already we seem to have slipped outside of its limits. We recall the meaning of the secular as what is withdrawn from service to the sacred.[13] But this is not only a matter of historical or conceptual significance. It arises from within the secular dynamic itself. The world that would brook no interference from any extraneous source beyond it begins to realize that even that assertion is one that cannot simply be adduced as secular. The freedom and independence of reason is not guaranteed by reason itself. It is authorized by the reason of reason. The world is continually transcended by that which preserves it as world. To guard the secular is already to depart from it. Such a strategy is needed not only to preserve the secular from its own excesses, but, more fundamentally, as an affirmation of what the secular truly is. It is not a realm that scrubs itself clean of transcendent reference, in order to ostensibly allow the bearers of faith to cling to their private convictions. This neutral conception betrays a subtle hostility or indifference to faith that has been a source of much misunderstanding. It may well be that disdain for religion characterizes much elite secular opinion, justifying its characterization as a "culture of disbelief."[14] The secular ethos must, however, be judged, not by the most minimal sentiments to which it gives rise, but by the most elevated expressions of its spirit. In this regard, the reaction of John Rawls to the view that his notion of "public reason" is hostile to religion is a good indication. He seemed genuinely taken aback by the suggestion.[15] Unlike many of his fellow secularists, he did not consider exclusion of religion from the public sphere as a negative aspersion. To the contrary, secular reason was precisely what was most favorable to faith. Like Tocqueville, he thought that the absence of official endorsement left religion free to make its way unhindered. It is, in other words, out of due regard for what transcends it that the secular confines itself within the secular. The world from which God is absent may simultaneously be the world that reverences him most profoundly.

The secular is defined by the awareness of its distance from the divine. It declares that nothing can represent God but God himself. He is nowhere present in the world and therefore can only be found within himself. Secular neutrality turns out to be anything but neutral. Not only does it hold itself back, opening a space for the sacred, but it thereby affirms what is beyond it. This is well known in the guarantee of the freedom of religion that is often regarded as the first freedom, without which no other freedom means anything. Even when it is formulated as the freedom of conscience the result is the same. The state puts itself in relation to what is beyond it, what it can properly acknowledge only by submitting to its imperative. It declares that nothing is more important than the relationship we hold toward the transcendent. At the same time the state concedes that nothing within it provides access to that which exceeds all reality. Only the transcendence enacted by each human being opens a path toward the transcendent. Each carries within a mystery that the secular realm cannot reach. To the extent that it is that relationship that is the source of their dignity, the state acknowledges what it cannot comprehend. This has nothing to do with such "metaphysical" notions as souls and immortality that are in many respects an afterthought. They are a retrospective terminology for what initially escapes all naming. What is beyond is beyond naming. It is enough that the secular realm has thus confessed what it cannot confess. The language of rights, by which it too subsequently unfolds its intuition, can never plumb the depths from which it arises, that is, that rights are inexhaustible. There is no point at which the person ceases to matter. Each is the center of the whole but only because each carries the whole within. In reaching toward the transcendent, every person is more than all that is.[16] Even to themselves they are an inexhaustible mystery. This cannot be said in the language of secular finitude, but it can be said by not saying. That is the meaning of the guarantee of religious liberty. It affirms the mystery beyond it.

Atheism has become impossible in practice for the modern liberal state. It may not profess any religious order and, indeed, often understands itself as bound to eradicate any vestiges of the public confession of God. Sometimes the urge to maintain its secular purity has become so immoderate that it seems to make a religion of secularism itself.[17] But that is merely to put forward a substitute for what it knows it does not possess and thereby sets in motion the logic that overturns it. A secular religion is not just a contradiction in terms; it is self-defeating. By erecting a false reality, it prompts the demand for its true alternative. The very cogency of an order of rights depends on the truth that exceeds it, for the one principle that cannot be conceded is that rights are finite. Rights that can be quantified, divided, and exhausted are not rights. Inalienability is at their core. They are thus not rights that the state accords but ones that it acknowledges as defining its own deepest responsibility. Legislatively bestowed rights can be legislatively abrogated. If they are to retain their integrity, there must be no whiff of mutability. They must derive from what is impervious to negotiation or power. They must be absolutes that can only be limited by other absolutes. And nothing worldly can fit that requirement. If the reach of power is to be limited, there must be something that power cannot reach. But that means that power recognizes its worldly limits by virtue of what is beyond it. Rights must be capable of holding power in awe. They are the point at which power submits to what it knows but cannot say. It is this aura of the transcendent that still attaches to the seemingly secular language of rights. Often the resonances are quite unconscious. In the hands of a spiritually sensitive thinker like Rawls, however, they become explicit. This is why even though he left his religion behind, his spirituality could never finally be jettisoned. To do so would be to eliminate what a regime of rights sought to protect. Even though Rawls refused to say what that unspeakably precious core was, he knew that it remained indispensable.[18]

It is, he seemed to say, too great a treasure to be named. The refusal to appeal to any comprehensive philosophy attests to the freedom to appeal to comprehensive philosophies. Even the minimal justification he himself had provided in *A Theory of Justice* would have to be set aside in order to preserve the inviolability of each person to construct their own. Of course, it can be objected that this is itself a form of comprehensive worldview, but if it is, it is a remarkably self-effacing one. It is a comprehensive worldview that refuses to call itself such for the sake of not preempting the elaboration of worldviews by others. The extraordinary delicacy of Rawls's insistence on self-effacement has rarely been noticed. Most often it has been mistaken for an antifoundational turn of mind. Or it has been viewed as the furthest possible extension of his principle that the right is prior to the good. Even Rawls himself only gradually managed to grasp where his thought was leading, so it is perhaps not so surprising that it has been seen as ending in incoherence. I once thought as much myself.[19] But I have since come to see that it is the unconventional character of the project that has been the principal obstacle to its penetration. In a world where everything is said or, we are confident, can be said, what are we to make of the refusal to say? It seems to serve no purpose, until one realizes that it aims at what transcends all saying. The defect is not that we cannot say but that we seek to say more than we can say. Perhaps the liberal regime of rights is a variant of apophatic theology, and Rawls is not so much an unbeliever as a mystic. Such intriguing possibilities do not have to be resolved here. It is sufficient to note them as we struggle to unlock the meaning of the secular. Its publicly political language, at least in the hands of one of its preeminent theorists, suggests that it is far from what it appears to be.

The secular guards the transcendent. That may be a provocative way of presenting the Rawlsian viewpoint, but it does suggest its deepest spiritual inspiration. Whether that is intended or not is less significant. The liberal regime of rights has long been suspected of containing more than it says. The elevation of the person as the one infinity within a world of finitude is something of an open secret.[20] Like Rawls, liberal political society may be unwilling to confess what it believes, and that may well be the key to its success. By resonating transcendence, liberal politics no longer has to defend it. Certainly there is no need for a theological underpinning to justify the infinite worth of each human being. That has already been affirmed in practice. The regime of rights opens up the perspective of inexhaustibility and indivisibility that had previously been derived from the assurance of divine love. Convictions concerning the inviolable dignity and worth of each human being are rooted in the convictions themselves. Any metaphysical underpinning that might be adduced would be less reliable than the abiding intuition for which they are adduced. The guarantees are not imperiled by the lack of a rationale. Liberal regimes attest to the transcendent worth of every person as unique and irreplaceable. They do not have to justify what they take to be axiomatic.[21] Dispensing with foundations is not an eccentricity of Rawls's formulation of the priority of right but indicative of the broader consensus of liberal political society. It knows, even without a theoretical explanation, that its conviction of the infinite value of every person is beyond question. Rights and dignity may be endlessly discussed, but they are immune from the danger of abrogation. The extent and strength of such convictions is surely one of the most striking features of the contemporary world.

This is why the language of human rights has become a global legacy. Even regimes that evince little sympathy for their preservation still clothe their infractions within its discourse. None step forward in the name of subordinating the individual to the collective good. Somehow the person transcends the whole. We may not be able to fully explain the source of our conviction, but we know its rightness intuitively. Without possessing a philosophical means of articulating this astonishing thought, that the part is greater than the whole, we have managed to hold onto it as the lodestar of our political life. Even in a world riven by political disagreement, domestically and globally, we cannot abandon this core conviction. The measure of a regime is how it treats its most vulnerable members. Does it accord them the same immeasurable dignity and respect it assigns to its most powerful? The high and the low may not enjoy the same advantages, but they are entitled to be regarded as equally worthy. The priority of the person over the whole may be an elemental intuition in our daily interactions, but it would be difficult to give it public expression in the absence of the language of inalienable rights. In many ways that discourse functions as our most theologically charged medium. Certainly, its reach is beyond any theological limits. To say that it is secularized Christianity, as Nietzsche did, is perhaps not too far off the mark.[22] But that is also to imply that it is derivative and doomed to decline with the withdrawal of Christianity from the public realm. An alternative account would be that human rights is the sphere through which the spirit of Christ prevails within the secular world. The relationship may be interdependence rather than dependence. Whatever the case, the crucial aspect is that the language of rights enables a secular world to retain its hold on a transcendence that would otherwise elude it. Without it, we would live in a thoroughly mundane condition in which everything had its price and nothing was of value.

It is because that bleak prospect has not been realized that, even in its own terms, the secular is not an irrevocably closed universe. It remains open to the transcendence it inchoately preserves within it. Even when it vigorously professes agnosticism about ultimate reality, it cannot embrace the most dogmatic form of atheism. The secular cannot exclude the transcendent. Even if it could get over the self-contradiction, of pronouncing on what is beyond itself, the secular cannot afford to eject what is pivotal to its own most deeply held convictions. If each human being is to be regarded as an end-in-itself, outweighing in value the whole world, then we cannot afford to turn our backs on the transcendent as such. Once again, atheism has become impossible in practice. To profess it would be contrary to what we most affirm, the unspeakable preciousness of each person whom we are bound to regard as the center of the universe. We cannot simultaneously exalt the dignity of the person and assert that there is nothing of surpassing value in each. Acknowledgment of human dignity is the invisible path to its source. The language of dignity implicates dignity as such. This is why its invocation has long been regarded as a stepping-stone to the acknowledgment of God. The persistence and expansion of dignity discourse within the talk of rights is testament, not only to its inescapability, but also to its reciprocity. If the defense of human dignity is the greatest moral achievement of our secular world, it cannot admit what could fatally undermine it. Theism may not be possible, but atheism has become impossible. Resolute openness may be the highest spiritual affirmation of the secular, even if it is not the highest secular affirmation of the spiritual.

The Transcendent That Reveals the Transcendent

The transition to a truly post-secular age awaits a deeper awakening in which the distinction between the spiritual and the secular is grasped as correlative. Both sides revolve around the notion of transcendence. Without transcendence we would not have the idea of the secular. Both historically and conceptually, the secular world is dependent on what it is not. But equally, the sacred has no meaning if it is not set apart from the profane. It constitutes a realm only if it is a realm apart from the everyday. It is in following this logic that the transcendence of God is revealed as beyond and within the world. For the earliest humans, the world was full of gods. Everything seemed to manifest the divine. But then it gradually became clearer that the gods too were all manifestations of what itself was not manifested in any of them.[23] A world full of gods is also a world without God. What everything seeks to disclose has not been disclosed. No extent of speculation on the one who is hidden behind all the hierophanies could adequately reach what is sought. It was only then that the realization dawned that the seeking would not have been possible without already knowing what is sought. Yet that was not the great breakthrough. For that, human beings had to discover that they could not find what they sought because it was beyond all that they could know. Only the self-revelation of God could break the blockade. Then it was beheld that God is transcendent. Nothing in the world can be a vehicle for his disclosure. Only God himself can reveal who he is. The transcendent is that which cannot be known except by the gift of the transcendent itself. The invitation may have been there from the very earliest symbol formation, but the irruption of the transcendent into consciousness had to await its self-revelation as transcendent, that is, as what cannot be revealed. From that astonishing breakthrough begins the long human struggle to understand the relationship with the God who is beyond to all that he is beyond. In the differentiation of the transcendent, there is the simultaneous identification of the immanent. The secular is not a modern discovery but a vestige from the great axial turning point. The revelation of God is simultaneously the revelation of the world that is not God.

This has been the pivot of our thinking about God and the world that we have scarcely been able to absorb. That which makes it possible for us to think about an issue rarely becomes an issue. We pass over it without notice. Yet, for all that heedlessness, we do not escape its inescapability. This is why the objectifying language to which we turn defeats the sense of mastery toward which it aspires. God and the world are not objects we can hold apart from us, for they are the containers within which our thinking about them occurs. Normally only a vague sense of the incompleteness of the categories of our discourse is all that disturbs our self-confidence. We sense there is something not quite right, yet we cannot assign a particular source to it. A rumor of the uncanny is all that remains.[24] We fail to see that the only grasp we have of God and the world is what arises through our participation in them. Intimations of what we cannot behold reach us, and we have such intimations only because we live within them. No matter where we begin we always begin with some notion of God and the world that is already there before we begin. For most of the things we think about, the necessity of adopting a starting point within the order of things is not a particular problem. Interest and opportunity dictate what is of relevance at any given time. But what about when we want to think about relevance as such? Is there a deeper or broader understanding of relevance that can encompass it? Is all our thinking doomed to spiral in an abyss of incoherence? It is at that point that we grasp for whatever straws we can reach. We begin to see that the relevance of what we seek is not so totally incomprehensible but is rooted in a deeper relevance we may never be able to plumb. We may not be able to exhaustively elaborate the source of its hold upon us, but we cannot deny its validity. We know more than we can say and acknowledge that all saying originates in that intuition. That is why terms like sacred and secular, transcendent and immanent, are not so much tools of our thought as the parameters that make all such tools possible. The differentiation of God and the world is the maximal clarity we can reach concerning the whole within which we exist.

Even then we only catch a glimpse of what it is we think we know. God and the world are the limits, not the content, of it. This is why we cannot "explain" the secular age, especially when explanations overlook the growing convergence of God and the world within an intensifying drive for perfection. It is possible to explain such a development without taking a stand on its validity. Should it be affirmed or resisted? And how can we render a judgment without situating ourselves within its tensions? Is there a way to discuss secularization that can ignore the implications for our own lives? Even how we understand secularization, whether as departure from the divine or increasing assimilation of it, turns on our response to it.[25] If we approve of the process, then we will be inclined to view it as an inevitable removal of the divine from the natural. If we disapprove, then we will be more willing to explore the notion that it amounts to an immanentization of the religious impulse. We may find ourselves untroubled by the notion of a world that stands on its own, without a source beyond it. But if we regard the project as a specious absorption of what cannot be absorbed, the transcendent, then we must look toward a radical reordering of spirituality. The inversion must be remedied by a reversion to its original form. Either we can live without a longing for transfiguration or the aspiration points toward its true realization. Untangling the dynamics that have been at the heart of the modern world cannot be undertaken in a purely scientific fashion. In this case, science must include the condition of its own possibility. The observer is included in the lines of meaning of the investigation. Even what science is depends on whether there is an immanent order of explanation.[26] But science can only be preserved if it recognizes that it cannot pronounce on what lies beyond the empirical realm. As with all investigation of the human world, we remain at the boundary that existence must cross continually. Thinking cannot find its bearings until we have determined whether we are God or apart from God.

Even to pose it as a question already implies its answer, for it arises from the sentiment of not being God and the presentiment of God as somehow other. We realize that there is no returning to a moment when the distinction was not inchoately present. No matter how confused, we still knew that God is other. But who is this Other? That requires more reflection, and we are poorly prepared to undertake it. Initially, we possess only the question itself. Only slowly do we realize that the question reflects more than our ignorance. It is already a knowledge of what we are not. So, although it is a negation of knowledge, it is a knowledge of what negates. We know what it is for which we search. The question arises from the answer already given within it. In some sense the question is not really ours for it is what enables us to raise it. We do not contain it; it contains us. It is within the unfolding of the question that we encounter both the question and its answer. Not only is the answer given to us but the question is too. Revelation is the structure of our questioning. As yet, however, this is not revelation as such, for we do not know it as revelation. It is simply a movement whose origin we only dimly perceive. All we have is a direction, not a source. For it to unfold into a revelation, something more is required. There must be a rupturing of what we know. The limits must be breached, so that we encounter the limitless. But no revelation would be possible unless we were prepared to receive it. We must be capable of recognizing what we had not known. The forgotten must be remembered because it was ultimately never forgotten. Revelation prepares the way for revelation, when the question is raised from within its movement. At no point do we elude the undertow drawing us into what is beyond us.

The break, however, does occur when we realize that we are not the source of the revelation. It is Other. Then we know it as a revelation, as the revealing of what cannot be revealed. Certainly it cannot be revealed by anything else that we know. Transcendence has occurred, and we have become its recipients. All previous routine, with its rhythms and regularities, has been shattered. We confront that which is beyond it all and fashion the language of transcendence to denote it. The cosmos, the whole that contained all, is no longer the reassuring permanence of order. Now all that *is* is grounded in that which is not. The effect is destabilizing, requiring a very different way of conceiving things. We are compelled to undertake a radical reorientation of our lives. In the most dramatic versions we undertake an exodus from Egypt, but even in the less dramatic forms the paradigm of authority is overturned. Those who have left the cosmos behind possess a new criterion of the really real. The world comes into focus as merely the "world," and we behold it in the diminished status from which enchantment has fallen away. We live in a secular world now experienced in all its unendurable finitude. It is precisely that from which God is absent. He must be found elsewhere, beyond it. The cosmos can no longer mediate the marvelous by which it intimates more than it can say. As the world, it is shorn of the transcendence that had been its shimmering boundary. Analogy is exposed as incapable of conveying what has no analog. This is the epochal turning point of history, the moment in which the spiritual outbursts generate the world religions and indelibly stamp the world as secular. We live within the rupture of transcendence that exceeds our comprehension. It is the event that cannot be located within a historical framework except by way of the traces that are the effects it leaves behind. The cause itself is beyond causality.

Yet somehow we know about it. Perhaps that is the most remarkable of all. The revelation of what is beyond all revelation is nevertheless received. How that is possible has not always been given the attention it deserves. We take it for granted and thereby diminish what has been granted. We do not see that even for God it must surely be a challenge to communicate his incommunicability. How does he accomplish it? A burning bush or a flash of lightning would be relatively easy. But how do we know that God is not in the thunder or the earthquake? The still small voice seems closer to what is disclosed, but, even then, there is a pointing beyond what is not. A voice is, after all, merely a sound, a frequency vibrating in the air. Unless it is a sound that is soundless? Perhaps what is heard is only heard within. No eruption of cosmic fireworks can say what it seeks to say. For that there must be more than hearing. There must be the listening that catches what cannot be heard, that is, the voice of the other. The transcendent that exists nowhere and cannot be manifest in anything must nevertheless reveal itself. This can occur only when it is known inwardly as itself another inwardness. Then we know God as he is in himself, as a self. The revelation of God as transcendent is simultaneously the revelation of a personal God. There is no transcendent ground as a vague impersonal reality beyond revelation. There is only the personal depth that is the person who is irretrievably deep.[27] A depth unspoken is the person who speaks. That is what makes it possible for God to communicate the incommunicable, for he reveals himself as a person. All revelation is personal. It is always of what is beyond revelation but is nevertheless revealed. Persons always say more than they say because they disclose themselves. Transcendence is the inwardness in which all is contained. To go beyond the world and all that is within it is to enter into the heart of the person.[28] That is the event of revelation, an event that is contained nowhere but within itself. Persons who transcend are capable of reaching the transcendent. To say that we thus discover ourselves as the image of God is still to revert to a mere image. The truth is that we here advert to what is beyond all imaging. That which apprehends cannot be apprehended. It is the meeting of persons who cannot be contained in any of the circumstances of their meeting.

God is encountered as not being in anything said, for he is always more than that. It is the "more than" that is accessed. We know it directly in the way that persons know one another. Absence is *known* as absence. The problem of the absence of God is thus not a uniquely modern concern. It is there from the very beginning. Nor do we overcome it by finding God in something else, for he can be found only if he is found in himself. That is to know God as a person. He must be known as transcending all, because only then is he known apart from everything, as he really is in himself. The encounter is an encounter with nothing, although the nothing embraces everything within it. The language of theology that makes God into a being, or substance, or the One is not inaccurate, but it does depart from the source of its own terminology. The meaning of such terms derives from what it means to be a person, that is, as one who is transcendent, beyond all and containing all. This is what it means to be a person. To say such things of God is to say that he is a person. It is also to say that he cannot be known by any of those aspects, for if he is known it can only be as he is within himself. Metaphysics and the language it provides to theology cannot convey what is most essential. It is not just that we need a personal experience of God to know him, for strictly speaking there is nothing to experience. What we most need to know about God is God himself.[29] What is it like to be God? To know the inner person is really to know the person; everything else belongs to the incidental. To know that is to go beyond all that is given, to reach the heart of God. How we do this is as mysterious as knowing any other person. We cannot say, except that the other lies open to us. To be a person is to possess an inwardness that can connect with the inwardness of another, of all others. It is not that we infer from some outer evidence to the presence of the other. It is that the priority of the other is already what makes it possible for such inferences to occur. Otherwise no amount of speculation would enable us to make the leap from what is visible to what is invisible. This is why proofs for the "existence" of God are notoriously circular.[30] They end up bringing us back to the starting point we already knew. At best they consist in the recognition of God who is otherwise unrecognizable in any of the trail of evidence. In knowing God, we know beyond all knowing.

This has often been referred to as a mystical knowledge, but it is far from hidden or secret as the term suggests. It is the same as the knowledge we have of other persons who are in no way visible, or at least not in their most central aspect. Their inwardness is a pure absence, yet it is more fully present to us than we are to ourselves. We cannot doubt that they are other selves. Descartes's famous *cogito ergo sum* seemed to make the self the basis for everything, but that was to overlook the realization that it is awareness of the other that makes it possible for me to know myself. Relation to the other is prior to the relation to myself. We know what is transcendent before we know anything immanent. Descartes also initiated this correction when he went on in his Third Meditation to say that knowledge of the infinite is what makes it possible to know the finite. This is the theme I have been mining in the previous chapters in suggesting that the secular is derivative from the sacred. When we begin with the finite and the secular, as worldly convention powerfully suggests, then it is always difficult to find a place for the sacred. Nothing in the material seems to yield a place for spirit. The secular imagination is incapable of thinking beyond its boundary. It is only when we begin to turn our attention to the boundary as such, to notice that in becoming aware of it we leave the secular world behind, that we gain the alternative perspective that brings our existence into focus. Then we see that transcendence is not an alien or hidden reality but the condition of possibility within which we live. Just as we could not know other persons unless we already knew them, so we cannot know God unless we already know who it is that we seek. To attempt to prove either one is not only impossible; it is also unseemly. It is as if to say that they are merely factual, when in truth they overwhelm all facts. Nothing is sufficient to demonstrate the existence of the other, human or divine, for they cannot be contained in what merely is. The absence that is their presence is not an emptiness but a superabundance that overflows all limits. Transcendence is what cannot be contained.

That is the deepest meaning of the secular world, although it has yet to awaken to it. The secular resists the inclusion of the divine within it and thereby affirms divinity as such. It proclaims its own incapacity to be a vessel of the divine presence. In that way it announces the divine presence as a pure absence. God is to be found nowhere within the world, for God is to be found only within God. As yet the secular world has not reached the latter affirmation. It only dimly intuits the nonexistence of God. It knows that he is not among the things that exist. But it has also not been able to completely shake off the intimation of its positive affirmation. The secular knows the uncanny that uncannily clings to it. This is why it has begun to raise the question of its status and to contemplate the possibility that it is entering upon a "post-secular" phase. Within that concession there is a discernible awareness of having stepped beyond its own boundary. The question of the secular is not a secular question. It is an attempt to locate itself within an unbounded region. Confusion reigns but gradually begins to dissolve with the growing awareness that the boundary cannot be included within the field of vision it opens up. Consciousness of the transcendent hovers, as that of which we cannot have any consciousness. None, that is, except the sideways glance that enables us to glimpse wherein we are. We are located in that which cannot itself be located within anything else. That is what is meant by the name of God. It is in this way that God is at home in the world, by not being at home in it. The only question is whether the world can be at home in God. Can the secular world understand itself as not only separate from God but also as most faithful to him?

The Secular Opens on the Transcendent

At the point of maximum openness the secular ceases to be simply secular. It would more properly present its self-limitation as a mark of respect for what it is not. Aware of the distance that separates it from the transcendent, the secular world would thereby gain the deepest understanding of itself. The fog that for so long enveloped it would begin to lift as it grasped whence it had come. Where previously it had drifted away from what it could no longer remember or rebelled against what it did not know, now it can recognize the boundaries by which it is constituted.

It can see that there is no boundary apart from what is beyond it. The world cannot contain itself. It cannot even be a world without intuiting its transcendence. But this is more than a conceptual clarification. It is simultaneously a liberation. The secular world is free to be itself. It does not have to reoccupy or replace what it is aware of missing.[31] It can simply be finite and limited, without any dissatisfaction concerning its status. It does not have to promise or claim to be more than it is. The burden of transcendence has been lifted from it, a burden that had always been impossible to sustain. With it there also evaporates the tissue of subterfuge by which the secular world had sought to deny its own inescapable shortcomings. Without having to promise more than it could deliver, the secular outlook can acknowledge itself as it really is. Free from the impossible, it can now give itself fully to the possible. When perfection has become unattainable the good can be adequately served. The breakthrough to the secular as secular is both an advance in self-understanding and an advance in the restraint of action within its unsurpassable limits. It may simply never be possible for human beings to walk on Mars, just as they may never be able to defeat death. And it makes even less sense for them to expend their precious lives in pursuit of projects rendered futile by their own mortality. Far better to live within an acceptance of limits that is always more than mere resignation. It is the discovery of joy within the boundaries assigned to us. A whole universe is contained in the smallest gesture of love. Gone is the forced hilarity when true laughter bursts upon us. The ephemeral nature of all existence can now be embraced when overtaken by the joy that utterly surpasses it. Finite reality is touched by the infinite.

It may not yet see itself as the proper affirmation of what is beyond it. The secular knows it is not the divine and may even be relieved by acknowledging its nonultimate status. It knows it is free simply to be, to be itself. What remains is the discovery that thereby points most profoundly to what it cannot say. In that sense the secular is included within the transcendent. The self-restraint by which it refuses to go beyond its own finite range is, at the same time, the acknowledgment of what it is not. Not saying is never simply not saying at all. It is the affirmation of what cannot be said and thus its most powerful attestation. The inner meaning of the secular world is disclosed, even as a meaning that radically exceeds it. Just as the boundary cannot be included within the bounded, the world cannot contain the divine although that noncontaining is already a glimpse beyond it. The mystery within which it exists, the uncanny that had continually eluded its grasp, begins to be discerned. The transcendent seeps into the immanent without breaching the barrier between them. Yet something momentous has occurred. What had seemed impossible has nonetheless occurred. The miraculous has broken through. The secular is no longer secular when it guards the boundary that opens upon the transcendent. This may well be the turning point of a civilization that had sought so forcefully to absorb the transcendent within it, even while it knew the futility of the task. Now it intimates the possibility of overleaping the impossibility. The transcendent may not be absorbed, but it is unmistakably welcomed as the condition of possibility of the secular as such. Eternal and temporal enter upon a mutuality that sweeps away prior opposition. Now sacred and profane become virtually continuous.

But they have renounced identity. In that proscription is the key to the secular affirmation of the transcendent. No longer a mere rejection of the sacred, the secular has assumed the far more positive role of preserving the proper distance from it. Separation is still the reality, but it is at the same time a conjunction, a unity in difference. The awareness of what is missing, the uncanny that Marx sensed and Nietzsche voiced, is no longer so incomprehensible. Now it has become an absence that cannot be filled, not because of incapacity on the part of the secular, but out of reverence for what it can never make present within it. What is missing is still missed, but it has also been found in the acknowledgment of it as missing. Far from confrontation or hostility, the division is overcome in a Hegelian grasp of its necessity. The secular can never absorb the sacred without thereby losing it.[32] Their relationship is now defined by a distinction that cannot be abolished because it has become their permanent condition. The separation renders them inseparable. That is the meaning of a secular civilization. God may be forgotten and faith may have ebbed, but that is not the deepest realization at which the secular ethos aims. To really be true to itself it must simultaneously affirm what it cannot contain. It does this by not containing it. The absence has become a deeper form of presence. Amnesia is never sheer loss. Forgetting is only a possibility for those who remember, and we cannot forget without remembering. That is the deepest layer of irony hidden within Marx's remark about the impossibility of atheism. The secular world cannot be without ceasing to be secular. The revolution, within which it finds itself, finally reveals its inexorability. The leap beyond itself into what it is not is almost palpable. This is the mystery that compelled a thinker like Habermas to poignantly struggle against his own reluctance.

Atheism has become impossible in practice. Yet the concession is neither the triumph of the secular, as Marx envisioned, nor the demise of it, as Habermas feared. It is the transformation of the relationship between the immanent and the transcendent that has been under way ever since the first revelatory outburst. Nothing in the world can represent that which is beyond it. What has changed today is that the world, which understands itself by virtue of that separation, has now begun to understand and embrace the condition of its own genesis. This cannot occur without an acknowledgment of what transcends it. In its most secular moment it becomes aware of what it is not. The uncanny that it harbored within has been understood in its source. It has ceased to be uncanny. To retain the insight, however, it must go beyond that first halting intimation. The secular must see itself, not only as derived from the sacred, but as its most faithful depiction. The transcendent that cannot be known through anything else must be glimpsed through itself. That is, the transcendent must be present as the transcendent, as that which cannot be present and therefore must be present. Overcoming the paradox is the purpose of the secular.[33] By refusing to mediate that which cannot be mediated, it has thereby mediated it. The transcendent is present more faithfully than in any other form, for it can now be present only through itself. God can be known only through God. The distance a secular order places between itself and the divine is the highest reverence that can be offered to God. That which cannot be conveyed is conveyed more inwardly than all the familiar pathways religion had mapped toward it. By making God accessible, religion has made God inaccessible.[34] The secular, in contrast, by marking the transcendent as beyond, has secured its place more firmly within it. As a consequence, the secular has more thoroughly displaced its own secularity than any of its promoters could ever have expected. Perhaps this is the ultimate irony within the many layers of Marx's guiding observation. Where Marx wanted to have done with the theistic remnants against which atheism raged, we realize not only the impossibility of his determination but also the impossibility of its conception. The secular can only maintain itself by virtue of the separation from the divine that sustains it. But that separation finds its deepest affirmation within the preservation of the transcendent as transcendent. A secular world is not only open to God, but indispensable to the acknowledgment of his divinity. The secular knows that God is transcendent. Atheism *is* impossible in practice.

CHAPTER FIVE

God beyond Being

The secular world has at last secured the transcendence of God. That is its paradoxical result. Without intending it, the secular has made room for the sacred. Admittedly, it has not provided a space for the sacred within it, but it has ensured that the sacred remains properly itself. God is contained within God and nowhere else. Those who approach him must do so by going through God. The transcendent, no longer mingled with the mundane, prevails within transcendence. Of course, that also means forgetting, the absence of God, from which talk of the death of God has persistently arisen. An era whose massive this-worldliness displaces even the possibility of recognizing its own character makes the opening toward God difficult in practice too. Yet we have seen how the naturalistic outlook has nevertheless been unable to shake a sense of the uncanny, because it cannot remain what it is without glimpsing what is beyond it. Now we must take the step of pondering how that indefinable opening might yet burst forth within our secular world. How can that which can never be present make itself present? How is absence a mode of presence? This is more than the question of how God can be represented in an age that eschews the metaphysical, although that is certainly included within it. The deeper challenge is to understand how the secular is at its core an affirmation of God. We are possibly on the brink of a profoundly new concept of revelation. Or, perhaps, it would be more accurate to say that we are regaining a sense of what revelation has always been.

Can the Transcendent Be Revealed?

Despite the strongly visual narrative in which the revelation of God has historically been couched, we have begun to suspect that the reality was not like that. How could a burning bush disclose what is infinitely beyond it? How can a voice convey what cannot be voiced because it is before all saying? Could it be that those who received the message of God were no better informed of who they had encountered than we are? It is no wonder they were inclined to assimilate the symbol to the source. Faced, as Moses was, with the need to explain who it was that sent him, it was remarkable that he preserved the unexpected character of the event in the "I AM."[1] Precisely at the point when he needed to communicate it to the Hebrew clans he departed from what they knew. The story is so familiar that we scarcely note the incongruity of the suggestion that they leave Egypt to serve a God whom they had never named. Moses asks his name for that reason. Even he does not know who it is that has called him. How then was it possible to convey who this astonishing divinity is to those who had not yet encountered him? The real miracle of the Exodus is not that the Egyptians let them go but that the Israelites accepted the invitation of departure. The exodus occurs inwardly before it unfolds historically. Merely suggesting that this was the God of the fathers was hardly enough to convince them of his incompatibility with the gods of the Egyptians. Why could they not stay? It was because they could no longer live in relation to the cosmos and its gods. They had been called to live in relation to what is beyond it, to what cannot be encountered within space and time. What evidence is sufficient for that realization?

The more we ponder the biblical narrative, the more its incomprehensibility strikes us. None of the historical factors are sufficient to explain what amounts to a radical departure from history. The encounter is with what exceeds all tangibility within space and time. When we think of the Mosaic revelation in those terms we realize that the situation was not so radically different from our own. The world from which God is absent is precisely the experience on which the revelation turns. Transcendence and immanence are correlative. The problem is to explain how we come to know what they signify. While living within the world we must be capable of apprehending what is utterly beyond it. Surely this is as great a wonder as the bush that burned without being consumed. That is, Moses recognized the God who spoke to him as the one who is beyond all, the one who can be neither in the bush nor in the voice. The visible discloses the invisible. But how do we grasp what is thus beyond visibility? The Israelites too must have carried some inchoate sense of the transcendent, for they could intuit who it was that Moses recounted to them. We too must be borne along by the same indefinable awareness if we are to take the record of the encounter as one to which we also must respond. In other words, it is not closeness to the events that is the decisive factor but the equidistance of all of us with respect to what the events signify. We could know nothing about the meaning of what had transpired if we did not already carry within an intimation of the transcendent. Even the Egyptians, whose monumentally present divinities provided the solid underpinning of their lives, must have sensed a beyond of what they held onto so firmly. No matter how far back we trace the record of our conception of the gods, we know that the shaft of transcendence accompanies it from the beginning. Even the Paleolithic cave painters were aware that the images, while they drew upon the cosmos, came from what was beyond it.[2] Their own work testified to their capacity to stand outside of it. The depth from which everything arises could not be included in what arises. While living within the cosmos, they could not depict the cosmos. Transcendence is the ineliminable horizon. It was simply that, with Moses and the Israelites, it had become differentiated as such.

To recognize what transpired is of course not to explain it, for we can only grasp its character because we too live within the same horizon. Without our own glimpse of transcendence, we would be fumbling with worldly causes of the Exodus, along with naturalistic explanations of the plagues and the Red Sea.[3] We would be clueless as to what the revelation was. Thinking it was about the commandments, we would fail to apprehend their source. Even opting for the explanation that the biblical text itself offers, that it marked the establishment of the covenant between God and his people, would still overlook who it was with whom the covenant had been made. Besides, the character of the commandments and the covenant can only be grasped if they are seen in the context of the relationship that underpins them. Nothing can come into focus until we realize that this was the moment when human beings grasped what they could not grasp. The God who is beyond revelation had revealed himself to them. Beyond all that he said and all that he did, they apprehended God as he is in himself. The transcendence of God had moved from the periphery of their awareness to their focus. Now they encountered God, not through any intermediaries or representations, but through himself. They knew God as Other, as the One who cannot be manifested because he is entirely himself. It is not that Yahweh became a personal God to them but that they realized that God cannot be anything other than a person. Only a person is transcendent, untouched by all that touches and emanates from him, because he is wholly within himself. Holding his being within himself, God is unscathed by all else that is. Contained only within himself, God exemplifies what it is to be a person. It is for this reason that he can only be known by persons who come to know him as a person. Only God provides access to God.

Knowing about God is like knowing about someone one has never met. Much valuable information may be acquired in this way, but it is not comparable to knowing God himself. Then one knows whereof one talks, and without it no amount of talking will suffice to convey what cannot be conveyed. The person transcends all saying, and God is preeminently a person. Whether there is more to the personhood of God awaits a deeper disclosure of the three persons who contain the being of God. But initially, it is the transcendence of God that reveals his personhood. We might even say that transcendence is the disclosure of a person. Now we begin to see how it was possible for Moses to communicate the incommunicable. It could only be grasped by persons who are themselves constituted by the awareness of what it means to be a person. Persons live within the horizon of transcendence, even when they have not made their apprehension explicit, because they live within the awareness of what it means to be a person and to encounter persons. Personhood is the medium within which they move. They know that nothing they say can exhaustively convey who they are, nor can they succeed in reaching the other no matter how extensive the disclosure. Yet they routinely encounter one another as the transcendence of all discourse. Persons know persons as persons. It is because they transcend all that *is* that they can reach what is beyond being. They can know God because, like God, they transcend all. The biblical phrase is that they are "made in the image of God." But even that formulation derives from a realm beyond all images in which persons encounter one another as persons, in themselves and beyond all manifestations. It is their participation in the same being as God that enables them to know the being of God. In this sense, they are more than an image of God for they are in the same way as God is, in being persons. They are the pivot of the analogy of being, for, as St. Thomas asserted, persons are the highest reality there is.[4]

They are not of course identical with God, but they are called to enter into union with God. This is only possible for persons who alone can give themselves personally to God. Then they know God because they know him as a person. Where does this take place? Nowhere but within the persons, God and man, who know one another as persons. To know God is to know him as what cannot be known, yet somehow is known in the way that persons know one another as unknowable. It is to know God in himself and not in any other reality. Transcendence is the heart of what persons disclose to one another. Each is a unique other who cannot be contained in anything but themselves. That is why they cannot be known in any other way but personally. To know a person is to know nothing about that person. What is known is the person who is beyond all other expressions of the person. The person is known without any added information being known. It is what personal knowledge is. The same is true of the knowledge of God, even when he reveals himself to us. Beyond what is said is the one who says and who, for that reason, is never simply contained in what is said. Even God's will as elaborated in his commandments is not the same as God, for he remains ready to disclose his deeper will as mercy. We are not called to meet the requirements of the law but to go beyond the law in meeting the one who already is beyond it. Obligation and fulfillment are a path only for those who are not simply confined to it. They listen, not just to the call of the law, but to the call of the One who is ever beyond the law. This is the great insight of Kierkegaard in his singular analysis of Abraham's sacrifice of Isaac. The individual exceeds the universal.[5]

Both the one who responds and the One to whom response is made are prior to all that is. It is for this reason that obligation can have no incentive. What is owed is already owed to the other before there can be any calculation of what is owed. The debt cannot be amortized because there is no point at which the other ceases to be other. There can be no reduction to a finite measure. The relationship is shot through with transcendence. Fidelity to the commandments is not enough, for we are commanded to perform the impossible. Entry to the promised land cannot satisfy the unlimited promise from which it beckons. Nothing less than mutual self-giving can constitute the relationship that is already so constituted. This is why the cosmos could no longer contain the mutuality of persons who can recognize it as such. Revelation is that irruption of an awareness of what had always inhabited the horizon of human existence but that now bursts forth in all its explicitness. It is the turning point of history because in it everything merely historical has been exposed. The search for explanations, for the cause of what exceeds causation, has been irrevocably surpassed in the realization that being can never contain what is beyond being. What merely exists can never establish what is prior to existence. Just as reason cannot demonstrate its own validity, so it cannot demonstrate its condition of possibility. No accumulation of evidence can sufficiently attest the God who has revealed that nothing is sufficient to attest to him. Nothing in nature can disclose the One who is its source.[6] Everything in time has a precedent that explains its genesis, but nothing can explain that which has no genesis because it always is. Only that realization requires some explanation, but none can be given for it, except the sideways glance at its own emergence. Revelation is simultaneously the revelation of persons who can apprehend the revelation of what is personal. It is only persons who can glimpse the prior openness by which they glimpse everything else.

No matter where they begin they can always ask, "Is this where I begin?" Whatever criterion of goodness is adduced, they can step back to consider whether it too is good. Very often this realization is presented as the unlimited openness of questioning, but it is far more than a capacity. It is a mode of being. We do not initiate questions but stand within them. We are that openness that precedes what is, and it is from this that the possibility of questioning arises. Man is a questioner because questions precede his existence.[7] This is how it is possible for us to glimpse what cannot be glimpsed because it is beyond all that is. The transcendent that exists nowhere is the condition of the possibility of grasping all that merely is. To acknowledge this is not to depart from reason but to realize the unlimited movement that reason itself is. What explains everything cannot itself be explained, for it has already stepped outside of all explanations. Reason as an instrument is thus derived from revelation, the moment in which what is beyond reason discloses reason to itself. As a movement that cannot contain itself, we may more properly characterize reason as faith. It believes what it cannot say. Far from this constituting a leap, least of all a blind leap, it is the progressive deepening from which reason lives. To be reasonable is to stand within the transcendence of all that merely is. Immanence, the realm of causes, can be apprehended as such because we are capable of standing outside of it. Reason is in this sense an irruption of transcendence within immanence. It itself cannot be explained because it is without cause. That does not mean that human beings create themselves but that they participate within uncreated being.

That is what it means to be made like God. Reason stands within the nonbeing of God. The integrity of reason turns on its capacity to resist the assimilation of itself to what merely is. It must not collapse the transcendence that is the possibility of a secular world into the facticity that is that world.

A sign of that tendency is the demand that God's existence be proved. Despite the refusal of the whole philosophic tradition to enter upon such an impossible task, the suggestion continues to hold traction in a world that has forgotten it is a world. It demands that God demonstrate his veracity while the question itself eludes the same demand. The questioner stands outside of all things while insisting that the source of all things be found within them. Self-oblivion seems insurmountable. It is only when we begin to realize that God is not the object of a question but the condition of its possibility that the confusion begins to dissolve. Transcendence cannot be contained within our perspective because it is that which opens a perspective. God can only be interrogated because we stand within the transcendence of God. Our ordinary application of reason to objects can overlook its continuity with what it contemplates. It is different when reason must consider that which includes it itself. This has been well known for two millennia, but it is only in the past two centuries that it has begun to find a means of articulation, and, even then, it has not found the unwavering clarity that could eliminate the demand for divine irrefutability. It may even be that the secular ethos is the best hope of such a definitive realization. Lacking any means of providing its own foundation, that world can only acknowledge that it proceeds from what it is not. Transcendence that is utterly absent is nevertheless present as what enables the world to be what it is. The secular establishes that transcendence can only come from itself.

The Secular as the Revelation of the Transcendent

When everything is required to give an account of itself in terms of something else the process itself is unaccountable. It escapes the net of immanence. Only that which stands outside of all time and space can adequately consider time and space. Science is possible only because science itself cannot be included within science. This was Einstein's observation that the only thing that could not be comprehended was comprehensibility itself. Why should there be somewhere in the universe that one speck from which it can all be considered? "A theory of everything," to draw on Stephen Hawking's memorable phrase, cannot include the theory itself.[8] The process as a whole is only impenetrable because we assume that there can only be finite entities within reality. When we are engaged in the activity of knowing, nothing seems more natural than that we should be able to grasp the structure of things. The challenge is always to realize that grasping itself cannot be included within the structures. To reach that realization we have only to advert to the opening to truth that is entailed. Truth can be grasped because it cannot be grasped by anything else. Opening to truth cannot be compelled because truth stands radically outside of all compulsion. We can of course be forced to say something is true, but we know that that does not make it true. That awareness marks the imperviousness of truth. Truth can only arise from truth. Nothing comes before it. Even the truth of God initially requires a stance beyond God, for how else can we know that God is true? It is only gradually that we come to see that the question of God can only come from God himself. The stance of truth, reaching utterly beyond all viewpoints and boundaries, is the stance of God.

This was the insight of Grotius in his nonchalant concession to atheism. It scarcely troubled him because, contrary to the horror with which his remark has often been greeted, he remained close to the consciousness of God from which it emanated. We might say, as Nietzsche almost does, that it is God who is the first atheist.[9] To be God is perhaps most of all to set God aside. This is a sentiment that would hardly strike Christians as so far from the mark. The God who dies is the point from which the theme of the death of God arises. My God, my God, why have you forsaken me?, is, after all, the cry of God. Only timidity, and a certain mental confusion, has prevented Christians from taking the full measure of what their faith entails. The logic of Grotius's "even if" has, however, not completely escaped the tradition as a whole. This is attested by the numerous predecessors who invoked the same liminal imperative.[10] The law of God would hold even if there was no God. This is because, as Christ proclaims in extremis, we must remain faithful to God even when we can no longer know if he remains faithful to us. The dark night of the soul is far from a later or occasional phenomenon. It is there from the very beginning with Christ himself. And it remains with us up to the latest exemplars of holiness. Mother Teresa of Calcutta poured out in private the sense of distance she experienced from God.[11] St. John Paul II was so conscious of its contemporary relevance that he made John of the Cross's account of the Dark Night of the Soul the topic of his doctoral study.[12] Far from being only a feature of our secular age, it would seem that the absence of God is an accompaniment of divine transcendence from the beginning. Certainly it was there with the psalmist who complained of the fool who said in his heart, "there is no God," and the prophets bore more than passing familiarity with the Israelite defections from a God who remains hidden.

Indeed, to be transcendent is to have relinquished presence. It is what makes the secular, as that which is not transcendent, possible. But it is the movement between them that really constitutes the relationship. Neither can be without the other, and they can come together, not by abolishing distance, but by overtaking it. This was the significance of Grotius's remark. It was seized upon precisely because it penetrated to the heart of the secular project. In contrast to the skeptical overtones detectable in his English contemporary, Hobbes, Grotius remained so profoundly Christian that he could embrace the secular emergence without a trace of irony. A faithful Christian would uphold the law of God even if there were no God.[13] Fidelity to God is demonstrated by the readiness to set everything aside, even God himself, if it comes before service to God. The God who sets himself aside for the sake of man already points the way. Transcendence arises from the imperative that forsakes every incentive but itself. This is the meaning of the *estsiamsi daremus*. Nothing stands higher than the imprescriptible force of what is right.[14] How could every consequence be evaluated except in light of what lies beyond all consequences? What can provide a reason for justice other than justice itself? Would it not be to slide into injustice, that which deflects us from justice, if it were to furnish a justification? Going back to Plato's *Republic*, that was the question that set the dialogue in motion. What is justice in itself, and is it worth following, apart from its consequences? Glaucon and Adeimantus asked Socrates to show them what justice is in the soul, but this turned out to be more paradoxical than it appeared. The soul itself could hardly be seen apart from justice. It is justice that contains the soul rather than the other way around. Only justice can provide a rationale for justice. Every proposed definition must confront the question of whether it too is just. This is why it is only in relation to the good that it can be seen rightly.[15]

No reasons can be adduced for the imprescriptibility of right, for every reason must be judged as right. The law and its justice are primordial. Even God does not come before it. That is what is intimated in Grotius's infamous remark. In that respect it carries within it the germ of the notorious revolt against God in the name of justice that would mark the later centuries. But Grotius was far from the murmuring that spilled over into revolt in Ivan Karamazov. He was sufficiently close to the tradition to know that God cannot be charged with injustice for he has already clothed himself with the full suffering of injustice. His justice surpasses any finite scale of measurement. Of course, that intimation did not entirely escape the perceptive Ivan, as he allows the indictment of the Grand Inquisitor to be answered by Christ with a kiss. Justice remains unconditional. It cannot be premised on reciprocation by others. This is why justice in the end requires the transcendence of justice. It is not sufficient to demand justice, an eye for an eye, for justice can only be established by the forgiveness that suffers even to the limit of injustice. This is an implication that was quite familiar to Grotius in the distinction he made between "expletive" or explicit justice and the "attributive" justice that attributes or builds the justice that is lacking.[16] Justice always requires more than justice. You have heard it said . . . but I say unto you. The dynamic is inexorable because justice never arises from what merely exists. As a transcendent imperative, justice continually heads beyond the stasis of being. It is transfigurative. Redemption is embedded in it.

The Transcendent Cannot Be Transcended

Yet that indefeasibility of justice is more often overlooked. An awareness of it may hover mutely in the background without becoming thematic. We know there is nothing more powerful and nothing that can displace it for, even when justice is defeated, its demand prevails implacably. Out of that inextinguishable call we may, as Kant suggested, fashion the notion of an afterlife.[17] It is not, however, a mere continuation of this life, the opening of an expanse of time in which new injustices may be perpetrated. No, an afterlife is distinguished by the absolute foreclosure of possibility within it. In this sense it is not life in our ordinary sense but the moment in which life is contained. Within it, justice and injustice are rendered irrevocable. In religious language it is the event of judgment. Eternity is thus not an endless expanse of time but the moment in which time is abolished. We know about it only because the indefeasibility of justice requires it. Justice cannot be without eternity. This is not because we demand rewards and punishment in some future life but because justice itself cannot support anything less. The defeat of justice, we know, is an all too common occurrence. Often there is nothing available to defend justice but justice itself. But therein lies its power. Justice is indefeasible because it endures beyond defeat. Neither the passage of time nor the disappearance of memory can touch its impassability.[18] When everything else has passed away, justice remains as what cannot pass. This is why it is outside of time. Its inexorability is not of this world. In engaging with justice and its implacability, we touch the immortal. This is why it holds "even if we grant" the passing away of heaven and earth.[19] In its transcendence justice is inextinguishable.

It is the judgment under which all existence lies, including our own reflection on that very process. Even what we think must be examined by the light of justice. We cannot think outside of its parameters. Can there be a thinking of justice that deviates from justice? How can it be a thinking of justice if we fail to be just? In that sense we cannot, as Socrates showed, reach a definition of justice. Mastery of justice escapes us for we are called to submit to its mandate. This is why the definition of justice reached in the *Republic* is no more than a way station toward that deeper realization. Justice as a harmony of the parts is, after all, no more than an external characterization of a reality that can only be apprehended from within. The justice that creates harmony can only be known through submission to it. This is reached in the vision of the Good as what makes justice just. The transcendent cannot be transcended. This is finally the achievement of Plato's most famous dialogue, even if the voluminous commentary on it largely succeeds in missing this central epiphany. And who can blame them, for there is hardly anything more invisible than visibility itself? By remaining so thoroughly within justice, we miss the immovability that it is. Of course, we know that justice that can be bought, the mere shell of respectability of which Glaucon and Adeimantus complain, cannot be taken as the real thing. But how do we know the source of that recognition? It is as if justice is there before we begin to think about it. As the boundary of our thinking about justice, justice is unsurpassable. The challenge is to include that insight within the thought of justice itself. This was the notorious source of difficulty in the dialogue as the interlocutors struggle to determine whether the city in speech, the just city, is the true one or not. Was it only an ideal? Even that language derives from Plato, who could not settle the question of where his most beautiful creation was located. The irresolvability of the ensuing debates was sufficient to prompt Hugo Grotius to hazard a more provocative strategy. Instead of linking justice with the order of being, perhaps more might be gained by regarding justice as the opening upon being. The etsiamsi daremus reversed the priority of ontology to ethics.

Rather than see God as the foundation of law, now law becomes the path by which we arrive at God. Law, we discover, is not an externality drawn from God or nature or human will but the condition of its own possibility. We do not know about law and its imperative except by entering upon it. And we bear the possibility of submission to its mandate because we are already contained within the mandate. The law of justice and the justice of law is the decree within which we find ourselves. Nothing is higher. In entering upon the imperative of law, we already reach the shore of the transcendent. We do not have to await a demonstration of its validity, no more than we require an authentication of the reality of God. Law would hold, we are prepared to say with Grotius, even if there was no God. Not even God can stand in the way of its unassailable force. In setting aside even God, we have reached the God who empties himself so completely on our behalf that he is no longer God. Of course, in doing so he is God even more completely, or at least reveals himself even more completely. That is the paradoxical movement of transcendence that *is* by not being what it is. Grotius, by risking the loss of God, has reached an even deeper affirmation of God. By losing all, he has gained all. Therein lies the salience of Grotius's passing remark, which, despite the extensive anticipations before his time, was uniquely seized upon by the modern world as a remark that it could not pass over.[20]

Contrary to the commonly received impression that Grotius's notorious aside marked the demise of faith, it should be regarded as the point at which its interior movement is apprehended most profoundly.[21] While Thomas Hobbes seemed to be enlisting faith in the utilitarian cause of civil peace, Grotius already grasped the futility of that enterprise. Faith could never be of use in this life if it did not arise from what is beyond utility. The modern anxiety at the prospect of the withdrawal of faith from human life was real.[22] The seventeenth century was certainly the time when concern with the abyss of atheism begins its long preoccupation up to the present. But the answer could never be found in an alliance with earthly power. Sovereigns may have needed faith, but faith did not need their dominion. Initially it may have seemed as if the moral underpinning of society could not survive the disappearance of its transcendent authorization. What would there be to restrain human beings when they could engage in wrongdoing without an ever-watchful judge?[23] Why would they remain faithful to their pledges when they no longer served their interests? The social covenant seemed to require it, for, even if it had been entered upon for the sake of the benefits it could generate, it was only if it endured in the face of the total loss of benefits that it could be counted on to remain and deliver them. Without God, what force could keep men from breaking their word when death is about to strike them? Could any purely mundane calculation sustain them when all is lost? That was the anxiety that gripped and continues to permeate the unfolding secular civilization. In the early modern period Grotius is almost alone in contemplating the crisis with equanimity. He gives no hint of losing faith in faith. He knew that it rested on a foundation impregnable to the slings and arrows of outrageous fortune. Otherwise, it would not be faith.

The anxieties had been misplaced. Eventually the world would agree with the intuition of Grotius that unsupported faith need not be a source of concern. It realized, with Tocqueville, that faith can best be preserved and deepened when it is left free from all official endorsement. Then faith can arise from within its own interior movement. There may still be a role for public alliance with religion, for it is never a wholly interior reality, but even that official support must acknowledge that faith has no other beginning than free assent. It can never be compelled because it is in the nature of faith that it lives within and of its own right. Not even concern that the natural law might not bind human conscience is sufficient warrant for preempting irrevocable freedom. Later in the seventeenth century, John Locke saw this clearly as "the principal consideration" in his enunciation of the idea of toleration.[24] His pivotal letter transformed the meaning of toleration from a grudging concession to a noble affirmation. Yet even Locke had not reached his conviction by exposing himself to the complete loss of faith. He drew his principle from the logic of faith but not from faith itself. Grotius is the one who saw that faith, when it is lost, cannot finally be lost. There still remains faith in faith. Loss, we may say, is the path of faith. This is why he could hazard the etsiamsi daremus, that most daring speculation that has repeatedly been seized upon for its audacity. Somehow we sense, not just that it is a recognition of the abyss, but that in it the abyss already opens a glimpse of its own impossibility. Natural law would hold. That is the faith of Grotius.

Even when it is lost, natural law cannot be lost. Grotius thinks the unthinkable, not because it plays any role in the arguments about law that follow, but because it frames the arguments in an unsurpassable way. The *Law of War and Peace* is a great exposition of this faith in natural law and the great dissemination of natural law in the modern period, but the faith itself cannot be captured. It is what makes the exposition possible and thus cannot be included within it. He utters his most memorable exclamation in a prologue to the whole work. Like all prefaces, it tries to say what the author has not been able to say. This is of course why prefaces are so important in the books to which they are separately appended. No text can include itself. But somehow an author must attempt to say what cannot be said. "That is how I came to write the work." Grotius is thus more successful than most authors, and the secret was his willingness to seize upon the most provocative formulation of his position. He couches his raid on the inarticulate with many self-admonitions against it, for he is aware of the characteristically modern tendency to take contemplation of the abyss as an embrace of it. Nietzsche was only the most striking case of that inclination. It is notable that none of the earlier occurrences of the etsiamsi, many of which he undoubtedly knew, had provoked a similar suspicion of endorsing atheism. Yet only Grotius was so misread, and one is inclined to think that he had an inkling of the misperception he was setting in motion. However, he persevered because he knew his remark was in continuity with the preceding speculations on the dreaded loss of God as the surest path to his recovery. He was engaged in a great act of faith that sought faith on the other side of its loss. Then faith cannot be lost.

Faith beyond Loss

This faith was a signal benefaction for the modern era that Grotius was also conscious of inaugurating. It meant that the abyss of atheism could be surmounted even before it had opened. Faith would remain even when it had been lost. Perhaps then most of all. The faith that natural law entailed was evinced most of all when it was needed most, for then it would become plain that faith could not be lost. There is nothing prior or deeper than faith. Whatever is before faith can only be reached by way of faith. It is not that natural law cannot dispense with God but that even when it has dispensed with him it has not so absolved itself of God.[25] It still stands before God as the one from whom it cannot turn away. Even when it says no, it fails to say no. Natural law still holds, and it holds with the same force. In many ways its hold is deepened by the knowledge that it retains even if we say there is no God. Irrespective of God, natural law binds because it stands in the place of God.[26] Nothing is higher. It is divine or puts us in touch with what prevails in the same way as God prevails. This is the enduring reality that natural law is. To follow it is to go beyond even God, which is to arrive at what God is. The transcendence of all considerations and calculations, to realize what is right for its own sake, is to reach the transcendent. It is the reality of God even if there is no God. Atheism has become, in a reverse echo of Marx, impossible in practice. How can there be atheism when even the readiness to transcend all, including the approval of God, has brought us to God? Grotius has in this way made the transcending reality of law clearer than it would be if it were derived from the transcendent itself. We already move within God rather than move toward him.

Later Kant would refer to this structure as a transcendental. That is, a category we must think within because it could not be thought outside of itself. But Kant would miss the full force of his own insight for he lacked that last degree of boldness evident in Grotius's unforgettable remark. For Kant a transcendental is an intellectual category, but for Grotius it discloses our participation in the transcendent. That may not have gained full explication in the passage, but it is the only thing that captures the fearlessness that lies behind it. Kant was afraid to lose God and famously referred to him as a postulate.[27] Grotius was certain of God in a way that precluded fear of his loss. Etsiamsi daremus could only be pronounced by a man of unshakable faith. God could not be lost because he is always there. He provides not only the object of our thinking, but the path within which thinking abides. The condition of the possibility of thought cannot be lost because it is built into its very being. Neither the beginning nor the end, God is that which prevails in all thought about him. Theology is left aside when we think *within* God. That is what natural law is and the categorical force of its imperative, to enlist the Kantian formulation. Ends may be presented, but they must arise within the framework of what makes all consideration possible. Even when we fail to live up to the unsurpassable demand, we know it as the unsurpassable.[28] Simply because we do not fully live the life of transcendence does not mean that we fail to be touched by it. In that sense even our failures are a participation in the transcending. It is closer to us than we are to ourselves. Defection from it is possible only because it cannot defect from us. Transcendental imperatives, especially as intimated by Grotius's ever turning remark, provide natural law with a foundation that previously could only be desired.

That is the paradoxical result of avoiding the fruitless quest for foundations. This reassessment of Grotius's achievement casts a different light on the numerous attempts to reach a nonfoundational morality in the succeeding centuries. At the same time, it begins to illuminate the mystery of a secular order that cannot account for its own moral and existential viability. Does secular society possess the spiritual resources to assure its own survival? This familiar question was what prompted the conversation between an enlightened intellectual and a future pope, Habermas and Ratzinger.[29] Neither partner yielded his starting points, but they converged in the cordial desire to see the secular world succeed on its own terms. The absence of any need to install their respective positions and their submission to the common project is in the end the most striking quality of the encounter. No new ground had been broken, yet they occupied the same ground. That remarkable mutuality suggests that the secular ethos does indeed contain resources it can scarcely articulate. Even its best, most acute observers struggle to lay their finger on it. Yet it remains as the invisible source of authority within it. The interlocutors, Habermas and Ratzinger, circled around it without seeking to impose their respective presuppositions, of reason and God. It was enough that they shared the unspoken openness that made their discussion possible and acknowledged as much in their conclusions. What they could not do is recognize that they had thereby moved beyond the positions that separated them within the conversation. To do so would be to admit that they were no more than starting points that the conversation would of necessity step beyond.

When we consider God or reason as the basis for an order, then we have considered them both from a distance not coincident with them. Conversation has an openness precisely because it is not tied to the fixities from which it begins. Modulation away from what is said is of its very essence. It has no essence. Neither secular reason nor divine transcendence can remain what it is for, by talking about them, they have been placed within a wider horizon. What that horizon is may be a bit more elusive, even though it is inescapably real. Our problem is that we can scarcely discern the boundary while we think and live within it. Topics of conversation are well demarcated, but the conversation itself possesses an indefinable extension. It cannot be characterized as a secular or a religious exchange, since it includes both and, thus, is neither. As a consequence, the conversation itself begins to unsettle the fixities with which it began. The pattern is displayed in an even more famous conversation that Jean Bodin imagined in the sixteenth century, as a symposium between representatives of the various denominations and religions, including none, that was intended as a probing of the truth or falsity within each of them. Without winners or losers, this celebrated *Colloquium of the Seven* succeeded in acknowledging the conversation itself as their ultimate truth.[30] From this lived mutuality we derive a substantive notion of tolerance far above procedural legality. Tolerance is only of value if it values what it tolerates. Permission of the indifferent undermines what it permits. Tolerance is not only a condition for the exercise of reason and faith. It is included within them as the most profound affirmation of what they are about. Without acknowledgment of the value of what they pursue their pursuit could not be sustained. Tolerance is reverence.

That realization is what gave Grotius the confidence to ponder, even if cautiously and fleetingly, the absence of God. Even if there was no God, there would still be a God within the imperative of natural law. Theology might fail, but its mandate could not fail. He knew that by living within it. It is the absent presence or the present absence that so pervades a secular age that it scarcely rises to self-awareness. This is what makes Grotius its leading exponent. Within his pithy formulation is contained the revolving thought that characterizes a world that is neither secular nor sacred. Instead it moves from one pole to the other and back again in a circle that never rests at any one point on its arc, to finally fix what it is. The difficulty arises because no condition of possibility can contain itself. We cannot see that wherein all our seeing occurs. The best that might be achieved is a passing glimpse of what contains us. We are not so self-contained as we at first appear to be. There is yet the possibility of piercing the limits of possibility. That is what Grotius accomplished in his speculative exclamation. It neither affirmed that there is a God nor denied that he is but, instead, unfolded within that polarity. God when he is absent is even more present, and he is more absent when he is present. That was the meaning he circled around, a meaning that could not be expressed without overturning it. The God who is absent lays upon us, ever more profoundly, the mission of remaining faithful to his law, and, in doing so, we approach even more faithfully the divine being. Long before Kant had elaborated a notion of the transcendental, that which contains the condition of possibility that cannot be surpassed, Grotius had arrived at the seminal instance of it. It is for this reason that we can regard the etsiamsi as not only an equivalent to the transcendentals of truth and goodness and beauty, but as itself a transcendental. Etsiamsi daremus is the transcendental of the secular age. It is the secular age in its transcendental aspect as, in Simone Weil's equally memorable formulation, a waiting for God.[31]

The Condition of Possibility of a Secular Age

That which the secular world cannot ground because it is presupposed is thereby glimpsed. Its secret is that it would continue to obey the natural law even if there was no God. Nietzsche too had a similar insight into the uncanniness of the age, although in his case he was inclined to dismiss it as a residue destined to eventually disappear. Yet even he did not have the daring to look the negative in the face. He could not acknowledge the miracle before him, that is, that morality could endure even in the face of the loss of God. The dark night of the soul was simply too dark for him, despite the formidable resistance he mounted against it. In the end it was only a believer, like Grotius, who could find the fortitude to endure the darkness of divine absence. This was because for him, the absence was not a sheer vacuum but the nonpresence that betokens presence.[32] He was sufficiently familiar with presence in the mode of absence not to become unnerved by the prospect of a world without God. That may not be the case for believers in general, who are often so attached to the tokens of faith that they are not ready to endure the journey without them. In contrast to their disorientation, Grotius would persevere in the absence of the contours that had guided him. He had asked the question that should not be asked and had contemplated what should not be contemplated. Would the moral law hold without a divine foundation? It was a risky venture, as he conceded, to hazard the arrival of what was later termed the advent of nihilism. But the reward for confronting total loss is, if not total victory, a kind of victory that possesses a newfound durability. When one sees that the moral law retains its full force even absent a transcendent sanction, then one has found an impressively solid foundation.[33] How can that which has been so utterly dislodged hold nevertheless? Now it endures beyond the uncertainties and contentions that forever circle around it. The question of God can perhaps never be settled within a secular age, but it can be saved from the superficiality of the discourse in which it is conventionally posed.

That is no small achievement. It explains the enormous hold that Grotius's passage exercises on the modern mind. We return to it again and again in order to draw forth the reassurance that the rule of law that emerges from it is not the impossible house of cards it is often suspected of being. Without being able to explain how, we sense that Grotius has put his finger on the formidable source of truth that sustains our secular world. We know the incoherencies, the contradictions, the fragility, that seem to permeate our ethos. Yet we continue to live within it and depend on its reliability. For all of its disastrous breakdowns, modern civilization has evinced impressive powers of reaffirmation. The truncated language of secular discourse is incapable of explaining to itself how a world lacking any permanence in the order of being has nevertheless been able to endure. At this stage predictions of an imminent collapse seem especially unjustified. Only Grotius with his self-overturning speculation seems equipped to plumb the interior movement of the spirit that marks a secular age, that is, that it exceeds all that it claims to be. It continues to live as if there was a God while it asserts there is no God, and, thus, it overturns in its action what it says in its words. It lives in relation to the God it does not know. All that needs to be explained is what it knows when it does so. That last step was one that Grotius could not undertake and, it must be conceded, remains to be reached despite a considerable philosophical investment in it. The fact that we can, however, shed a little light on it is due to the significant enlargement of horizon taking place since Grotius's time. At least we can gain a better appreciation of what his intuitive insight accomplished.

It was nothing less than to suggest how an invisible authority can reign over the realm of visibility. Contrary to all appearances, the secular is not truly secular for it remains open to the transcendent. Indeed, it is defined by that relationship. By not believing in God, it believes in him. Nonbeing is the way of being. The abyss has become the path by which fulfillment is reached. A harrowing experience of emptiness that would be repeated in the modern period, and perhaps never so intensely as within the totalitarian annihilation of existence, became the way that the secular world reached what could not be lost. Transcendence is not only the end but also the way toward it. By yielding all, even the presence of God, God is reached more surely. The invisible wields its formidable authority because it arises beyond death. What has died cannot be extinguished. That is the path on which Grotius launched, perhaps unknowingly and certainly without a full realization of what it entailed, our modern secular self-understanding. In that sense he overturned the secular presumption of a limit to reality before it had even been expressed. At its very inception our age had been seen as an age that must continually transcend itself. It did not need to hold onto vestiges of divine presence or divine consolation because it had already gone beyond its need for such assurance.[34] What else does the vow to remain with natural law without God mean if not that fidelity to it exceeds even God himself? The only remaining step to take is the realization that this is what it is to be like God. Even God does not wish to remain with God if it means relinquishing any element of what is required of him. He is prepared to leave God behind in the complete outpouring of self that opens the meaning of love. To say that God is love is to recognize that he has left God behind. How else can persons love if not by giving themselves unreservedly? That is what the divine life is within the mutual self-giving that is the life of the Trinity. We behold it within the sacrifice of Christ who yields himself up completely on our behalf. Grotius dwelled on the significance of Christ's atoning sacrifice and recognized it as the path that human beings and human society must follow. Behind the law there remains the fulfillment that abolishes it. The judge puts himself in place of the accused. This is why Grotius devoted such attention to the enlargement of the notion of justice around which law always revolves. Law is in essence an order of justice, of what is owed of right. But it cannot remain within the limits of law. Eventually it must be exceeded as the generosity that goes beyond law. Forgiveness and atonement are as inexorable as redress and punishment.[35] Only then can law have a beginning for, without that unmerited act of grace, violation of law and its consequences repeat to infinity. A new beginning occurs when lawbreaking has been wiped out. The burden of law must be assumed by those to whom it has not been assigned. Forgiveness is that leap outside of being from which being originates. Grotius nurtured a deep appreciation of the self-overturning that was inherent in the notion of law. He sensed the reverberations within the sacrifice of Christ. What he did not do was connect it with the very being of God and thereby with the character of being as a whole. The unmerited love of Christ is the arc on which all that *is* is drawn.

That is the step he gingerly took in his most provocative exclamation. Hesitation was already built into it, even though it could draw support from the example of Christ himself. The implication of blasphemy within it would immediately have to be reversed. To gain any more confidence, something more than the forsakenness of Jesus on the cross would have to be adduced. Somehow the imperative of transcendence, even of God himself, would have to be embedded in the idea of God. Then the implied revolt against God would be overcome for then it would be apprehended as not only the way to God, but as the way of God. Transcendence of God would have to be discovered as the being of God. Not only did Christ in extremis acknowledge his separation from God, but God would have to be recognized as in himself a process of separation from himself. To say that this is a modern discovery is not quite accurate for it could hardly be discovered if it were not so from the beginning. From the earliest revelation, God is glimpsed as the one who reveals and, in revealing, goes beyond himself. He is the one who pours himself out. Christ may be the definitive revelation, but he is the revelation of what God has always been. We recognize God in Christ and Christ in God. What has been lacking is not the perception that God is a process of self-transcendence but the linguistic means of saying what is a virtual impossibility within a world of finite entities. How can anything that *is* give itself away to the point of complete self-giving? That is the mystery that overhangs the insight in Grotius's etsiamsi. This is why it had to assume the form of a hypothetical. It could become a categorical statement only if we possessed the means of confirming that it is possible to go beyond being. Is there a being beyond being? Some element of that suggestion is contained within the idea of transcendence from its first application by Plato, who characterizes the good as beyond being in dignity and power. How can anything be beyond being? That is the obstacle that has blocked the path of Western metaphysics ever since its Greek beginning. Even the advent of Christianity, with its supererogation of divine outpouring, was not enough to open a path toward the transcendent.

The whole great secular world itself can be taken as testament to its impossibility. Being is what prevails, not what yields itself up. To be is to cling to being. How can that *be* that willingly goes beyond its being? It is an offense to the very idea of being. Only the words of Christ counsel us not to be scandalized at those who give up their lives for his sake. We still lack a paradigm of what such a reality would be. Perhaps, we begin to suspect, there may be a deeper layer to the endlessly fascinating thought Grotius injected into the history of our thought. Besides drawing on the deepest level of what is disclosed in the redemptive outpouring of Christ, it leads us toward an even more profound account of the God who is disclosed within Christ. Much has been made about how the medieval distinction between reason and will in God led to the nominalist account of divine power that paved the way for the later emergence of nihilism.[36] But what if there is an alternate theological path making its way through the early modern centuries and that it approaches its most self-conscious statement in Grotius's etsiamsi? This would appear to be a particularly apposite suggestion given that Grotius's observation moves in the direction of a deeper grounding of the law, while the nominalist-nihilist axis veers toward the antinomian impulse that unhinges law from any foundation. Moreover, the Grotian formulation would seem to be the perfect antidote to the latter. As the meditation that has emerged from the abyss by going through it, the etsiamsi endures as the most unscathed account of law impervious to loss. How can what has lost everything lose any more? It would thus not be too surprising to discover that, just as the disintegration of the modern world can be traced to a certain theological dislocation, so the contrary path out of the disintegration may also have its roots within a correspondingly profound revision in our notion of divine being. The God who has become a being and therefore no longer guides being may be replaced by the God who can more thoroughly contain being since he lies definitively beyond it.[37]

God beyond Being

Transcendence has at last found its adequate formulation within Western metaphysics. This may seem a curious consequence of the advent of a secular age, but, as I have been suggesting, they remain correlatives. The notion of the secular hinges on the transcendent, as that which it is not, in order to define itself. Yet the secular cannot find a place within the transcendent, wherein it might behold the other who remains so crucial to its self-understanding. Only if the transcendent can immunize itself against encroachment on the space of the secular will it endure as transcendent. The history of the sacred, ever since the millennial breakthrough of revelation that brought the glimpse of transcendence within human consciousness, has been the history of its repeated intermingling with immanence. A notion of transcendence adequate to its truth has eluded historical unfolding. Yet Grotius pointed the way in the etsiamsi that freely relinquishes the claim of the transcendent to presence within the world. Without fully developing it, he has intuited a transcendence that is sufficiently transcendent. He has invoked the God who is beyond being.[38] That more technical later formulation, which is also not without its communicative difficulties, is nevertheless close to that at which Grotius aims. When God too partakes of the etsiamsi it secures it against the charge of empty paradox often lodged against it. The intimation that it is not just Grotius but the whole of reality too that strains toward transcendence of itself, begins to alter the scale of measurement within a secular universe. Everything remains what it is. Its secularity is intact. But it no longer prevails as the exclusive criterion for what is real. Beyond what is here, and surpassing it, is the movement beyond what is here. The difference is that now the accent of reality has shifted. No longer is the movement of transcendence a merely subjective longing, a romantic outburst from within the closure of the secular, but the very heart of what is present in everything. The God who is beyond being reveals the character of being. The absence of God turns out to coincide with the only way that God can be present: as absence, a mode of waiting.[39]

The uncertainty of the hold on being that haunts a secular world now finds its answer. To the extent that the secular paradigm of reality no longer holds exclusive sway, it can find a way of accepting the transitoriness that pervades all that is within it. The great disquiet of the secular age has always been the question whether it can be maintained, in the face of its evident futility. Only so much confidence can be placed in the longevity of human achievements. And they never serve, as Kant conceded, the lifetime fulfillment of any single one of us.[40] At best we are passing sacrifices on the altar of human progress. In our individual particularity we are deprived of any final satisfaction. Strategies of denial and distraction, as Pascal diagnosed them, can only be sustained for so long. Episodic convulsions that engulf modern societies may well be attributed to such recurrent outbursts of despair. The problem is familiar in the writings of secular intellectuals. The best of them find a way through their growing sense of despondency by reaching for that enlargement of the heart of which Tocqueville spoke.[41] He understood it as the secret of successful modern societies. However, even he did not grasp its interior constitution. He could not explain how it was possible for a human being to expend the whole of their existence without any prospect of sharing in the fulfillment of those efforts. How is a sacrificial existence possible? It is only if being is not what it seems to be. It does not consist in the vain struggle to preserve itself but is from the very beginning a movement beyond itself. It is by transcending its own finiteness that it touches what is infinite. How can a secular world understand that? Only if it glimpses that its cramped self-understanding does not contain the whole of reality. It must be capable of perceiving reality as, at its highest, a movement of love.[42] The secular ethos can sustain its own best impulse to transcend itself only when it sees that this is the way of being itself. God is beyond being, and we can attain the being of God only by following the same inexorability. He who loses his life will save it.

That is the invisible source of authority in a world blinded by visibility. Yet it is never so completely occluded that it cannot grasp its own status. However dimly, there remains the flickering awareness that this is not all. Even to regard the secular as secular, to acknowledge its limits, is to stand within a presentiment of what is unlimited. That inkling may have no claim on its locus within a secular world, but it is for that very reason all the more pervasive. What cannot be assigned anywhere is somehow everywhere. That which is so irrevocably forgotten is continually recalled. The uncanny of Nietzsche's deft reflection cannot be eliminated. This was the problem that the revolt against God always encountered, for it always served to bring God more unavoidably to mind. It always drew the invisible source of authority back into visibility. Marx thought he could resolve the issue by prohibiting the question of God altogether, although he only succeeded in demonstrating the impossibility of the task. The prohibition always presupposed the question. It is thus that his wish for atheism to become impossible in practice could only be taken in a completely ironic sense. The one thing a secular age cannot be is atheistic. Its very identity turns on it. The problem is that it cannot grasp the ground of its own possibility. Self-understanding eludes a secular universe for, without God, it cannot even call itself secular. It would simply be the universe, unbounded and uncertain of its status. Perhaps it is without fixed natures or limits and therefore incapable of the kind of regularity that science constantly presumes within it. Malleable and ill defined, as our technological picture of reality suggests, we begin to doubt whether science itself is possible. We may even end by regarding the universe as itself divine or lay claim to transfigurative powers ourselves. Then we embark on the hyperbole that has always hovered around the unlimited application of technology. This is the abyss of power without a purpose to guide it.

The fact that we have been able to articulate the danger is the most convincing evidence we have not yet succumbed to it. But that crucial restraint on the madness that proclaims endless possibility depends on a residual awareness of finitude, and of death. Nothing in this life is deathless, and any presumption of it engulfs all in death. Life that is lived rationally is lived within restraints. The Greeks who discovered reason knew this. Nothing too much. What made that principle possible was somewhat more mysterious, for it depended on knowing the separation of all things from the beyond of the cosmos. Distance from the transcendent made an order of limits within this world possible. To the extent that God is forgotten, it is more difficult to remember we are not God and can neither create nor perfect the order of the whole. Indeed, everything meaningful in human existence depends on the recognition that it is limits that preserve us. To be born without possibility of death would be to rob every event of our lives of significance. Nothing matters if it can be endlessly repeated.[43] To contemplate the duplication of human beings deprives them of the uniqueness that is each one's most distinctive feature. This is why a world without God is a world that increasingly loses its grip on what it is to be a world. To the extent that we still characterize our world as secular, we still preserve that distance from God. It has not yet become a simply secular world or, as it was in the great atheistic ideologies, a world that militantly seeks to separate itself from God. In either case, the result is the same. God remains even, or especially, when he is not.

We have not succumbed to the insanity that Nietzsche surmised within modernity. It is no accident that the proclamation of the death of God, as he pictured it, was uttered by a madman who bursts into the marketplace with a lantern.[44] To proclaim the death of God entails an overreaching that unhinges our connection with the rationality of limits. The excessiveness of the titanic saviors and secular messiahs of our world, who unleashed the totalitarian nightmare as well as the progressivist dream of perfection, is well recognized. But the loss of reason can also assume a more moderate form of pervasive disorientation. Without global militancy the draining of meaning can still continue. The shock of self-sacrificing generosity when it does return is greeted with incomprehension, as if it derived from an earlier era and now is no longer at home in the world. Mundane existence must struggle to maintain itself against the excess that destroys it and the enervation that dissipates it. The problem of course is that a secular world, by definition, cannot supply the equilibrium it lacks. And if it could, either the world would no longer be secular or the God it invokes would no longer be transcendent. Once again, we are navigating the boundaries of the finite and the infinite. Neither is readily equipped to provide the bridge that cannot simply be assimilated to one side or the other. This we may say was the imbalance of the medieval project of creating a pervasively Christian civilization. By contrast, modern civilization establishes its independence by dislodging the transcendence from which it began. What needs to be found is a linguistic means of moving from the immanent to the transcendent, and back again, without clinging to the designation as wholly on one side or the other. In many respects it has been the discovery of just such a way of expressing a faith at once ancient and new that has been the signal achievement of modern philosophy. It is nothing less than a formulation that does justice to a movement that itself assumes the shape of thought in motion. It must be a mode of discourse that in its very utterance engages in the process of its self-overturning. The notion is not entirely novel, as Kierkegaard recognized in his dissertation on Socratic irony.[45] But it was nowhere previously brought to the level of development reached in Kierkegaard's own identification of it as a language of paradox. What went by other names in other thinkers may all be regarded as reaching its apogee in his provocative conception. But the beginning of the pattern may well be ascribed to Grotius's celebrated etsiamsi.

Echoes of it go back to classical philosophy, as well as the Sermon on the Mount, although its elevation to a principle is a modern achievement. The uncanny that Nietzsche identified arises from the ceaselessly revolving nature of the formulations. No sooner has the death of God been pronounced than we are made aware of the God whose death is the path to life.[46] In a secular context what is dead is dead, but we are not confined to a finite scale of measurement. There is also the movement of transcendence itself that renders everything what it is. On that level death has been surpassed, not as an event within time, but as the event from which time begins. The choice is outside of time. That is what it affirms. Time is no more, because it never was. Proclamation of the death of God is fraught with all of the implications of resurrection. Only those who die can be reborn. Even from within time we know this because we are never simply within time. We are at the intersection. That is the point from which the entire movement of self-transcendence has occurred. It can be glimpsed because the glimpse is the still point of the turning world. Neither transcendent nor immanent, it partakes of both of them and can thus grasp the mediation between them. Perhaps nowhere was that developed as powerfully as in Grotius's etsiamsi with an echo that reverberates through the world that emanates from it. Far from an ominous sign of the secular gloom that would eclipse the age of faith, it opened a new possibility of faith within a civilizational arc we are still struggling to perceive. It is nothing less than the highest expression of the Christian paradox. The natural law that holds even if we grant that there is no God not only demonstrates its formidable depth, a depth beyond God, but it also reveals that in that moment it reaches even more profoundly the reality of God. God is where there is no God. Natural law does not rest on its own foundation but on the foundation that endures beyond annihilation. Neither human nor divine, it prevails within the movement between them. That is how the invisible source of authority shines visibly. It is beheld in invisibility.

CHAPTER SIX

The Invisible Source of Authority

The challenge of a secular world is to explain itself. Secure in its capacity to grasp all within its frame of reference the secular as such seems to escape it, for to explain the secular is to step beyond it. This has been the persistent instability we have noted in its self-conception. Now we must examine the status of that intermediate dynamic where, neither secular nor sacred, it partakes of both. How it is possible, to be in time yet retain a perspective that transcends it, has been one of the most elusive aspects of the experience. A vocabulary is lacking for the horizon within which our thinking unfolds. We know that we occupy the movement of reflection, but we cannot quite explain it to ourselves. Thought of thought defeats our thinking. Yet in thinking the limits, we have simultaneously exceeded them. None of the models we ordinarily apply can grasp the "more than" that has entered into our worldview. Without intending it, we have established our thinking on the basis of a far higher reality and have hesitantly begun to see that we have no choice in the matter. We are propelled inexorably toward transcendence. Only a more archaic terminology seems adequate to the apprehension by which we have been apprehended. Whence the imperative of transcending arises we cannot say. All we know is that its genesis is from before us. We receive it as a gift from we know not where and are borne aloft we know not how. To call it faith may seem perhaps too profound a word. Yet something like faith is the depth that decisively enlarges the limit of our thinking. Even we secular moderns live by faith. Certainly, there is no secular word for what overturns the secular word.

Faith as Primordial

Faith retains its hold even as it emerges from a vanished past that remains mysteriously present with us. While we no longer profess faith, we cannot do without it. We know more than we can say, even though the intimation rests uneasily within us. Indeed it is uneasiness that is the clearest point of contact with what so utterly eludes us. Faith is impossible when we have concluded its irrelevance. For us it is usually mastery, the knowledge that dispels uncertainty, that has taken its place. We do not need faith once we have reached certainty, and there is nothing that stands in the way of knowledge once we have removed all obstacles to it. Nature is compelled to yield up its secrets. Why not everything else in the order of being? We might even include the investigatory capacity itself within that limitless horizon of clarity and precision. The quest for certainty must be ringed with certainty. But then there arises the "horrid doubt" that it is impossible to so definitively guard the search for knowledge against error.[1] What epistemological safeguard shall we apply if it is not that with which we concurrently operate? The imperative of doubting all that can be doubted, the Cartesian prescription for certainty, cannot finally be inoculated against doubt. Only faith, the faith that sustained Descartes's own meditation, survives the winnowing scrutiny.[2]

This is because faith has already abandoned the claim to certainty. It knows it is not certain, but it knows that without faith no certainty is possible. Certainty must first be believed in as a possibility. In that sense faith is ineliminable. It cannot be lost because it has never asserted its possession of truth. It has only kept faith in it. This was the great overturning of the epistemological project initiated by Kant's Copernican revolution. Instead of finding reality in the mind, he suggested that mind might be found in reality. Once that had been conceded it was clear that priority must lie in what we bring to the understanding of reality, a priority that cannot be grounded in understanding itself. Knowledge irrevocably begins in faith.[3] This was why faith could not be ejected from a world that no longer invoked the language of faith. Instead faith would have to find its way back within a setting that regards it as incomprehensible. For the first time, faith would have to trace its genesis. It would have to show that faith rested on nothing but itself. Faith is primordial, and there is no getting beyond it to what can be established more securely. But this also means that faith cannot be lost. It is because faith does not rest on knowledge that it remains impervious to the vicissitudes of knowledge. Neither mistaken nor misled, faith, so long as it remains, is a faithful endurance, for only through faith can the missteps of knowledge be corrected. Knowledge requires faith in its own capacity if it is to function. Even when it is lost, faith has not been lost. It is only *we* who have lost faith, while *it* remains. At its heart faith is not faith in anything but faith itself. We may be mistaken in what we believe, but we cannot be mistaken in belief as such, otherwise there would be no possibility of attaining truth. The impossibility of demonstrating our capacity for truth is what we mean by faith. It remains a matter of faith. In the end faith is the relationship to reality in which we find ourselves, or lose ourselves, by turning away from it. The opening may be refused. That is the loss of faith. Before there is faith in anything or anyone, there is faith in faith. When it is gone, we find it impossible to restore what remains indispensable to any restoration. That is the abyss contemplated in Grotius's famous admission, and also the great affirmation that faith cannot be lost, even if, or especially, when it is lost.

We may lose faith, but faith cannot lose us. It is when it has ebbed, as Matthew Arnold failed to see on Dover Beach, that faith returns most of all. How can what has no precedence lose its precedence? How can that which *is* loss be lost? If faith is the realization that our knowledge rests on nothing more substantial than faith, how can its disappearance unhinge our understanding of things? We have simply confronted what we intuited all along. Our whole modern narrative from its beginning can be read as an illustration of this dynamic. The dark forebodings of the nineteenth century warn us of the abyss opened in a world without faith. The quest for a religious revival of some sort so spans the era following the French Revolution that it might be taken as the mark of the age.[4] The nineteenth century offers a proliferation of awakenings, restorations, and foundations that have played out over the period up to the present. Even if we grant the superficiality and the chaos thereby unleashed, including the ideologies of historical transformation, it cannot be denied that they drew on a longing of impressive spiritual depth. The major religious denominations, churches, and traditions experienced their most significant rejuvenation within this period. Even when the call for faith remained no more than a desideratum, as in the aspirational spirituality of Tocqueville and Mill, we can hardly attribute it to an afterglow of nostalgia. The search for faith itself arises from faith. It may be that they did not find what they sought, but that does not mean that they were untouched by it. The era remains, as Flannery O'Connor remarked of the South, "Christ haunted."[5]

The search for faith betokens faith. It is where faith is absent that it prevails all the more. This is why a secular age, an age defining itself by distance from God, is often where he is most intimately present. Present, that is, in the mode of absence that is the divine mode of presence. Faith is merely that apprehension. All that remains is the realization that this is what faith is. Instead, faith is misunderstood as if it were a discredited claim to knowledge. To acknowledge that faith is no more than the awareness of what is missing, to use Habermas's perceptive formulation, would be to restore its centrality in a secular age. Charles Taylor struggled mightily in the course of his tome on the subject to finally identify it as "immanent transcendence,"[6] without necessarily reaching a satisfactory articulation of what that meant. Largely overlooked in his lengthy interrogation is the realization that inconclusiveness is what faith is. It has no basis other than the awareness of what is missing that when it is brought to awareness is no longer missing or at least not in the same way.

The secular age is not an age from which God is absent but an age in which God's absence cannot be seen for what it is. Faith has not disappeared, but the realization of its disappearance has. Faith has lost the perception of itself. Now it wanders in ill-defined disquiet. Yet admission of absence is already the first word of faith and the first opening toward the One who is absent. It may not be the realization that the absent One remains more present than we have been able to realize, but it is a faint glimmering of that perception. From first to last, faith remains faith in faith. This is why its evanescence is not just a matter of religion, but a fatal step in which the whole of our modern existence seems to become unhinged. We cannot live without faith. Every undertaking originates in the movement of faith that underpins its possibility. To lose faith is not to withdraw from a particular outcome but to foreclose all possible outcomes. Reason cannot prevail without faith in reason.[7] A crisis of faith is in its nature not simply a religious affair, but inescapably a crisis of civilization. This is what lies behind the unending ruminations about our secular age.

Freedom Lives by Faith

The interminability of our bewilderment is surely an indication that the question has been launched from a mistaken starting point. Instead of dwelling on the unease from which the reflection arises, the debate leaps to the assumption that it is our task to dispel it. Faith cannot be found when it has been confused with mastery. It cannot be found when we are confident that we can find it, for it is not faith that has been lost. We are lost. Without faith we cannot find faith. There is no going back before there is faith to ensure the means of securing it. Instead, faith continues to elude us of little faith. Thinking we could dispense with faith, we have severed the only thread that could connect us with what we seek. The approach has been misconceived. Faith cannot be found because we have never really been in search of it. Our brimming self-confidence has dispelled the need for faith. We have not been lost, or, more accurately, we have not been able to perceive our lostness. That is what it means to be truly lost. Sensed as indefinable unease, it cannot be named or identified. Relatively few are prepared to hold onto an elusive prompting, to dwell in the waiting that is "the uncanny." To do so would be to concede that it is when faith is lost that it is needed most of all and that this is the most penetrating aspect of faith. If we had arrived at our destination there would be no need to behold it in faith. In the same way hope too would have evaporated in that moment of arrival. Only love, as St. Paul noted, would remain. But for now faith, hope, and love are required of us who find ourselves on the way. Faith is what directs the journey; it is needed most of all when our destination has receded. What we cannot behold, we must hold in faith.

The invisible saves us from the reign of the visible. Through faith we see what cannot be seen. But then it is not we who see but faith that sees through us. We see with the eyes of faith, not with the eyes in our head. In going beyond what is available to us, we have accepted the gift of going beyond. Faith is not ours but comes from we know-not-where, until its source is glimpsed through faith. The mystery by which we are held has opened within us the possibility of beholding. The realization that it does not derive from us is confirmed through our discovery of the impossibility of faith. It is in lack of faith that faith arises. Those who see clearly have no need for faith. Only we who are without faith can find the faith that saves from loss. This is what made the Grotian formulation so strikingly prescient. He foresaw that an age without faith would be the one in which faith would arise most profoundly. His vision has been confirmed in the totalitarian nightmare that engulfed the past century and still retains a residual hold on the present one. It was those who lost all, who were mercilessly flung into the maelstrom, who discovered the indispensability of faith.[8] When all is lost, faith cannot be lost. Whether they found God or belief in any conventional sense was less crucial compared to the discovery that their core humanity could only be preserved if they were held by the invisible thread. The most important part, the soul, as Solzhenitsyn referred to it, could only be saved if one steadily refused to compromise the voice of conscience that still reached him.[9] Through faith, the line of dissidents in every generation were saved, and in the process they gave an inestimable witness to faith. They regained faith in an age that seemed to have lost it irrevocably, or only retained it in its most conventional forms. Through their searing testament faith radiated in a world that sought to exclude faith from it.[10] Like the martyrs of the early church, and the ranks of their successors, they are the foundation on whom faith is built. Invisible truth can find no greater witness than in the sacrifice of those who hold it to the end. Faith prevails, most of all, when there is no basis for faith.

The mistake has always been to search for a foundation of faith, a search that like all searches presupposes the seed of faith. As the condition of possibility, faith cannot be set aside. We cannot simultaneously live by faith and become its controllers. All demonstration requires faith in its beginning, for there can be no beginning unless we entrust ourselves to it. A determination to guard against error cannot extend to the safeguards we erect. Engineering always builds in a fail-safe or a redundancy against failure. But no matter how far back we go, faith cannot obtain an impregnable guarantee. The engineer cannot be engineered. Even if we construct a system so perfect that, in the words of T. S. Eliot, "no one will need to be good," we would still be reliant on the goodness of the first designers of the system.[11] The possibility of a beginning, whether in the sense of the whole or in the sense of our individual part in it, requires that it originate in what is before a beginning. Freedom, that unbidden spring of action, cannot be eliminated. Nor can faith, the indispensable obverse of freedom, be pushed aside. Without faith, freedom would not be able to act, for every action attests to the faith that underpins it. Faith is the metaphysical anatomy of freedom. Normally, as with the metaphysical, faith is scarcely noticed in the enactments of freedom. It is only when it is opposed that the role of faith comes to the fore. Then it becomes clear that freedom is not like a weather vane but a compass that points toward its own direction. An assault on freedom is never simply a finite event, but a breach that marks a turn from the infinite as such. To block freedom is to break more than a link with what lies beyond it. It is to sap the root from which freedom is sustained. This is why the notion of rendering faith obsolete is also an assault on the lifeblood of freedom. To be free is to live by faith.

The rejection of faith is at the same time the rejection of freedom. In the same way as a conclusive demonstration would rob faith of its freedom, it would equally rob freedom of its faith.[12] Neither could be without the other. Faith and freedom are, if not correlates, at least correlated. They are modes of the primordial in human existence that without which we could not be full persons. Faith is the movement of freedom, just as freedom is the unfolding of faith. But this means they pervade our awareness so thoroughly that we are scarcely aware of them. It is only when they come under threat that we begin to sense the enormity of what might be lost. In the moment of danger what is in danger comes into view. This is especially the case when the danger arises from within. What could be more perilous than the threat that germinates when faith has been eclipsed by the freedom it made possible? How can we guard against a threat we have ourselves fomented? Faith would have to find a way of resisting the call to make itself redundant by giving reasons for faith. Too late we discover that mastery of faith in the name of certainty has expelled faith. The irony is that it was just such a demand for the deepening of faith that spawned a rationality that declared faith obsolete. This picture of an unintended reformation at the start of modernity is a revision in the historical narrative that is beginning to gain wider acceptance.[13] Less well confronted is the realization that faith has always contained within it the seeds of its own supersession. This is the uneasy implication our historical revisionism has not yet been sufficiently prepared to embrace. Few have had the temerity to dwell with the negative, as Nietzsche did, until it revolves into the uncanny. Faith cannot hold onto itself until it has, as Grotius surmised, gone through the death of God.

Freedom too has its awakening self-recognition. The trajectory follows the same intensifying demand for greater freedom. The "relief of man's estate" was the banner under which it enlarged the field of operation to include all that might come under its sway. Not only would the scarcities and diseases nature had inflicted be eliminated, but the limits that had for so long seemed natural would be indefinitely extended. What could stand in the way of this empire of freedom as it stood on the threshold of a momentous expansion? What could prevent it from taking that final fatal step as it contemplated taking charge of freedom itself? Why should freedom be the only thing left free? And what is freedom but subjection to the vagaries of genealogy and circumstance? Why not take a hand in designing ourselves and ensure our future against disappointment? The task was of such moment that it justified a willingness to discard outmoded inhibitions. Even genetic engineering and cloning were not a step too far. Freedom itself was the exalted stratum that now must be enhanced even if it entailed its own curtailment along the way.[14] A similar inexorability had already emerged in the social and political movements that aimed at universal emancipation. In the name of freedom much that had previously been regarded as integral to freedom would no longer be permitted. Property that had earlier seemed a bulwark for freedom must now be cast aside in the name of free enjoyment of property. The only difficulty was that property that had become universal was no longer the property of anyone. The abolition of property was indeed its abolition. Even within the more circumscribed language of individual rights, freedom, far from maintaining itself, has seen its erosion in the name of freedom. A right to die, like a right to be born or not to be born, carries overtones of a vertigo that suggests a lack of any parameters for the exercise or assertion of rights. That lack could just as easily include the right not to have any rights. We are dangerously close to the precipice from which we are helpless to save ourselves hurtling headlong. Freedom itself looms as the source of impending disaster.

Redemption Saves Freedom

Freedom, we discover, cannot include itself. If it were to take that fatal step, it would abolish the very meaning of freedom. How could there be freedom when it had set itself up to wield dominion over the one who is free? Could freedom be controlled from beyond itself without thereby ceasing to be free? Even God has renounced the abolition of our freedom in creating us. Freedom it turned out could not be preserved except by letting it be. Once we sought to take a hand in creating ourselves or defining the limits to our existence we ceased to be free. It meant the control of some human beings over other human beings, as C. S. Lewis had pointed out. There was a limit that freedom could not breach, for freedom demands the unassailability of the person who is free. Nothing should be done to violate the inviolable. Astonishingly, that imperative includes the putative possessor of freedom. It cannot be used to abandon our freedom. That troublesome source of discontent and discordance must not be sacrificed in the name of a freedom that, once attempted, will have evaporated. The abyss of power without purpose opens if it is no longer guided by the imperative of respecting and preserving the freedom of those on whose behalf it is wielded. The relief of man's estate cannot be bought at the price of our humanity itself. The functioning of freedom must be strictly confined within the limits of what is indispensable to freedom. The unassailable liberty of each person requires the imprescriptibility of each. In the end, the freedom to abandon freedom is not so much an exercise of freedom as a failure to exercise it. To relinquish freedom in the name of freedom is betrayal, for it says that freedom is not worth preserving. In the exercise of freedom we are not free, for freedom is already bound to the moral order it entails.[15] Freedom can never be a matter of free choice, and it can therefore never extend to itself. As the condition of its own possibility, freedom cannot include itself without abolishing its possibility. To be free means we have not stepped outside of the parameters of freedom. We have not killed ourselves.

We must keep faith with our freedom, and freedom must guard our faith. Their connection has long been intuited, for one cannot be without the other. Notable highlights in articulating it include Locke's *Letter on Toleration* (1689), in which he underlines the indispensability of freedom for faith. It was so powerful an exposition that it changed the meaning of the word *toleration*. Previously the word carried the negative connotation of putting up with what could not be suppressed, but subsequently it acquired its positive tonality of reverence for what is highest. Faith is most deeply affirmed in the commitment to its inviolability. Freedom and faith are coterminous in the recognition of their interdependence, an estimate that Locke declares in the opening to be the mark of the true church. An equally robust affirmation of the relationship is provided by Tocqueville whose interest in the religious underpinning of democracy drew him to the American experience. There he discovered that the vibrancy of American religion could be traced to the spirit of liberty under which it flourished. Unlike Europe where political authority had favored denominational establishment, America inclined toward a separation of church and state. Freedom, he concluded, was the distinguishing factor that had prompted the rejuvenation of faith, in contrast to its European decline. The alliance of faith and freedom was powerfully evident, at both the individual and the social level, for they are profoundly implicated in their mutual advancement. It is thus not surprising that religion, which had not always begun with an advocacy of liberty, should now find itself on its side. Nor is it remarkable that liberty should increasingly discover its own debt to religion, both as an inheritance and as its deepest realization.[16]

For Tocqueville, the affinity between them could hardly be more evident than if it had come from the mouth of God himself. In one notable presentation of course it did, the incomparable chapter on the Grand Inquisitor in *The Brothers Karamazov*. What made Dostoevsky's portrayal such an artistic triumph was that he managed to make Christ the pivot of freedom without his utterance of a word. It is the silent unaccusing Christ who most profoundly rebuts the Inquisitor's willingness to trade freedom for happiness. There is no need for him to pose the question whether human beings can be happy without freedom, for the Inquisitor's rationalizations expose the impossibility. Only by sinking below the human level can the exchange take place. But the implication also carries the conversation in the opposite direction. It shows that the defense of freedom cannot simply remain at the level of a utilitarian scheme. Human beings are free, not because that is the route to happiness or contentment, but because they are called to transcend themselves. The God-like quality of freedom is illuminated in that momentary lifting of the mundane veil. It becomes apparent that freedom cannot be defended or measured in purely finite terms. Only a God who loves unconditionally can affirm imprescriptible liberty. We realize that what had seemed a principle of purely secular affirmation is pervaded with transcendent significance. And yet it requires no theological elaboration. It must always be emphasized that Dostoevsky's Christ says nothing. He simply *is*, and we know him through the response of his interlocuter, the Inquisitor. The encounter is emblematic of the extent to which a secular world exists from what it does not and cannot affirm. If we were to ask how the transcendent can be present in a world from which it has been excluded, Dostoevsky's unspeaking Christ is the consummate example. We recognize what has been intuited all along. The transcendent can only speak through its absence. Not saying is its irrefutable way of saying.

The faith that underpins freedom does not have to occupy a ruling position. It can be just as manifest in the still small voice heard nowhere but within the faint stirrings of conscience. Indeed it is only there that it can be heard, for nothing mundane can contain its message. The transcendent transcends all earthly manifestations. That was the literary challenge Dostoevsky addressed and overcame. Christ could only be convincing by remaining within the transcendence of all saying and doing. But his authority was for all that not in the least diminished. We might conclude that it was heightened in the encounter with the most powerful political authority on the scene. The Inquisitor, who could seize anyone he wished, supreme in his power over life and death, had already dispatched Christ to the dungeon where the confrontation took place. Yet it was not the interrogator who emerged triumphant. It was Jesus who freely departed, after having left a kiss on the lips of his protagonist. The all-powerful executioner was powerless before the gaze of suffering love. How was this possible or plausible? It was because the Inquisitor knew it was he who stood under judgment. Christ did not need to indict, because the wizened old cardinal struggled to defend himself against charges that had not even been lodged against him. No need for Christ to accuse a man whose rationalizations already tacitly conceded his guilt. In the Inquisitor the judgment of the world, with all of its apparatus of power, stood under judgment. He sensed the mendacity of what he sought to defend. The Inquisitor knew his claim of serving human happiness was a lie and that far from loving human beings, he had reduced them to the level of slobbering beasts, utterly beneath his contempt. It was Christ alone who loved them with a love beyond all telling, a love that is unconditional. Only there would freedom find its fulfillment and its justification.

The intriguing aspect is that all of that could be unfolded from within the perspective of a complete unbeliever, for that is what the Cardinal Inquisitor is. When we strip away the trappings of vestments and office, we see he is no different from any absolutist. He intends to preserve power over others at all costs. Moreover, his project is nothing less than the elimination of Christ from Christianity. It is the saving message of Christ to which he objects most of all, because it cannot be accomplished and can only destroy human happiness. He may be a prince of the church, but his secret, as Alyosha Karamazov blurts out, is that he no longer believes in God.[17] As a thoroughgoing atheist he is ready to aim at the more finite goal of contentment. For all of the baroque setting, the Inquisitor is a conventional social engineer, prepared to enlist the full panoply of controls to implement his totalitarian goal. Dostoevsky well understood the shape of things to come once instrumental rationality had displaced faith. He knew that the application of power without purpose would lead to the nightmare in which "nothing is true and everything is permitted," a formulation he employed before Nietzsche.[18] Viewed from the perspective of its own logic, it was evident that a secular world was not simply a world from which God is absent, but one in which nothing stands in the way of an unlimited will to power. There are no limits that cannot be transgressed in the drive toward a dominance that is itself evacuated of all moral purpose. When mastery of nature has become so complete, then nothing in nature can function as a restraint or a guide. Without limits freedom itself is consumed in the maw. It devours itself. Respect for freedom, by contrast, depends on the conviction that there are limits inherent to its operation, most notably freedom itself. That is the vulnerability we are daily reminded of within a secular regime, for the secular is constituted without reference to limits.

The question of greatest moment is how a regime that does not recognize a higher authority can nevertheless remain bound by it. This is where the invisibility of a transcendent source is of utmost significance. In Dostoevsky's vision the putative master is brought to acknowledge his inescapable subordination. The manner in which it occurs is the most fascinating. It is not through the apocalyptic return of Christ in glory but in the unremarkable mildness with which he approaches the coffin entering the cathedral. The effect is to awaken the dead young man, although nothing disrupts the ordinary flow of worldly events. It is similar with the Inquisitor who is also confronted with the falsehood he has concealed within himself, for it could never be concealed *from* himself. He knows he is under a judgment from which no escape is possible and, in that, all the evasiveness of his life and his world is laid bare. It may be that he no longer believes in God, not because he cannot believe, but because he will not believe. How that is possible is the great confusion with which an adamantly secular world struggles. By rejecting God, it simultaneously affirms him, as every revolt against God attests. With every snarl of disdain it shows it is not what it seems to be, a secular world, but rather a world so driven to transcend itself that it aims at becoming God, even as it rejects him. The invisible source of authority prevails through its suppression most of all. A secular world that has separated itself from God cannot displace God without simultaneously displacing itself. It cannot be itself without God. That is the logic not only of its self-understanding as secular, but, more profoundly, of the aspiration of a God-given freedom that can have no other fulfillment. A merely secular exercise of freedom is either doomed to futility or doomed to the overreaching that abolishes it.

It is only saved from that fate by a transcendent love that pours itself out without limit. The burden of freedom is already assumed by the One whose perfect self-sacrifice has fully redeemed it. Nothing remains for freedom to do in order to justify itself. Everything has been said and everything has been suffered on its behalf. Freedom's source is revealed as expiation. Beyond tolerance, beyond the freedom granted to freedom, is the infinite suffering of all the misery it has perpetrated. Freedom it turns out cannot even be thrown away, for it has already been restored before it begins. It cannot lose faith in itself, for its faith has been more than affirmed. It has been fulfilled. The pledge that is identical with freedom has been satisfied without diminution or loss. What freedom could not do for itself—establish its bona fides or ensure its viability—has been accomplished. None of this means that freedom cannot be misused or even destroyed. But what it does do is declare that freedom as such can be neither lost nor abolished.[19] Even its most evil consequence cannot touch the goodness at its core, for it has been redeemed by a Love that is beyond all saying and doing. Freedom has been bought at an infinite price. That is the truth that lies hidden within, that Dostoevsky's tale sought to unfold. The insight may be ancient, but its retrieval required the modern provocation of freedom's vain self-mastery. The Grand Inquisitor may voice the consummate claim of freedom's self-salvation, but its accomplishment requires more than an assertion. What freedom cannot do is what the Inquisitor reveals most starkly. It cannot ground itself. Or it can only do so by way of professing the lie that it has been able to replace God as its creator. That which claims to be its own source is pervaded by the awareness that it is not. Only by accepting primordial freedom can it avoid the necessity of lying to itself. Then freedom can be freedom, a freedom that derives from its divine originator and is thus not compelled to replace it.

Vanished are all the misgivings that arise from the possibility that freedom may be botched. Is the experiment in liberty worth the risk? Even if it could be answered, we already sense that the question is misconceived. Surely it entails what it presupposes, as does any wider reflection that must take place within the horizon of freedom. How can what cannot establish itself be established? Validation must break through from a region beyond it. What freedom can neither taint nor damage must furnish its unassailability. Forgiveness, the word that wipes away every tear and tare, must be uttered from a source more primordial than the beginning. Its victory is certain for it has forgiven all who repent, without restriction or reservation. Neither injury nor death can reach that which has gone beyond them in complete self-giving. With nothing more to give there is nothing that can be deprived from it. Free from the assaults of freedom, it alone can indemnify freedom. Only the freedom that has received transcendent authorization can stand in the full light of freedom. Nothing that freedom could perpetrate can overturn the faith that has been placed in it. Our faith in freedom is only a pale reflection of that transcendent affirmation, but it is nevertheless a reflection. Just as we can only embark on the path of freedom by embracing the need for forgiveness, so we realize that freedom as a whole is undergirded by a mode of forgiveness that reaches wider and deeper than we can perceive. The genius of Dostoevsky's tale is not just that he grasped this imperative, but understood that it could not be recognized until it had become evident in the person whose very presence is already a disruption of the order of presence. The word of forgiveness must be pronounced by Christ who pronounces it most searingly in the gaze he turns toward each. It is as an icon of Christ that the tale functions at its highest artistic and spiritual level. Faith is encountered in the word of love that is the fulfillment of hope.

In the discovery that forgiveness is a person, we glimpse what it means to be a person. Freedom is not only the mark of the person, but the origin from which freedom derives. The faith that makes freedom possible is also the faith that sustains it from before its beginning. We share in the redemptive sacrifice. That is the meaning of faith. Freedom that requires faith in its imprescriptibility both receives and dispenses validation. It is because we live within the unfolding of freedom that we can catch a glimpse whence it arises and whereby it is sustained. As that which contains itself, we know that freedom is tantamount to the being that is its own source. From this glimpse there arises the perennial temptation of human freedom to dispense with its beginning, to become God. But then the overreaching this entails overwhelms the pride of freedom and tempts us to the despair of abandoning it. Both features are present in the Inquisitor's tale. Between revolt and despair is the path from which the tale itself is told. One is impossible and the other superfluous. The truth is even more wonderful. We are called to become God by uniting ourselves with the humility that is divine freedom. The path of redemptive outpouring is not only the way of God but also the way to God. Freedom receives its validation when it is seen as the divinization opened to those who take upon themselves the burden that is light. Putting the self aside, we make room for God. The transcendence that makes freedom possible is also its highest fulfillment. Through freedom we are not only like God, but we become even more united with him. Love is the goal of freedom. Complete self-giving is both the origin and the end of freedom. Giving without counting the cost is both the condition of the possibility of freedom and its culminating realization. As the life of God, freedom can be nothing other than the life of God.

Freedom as Transcendence

Freedom is transcendence. It derives from transcendence and returns to it. That is what reflection discovers when it goes beyond idle chatter about choice to contemplate the impossibility of freedom attaining its goal. The transcendence toward which freedom aspires is at best only partially reached and at worst utterly lost. How then can freedom be justified? It cannot be, in terms of its results. Besides, there would be no results unless we already trusted the finality of freedom. It must be affirmed even before it has begun. Faith, the faith that cannot be guaranteed in advance, is the condition for the possibility of its exercise. Nothing precedes freedom but the willingness to entrust freedom to itself. Freedom must remain free. But this also means that nothing can abolish freedom for it has no tangible existence in the world. It is what generates a multiplicity of finite actions and entities while it itself seems to have no beginning, or none that can become a target for elimination. Human beings may be killed but not the freedom from which all that they did and were arose. Transcendence is not only the direction of freedom but also its reality. That is, it has no reality but self-transcendence and is thus not subject to the law of existence. It cannot die. Freedom is deathless, as we would expect of what constitutes the core of the person. Even the satisfaction that modern philosophers derive from pointing out that when all is stripped away we do not discover a core of the person cannot diminish this realization.[20] Freedom is the core that is not a core. It is what is before and after the core and contains it as a whole. No doubt this is an elusive notion to unfold, confirming Walker Percy's observation that as we know more and more about the cosmos we know less and less about ourselves. The mystery of freedom cannot be comprehended. But it may be glimpsed, and that is what Dostoevsky attempted in recounting the return of Christ. It is in the moment of its unconditional affirmation that the meaning of freedom is intuited.

It is thus that faith apprehends what cannot be apprehended because we live within it. A vision has been granted of what cannot be envisioned, because it makes all seeing possible. The relationship was first apprehended by Plato when Socrates called our attention to the Good that makes it possible to know and yet is beyond knowing.[21] Like much else in Socratic wisdom, it begins in the awareness of its incapacity. Yet that self-limitation turns out to be wise and indeed to be the whole of the wisdom available to us. Even while not knowing, we know that we do not know, and thus know. Less well delineated in that classic account is any grasp of why this must be so. One of the notable features of the modern philosophical revolution is that it has meditated on the condition of possibility in order to realize the impossibility of any viewer or knower seeing or knowing himself. It is in the nature of our reason and our freedom that they must be exercised on the basis of faith. We cannot authorize them. But that does not mean they are not authorized. It is simply that the authorization is invisible, for if it were to step into the realm of visibility, it would no longer occupy the role of sustaining. Just as the eye cannot behold itself while seeing things, so freedom cannot be free in regard to itself. It cannot overstep the limits of freedom by which freedom is granted to it. That which releases cannot be released. Therein lies the intimate bond with a source that despite its closeness, indeed because of it, is continually in danger of being forgotten. Recollection too was a Platonic theme, but why it must be premised on forgetting eluded even him, except for the occasions when it surfaced in myth.[22] But myth, like faith, does not account for itself. That is a further philosophical problem on which Kant and his successors hazarded their best efforts. In itself, however, that was a signal development, for we have lived for millennia within the differentiation of transcendent Being without adverting to the necessity for its absence.

Now we are on the verge of an enlargement of perspective on what has eluded us for so long. It is not just recognition that the transcendent is absent or hidden, but the realization of why it must be so. Metaphysics, that misconceived term that suggests a realm beyond the physical, will finally be put to rest. It had always invited the objection that beyond the physical must lie a further reality that grounded it. The game of deferral could not, however, go on indefinitely. Instead we must acknowledge that meta-physics is impossible. There can be no other realm beyond the one in which we find ourselves because the sustaining cannot enter into what it sustains without abolishing itself.[23] Predestination would rob destination of its meaning. The end of history would destroy historical existence. Immanentization of the eschaton does not bring about the fulfillment of human life but robs it of its significance.[24] This has been the outcome of the militantly secular ideologies that sought a completely worldly happiness. Closing the distance between this world and the other not only eroded the very idea of a secular realm; it also demonstrated the impossibility of a secular fulfillment. It may be that much of our secular civilization still clings to the notion of happiness in this life as its best possibility, but only because it has not confronted the conclusion of its own logic. Occasionally there surfaces the awareness that life without death would be intolerable, but then it slips away again as we focus on the further extension of living. The truth of course is that it is because happiness cannot be obtained in this life that any happiness within it is possible. Aristotle had not quite captured this realization, but he intuited it in his observations about the undesirability of becoming a god.[25] Reaching the goal turns the rest of existence into endless vacuity. We literally have nothing for which to live. This awareness hovers in the background of much of our overhyped expectancy that cannot quite suppress the note of sadness within it. By pursuing happiness so completely, we sense we have lost it completely. Why this is the case is less easily explained in secular terms, although philosophy has begun to rise to the challenge. With Wittgenstein and Heidegger we have begun to see why all saying cannot say anything about itself. The possibility of saying cannot be said. As with Hellen Keller, the discovery that words signify is the great breakthrough for which words cannot prepare us.[26]

The invisible source cannot be drawn into visibility without making it impossible for us to see it. That which holds us cannot be held without becoming that which no longer holds. Contrary to the misimpression that modern philosophy has been focused on mere obstacles to communication, it has instead raised our awareness of the unsaid that can never be included in any saying. As in every meeting of persons, more is contained than can be expressed in all that passes between us. Mystery is not diminished but deepened by the widening awareness of what escapes our attention and yet is present in every attending. To draw the divine too massively into the world was always to attenuate its divinity. This is well known in the repeated pattern of the transcendent religions that seek to guard the holiest of holies they know cannot be disclosed. Disclosure would only reveal that there is nothing to reveal. The mystery consists of preserving the mystery. Now the secular world has provided an irrefutable demonstration of the impossibility of declaring itself sufficient, for the declaration would simultaneously expose its insufficiency. By completing itself, the world closes itself off from itself. Its premise depends on admitting its incompleteness. That is the paradox within which a secular world unfolds, and it is, therefore, not surprising that its philosophical self-reflection converges on the same realization. A secular world derives from what it is not, and can neither suppress nor consummate the relationship without destroying itself. The more we meditate on the condition of possibility, the more we bring the impossibility of suspending it into relief. A secular world is a world that unshakably affirms the transcendent. That is its faith, even as it grapples with the meaning of faith.

The nature of faith, however, is that it carries us forward even before we are aware of its momentum. We find ourselves there before we have arrived. Faith is both the condition of possibility and our access to it. We must have faith in faith in order to begin. It is only subsequently that we realize that we have faith, that we have received it and can begin to ask what it means. Faith is in advance of its meaning, as the history of the church's long reflection on dogma attests. Prayer life comes before its theological exposition.[27] The former is both the condition and the content of the latter. The secular world is no different, for it too is sustained by a faith it has not fully understood and yet seeks to understand. Faith seeking understanding remains the structure.[28] It is correlated with the understanding that seeks faith as the subject matter to which it opens. As with the church, faith exceeds its understanding, but the need for understanding is not in any way lessened. Faith has reached the end that understanding seeks and is thus the guarantee of the inexhaustibility of the search. What the secular world needs is assurance against premature attainment of its aspirations. It must be reminded of their inaccessability, of their transcendence, so that it can undertake the secular journey of their attenuation. In thus becoming aware of its status, the secular world is on the point of overturning that status. A world that recognizes itself as secular is no longer secular. It is no wonder that the nature of a secular age is a topic so widely discussed and already mooted as "post-secular." The boundary, in being more clearly marked, is a move beyond the boundary. But this is of far more than contemporary interest, for it brims with significance for the world religions whose genesis is tied to the revelation of the transcendent, the first and most pivotal hinge in history. Differentiation of the immanent and transcendent has been the axis of our thinking even before it was named by Jaspers as an axial age. Our secular age is thus only the latest chapter in a long unfolding from that break. It is continuous with the far-reaching struggle within history to find the appropriate means of representing what cannot be represented, that is, transcendent divinity and its order within time. Now we may well be at the turning point at which the self-limitation of the secular provides the most adequate means of symbolizing and, more importantly, of yielding space to the sacred within time. That is surely of millennial significance.

Whether our secular civilization finally grasps the meaning of its faith, of what sustains it despite itself, remains an open question. Here we are only concerned with following out the dynamic of the faith from which it unfolds. The faith of Grotius, in the law that would hold even if there was no God, drives toward the affirmation of what is beyond God. How can that be other than God? Echoes of the same moral imperative that reverberate from classical sources to the present are no accident. They attest to a spiritual-intellectual trajectory covering an extensive arc. Grotius is simply one of the noteworthy enunciators. But we recognize the same inexorability in Nietzsche's insistence that every moral code ends by transcending itself, just as it did in the Sermon on the Mount. The invisibility that accepts invisibility and sets itself aside so that it may shine even more brightly is surely the moral pivot of a secular age. Not only is it not secular in its composition, but its animating spirit derives from nothing so much as the self-concealment of its goodness. Let not your right hand know what the left is doing. When all that is done is done in secret, then we have been purified of all earthly motives. It may be that the Father in heaven who sees in secret still sees it, but he is the only one. We may be far away from the Greek notion that properly human action must display itself within the publicity of the polis, but we are not for all that within a strictly private realm. The action that is seen by the Father alone is nevertheless seen. We have traded the light of the political realm for the luminosity of the transcendent. The polis in the end never was the definitive setting for judgment, for there was no guarantee that it would either exist or judge rightly. The example of Socrates attests to the true forum of judgment as the realm of the dead.[29]

The secular world has only confirmed that realization. Just as the rule of law does not mean that law is without foundation, so it can equally assert that law does not include its foundation. Law points to what is beyond law. In that way it is always more than law but not in such a way that it either distorts the nature of the law or deforms what is beyond it within the parameters of law. This is the problem of Sharia, the law of God that masquerades as the law of a particular, albeit ecumenic, community. Law too requires a distance from that from which it derives, for only then can it illumine what is more than law. Everywhere we turn in a secular world there is the same pattern of self-limitation. While that is an admirable testament to modesty, it always carries resonances of far greater moment. By proclaiming what it is not, it nevertheless proclaims it, as what is properly beyond the secular. A secular world is by definition one-half of a dichotomy. What is less well appreciated is that in yielding space it makes space. The secular that recognizes itself as such is proclaiming its other, the transcendent, not in secular terms but in itself. This is why it may be the setting in which the transcendent most truly appears as the transcendent. When law refuses to go beyond the limits of law it affirms that which limits it as law.[30] By not requiring the transcendent to appear within the guise of the secular, it discloses the realm of the transcendent. We might say that a secular civilization is one in which the sacred is held most reverently. Perhaps more than any of the great spiritual civilizations of the past that, in the end, could not separate the transcendent from their immanent representations, a secular civilization is immunized against the danger. It may forget the transcendent, but it cannot distort it. That is a considerable advance. What renders it durable is that it rests on the imperative of not overstepping its bounds. Each testing of limits serves only to strengthen its sense of what it is that the limits venerate.

Nowhere is this more evident than in the unfolding of its morally authoritative principles. In a world without a source of authority, or without a visible source, the path of the invisible looms as its truth. But where can the invisible be perceived? It is nowhere but in the question itself. That which holds the question within is its opening. In the same way that the revelation of the transcendent correlated with the differentiation of inwardness, so the loss of the transcendent brings a deepening awareness of the region in which it may be found. When God has withdrawn, the way of opening toward him becomes even more precious. This is what accounts for the heightened attention to individual liberty. Mind is inviolable because it is the indispensable avenue to the transcendent. That which *is* nowhere is wholly within and is only encountered in that way. Religious liberty is often touted as the first liberty, but the reason is more than historical. The connection is far more intrinsic than circumstance would suggest. The primacy of conscience arises, not just from the sense that freedom of thought is the first condition of freedom, but from the intuition of that toward which mind reaches. Worship of God must take place in spirit and in truth, otherwise it hardly counts as worship. External sacrifice and verbal prayers are a long way from the encounter that can only be reached inwardly. When nothing material stands for the divine, the imperative of guarding interiority is deepened. An unforeseen consequence of the turn away from transcendence is surely that the enduring path of transcendence gains even greater salience. The correlation between a secular age and its theistic withdrawal is here exemplified within the logic of experience. A conceptual necessity gains living actuality. When God has been forgotten, the way of remembering assumes new centrality. Interiority assumes its undeniable primacy.

Rights as a Window on the Transcendent

That which is invisible remains within the invisibility within which we live. Not only is it more preciously guarded because of its invisibility, but it may be more venerated in its invisibility. We seem to be closer to its truth and possess a heightened sense of how the sacred prevails. A bemoaning of the secular world often overlooks this spiritual secret, that is, its confidence in more adequately securing the place of the divine when it is demarcated as transcendent. Nowhere is this more evident than in the determination to hold freedom of conscience inviolate. This indispensable freedom is not only the way that a secular world pays its respect to what is beyond it but also the principal way in which the transcendent shines in a world that has occluded it. By heightening reverence for the way, the end is correspondingly enlarged. Paradoxical and unintended as it may seem, the pattern begins to explain the vitality of religion in an age that has deemed it irrelevant.[31] Within the secular framework faith may be incomprehensible, but from the perspective of faith the secular appears as its appropriate precondition. I must decrease that God may increase. At some point the two perspectives may reach a moment of mutual recognition, but for now they move within the half-light by which they see just what is before them. They live by faith, trusting to the intimations from an unknown region they have yet to reach.[32] Religion may have the greater clarity in knowing that in which it has faith, but the secular should not for that reason be discounted. It may not have faith in God and, indeed, understands itself as not having such faith, but it retains its faith in faith. That is not inconsiderable for it precedes the opening of faith in the One who calls it forth. Faith in faith is a first step, one that for all its primordiality cannot be bypassed. A world without faith is one that nevertheless clings to faith and, in this, exemplifies it all the more vividly. This is the trail by which our secular history has placed increasing emphasis on the inviolability of the person, without acknowledging its implied opening beyond itself. Interiority, it has yet to discover, is both the path to God and the reality of God. Transcendence is directed toward what is transcendent.

For now, however, we live within a secular framework that fails to understand its faith. Having faith in faith, it exists purely on faith. We see this in the steady accumulation of rights that are pronounced inalienable while their source continues to elude us. Often the incoherence is so palpable that the entire scheme is dismissed as "rights talk" or "nonsense on stilts."[33] Skepticism abounds, and the project of providing a rationale to guide the application and balancing of rights is declared hopeless. The discourse of rights has itself modulated from the confident assertion of nature as their source to the admission of bare humanity as the justification. The Universal Declaration of Human Rights evades the debate about their source and meaning by consciously avoiding such questions.[34] Conflicting and competing rights claims are so constantly asserted that we could be forgiven for despairing of ever rendering them as a coherent whole. Rights are deemed mere subjective assertions that lack a foundation in nature or reason. An anarchic cacophony of claims is viewed as a house of cards doomed to fail. The only problem with this narrative is that history has refused to cooperate. For all of the incoherence and inconsistency evident within our regime of rights, the hold of its language has not diminished. Rather it has been strengthened and enlarged to demonstrate its historical staying power as the unrivaled moral discourse of the public arena. Rumors of its demise were greatly exaggerated. In addition, we observe that states that respect the rights of their citizens have the best prospects of long-term political success, while those who trample on them are incapable of securing the kind of support that guarantees their own continuance. Contrast the transfer of power within North and South Korea. Legitimacy is rooted in mutual guarantees that can neither be manipulated nor evaded.

Yet we lack a means of both explaining and creating that most beneficial political arrangement. The mere assertion of rights is not deemed sufficient, no more than a constitution stipulates its implementation. Documents do not enact themselves. For that human action is required, and this is the singular advantage of the tradition of individual rights. It arises precisely at the point at which the value and dignity of persons are under threat. Resistance is undertaken in the name of their preservation. Despotic regimes all over the world begin to be opposed by those who heroically undertake the defense of rights they sense to be indispensable to their humanity. But from where did that conviction arise, that they possessed a core that could not be alienated, a worth that could not be surrendered without losing everything that makes life of value?[35] Even those who had not previously thought much of their own inexhaustible value now discover that they are of surpassing worth. Previously all that mattered seemed to be defined in purely material terms, as the comforts or discomforts of everyday life. Even when the aggravations and deprivations were cataloged, as they were in the Declaration of Independence, they hardly amounted to more than a list of gripes. Yet on that occasion they burst into a crisis of extraordinary significance that required a more than ordinary response. Curtailments of liberty suddenly became an assault on its principle. How that realization occurred is not something the document discloses, even if it could. Like the signatories of Charter 77, or Charter 08, they could list the grievances but not explain why they constituted an assault on their humanity.[36] Why liberty is essential and why its curtailment insupportable could not easily be articulated. All that they knew is that the mission of its defense had completely absorbed them. It is only in relation to the threat that the danger becomes manifest. What had previously been taken for granted now became a consuming imperative.

They had been seized by faith, a faith they had scarcely suspected lay within them. Now it rose to a necessity for which they were prepared to give their lives. Why it must be so and what its source is they were less ready to explain; they only knew that it was a call from which they could not turn aside. As they entered more deeply into the struggle that drew them, they gained a deeper sense of what was at stake. It was nothing less than the whole of their existence, that whose loss would be incalculable for it would betoken an incalculable loss. They would lose their self-respect. Without it they would be deprived of all that is of value, for nothing can be of value to those who have ceased to value themselves. Even the regard of others, or their love, could not compensate an irreparable betrayal. Forgiveness might later arrive, but it would be offered for what is unforgivable. Besides, such an expiation would require a redemptive sacrifice beyond any we have a right to expect. For now, all that mattered is that the imperative of defending all that must be defended had brought into view the transcendent dimension of a human being. There are worse things than losing one's life, for one could also lose that which is worth more than life.[37] In that realization the scale of judgment became unmistakable. It had nothing to do with earthly fulfillment but with fidelity to what outweighs the whole world. In resisting that which must be resisted, they had discovered there is within them a measure that exceeds all finite measurement.[38] Without metaphysical language they discovered that they lived within an eternal horizon and not within the space-time limits hitherto marking their world. The secular had been shattered as the sacred had pierced it. This is why the commemoration of founders and heroes is inescapably tinged with sacral aspects. In this instant, however, it is without that momentous overtone and is simply a felt necessity of experience. What later emerges in the perspective of reflection is first present in the immediacy of practice. That is the nature of faith.

Practice knows more than it can say, for it lives by faith. What the content of that faith is it may never be fully able to say, although it inevitably must struggle to define what it is about. The language of rights, natural or human, is one such attempt. It asserts that there is a limit, and it marks the limit by asserting it. What cannot be surrendered is discerned more fully when it falls under threat of deprivation. Law, we know, furnishes us with rights under the law, but what about the rights that demarcate the limits of law? Are there boundaries to what law can grant or withhold? Whatever it is that law preserves must surely be immune to the application of law. There cannot be a law that would suspend law, for law too has its limits. What it is that constitutes those limits is less readily defined, but they arise from the immutability we sense as impervious to law. The inalienable cannot be alienated. Thus far and no further. This is the genesis of rights that are natural or human, meaning no political power can grant or deny what must be the measure of legitimate rule. When the Franciscans were asked to explain how it was possible to live on the basis of their renunciation of all property, they found it necessary to distinguish between a legal and a natural right.[39] All that they could renounce remained in the legal realm; what was in the natural realm was impossible to surrender. In confronting the limits of what they could do, they discovered that there were limits. From that point on the language became available as a barrier against the depredations to which all human beings are subject. The situation in extremis defined the extremes. A right cannot be lost even when it is lost. It remains as a rebuke against overreaching dominion. The human being who has surrendered everything or has been deprived of everything remains, more than all that is lost.[40] An unassailability endures at the core as nothing but that inviolability itself. It can be neither given away nor taken away, for it is the shaft of transcendence within which the person stands. The language of rights is an epiphany of the dignity it is intended to preserve.

This is nothing less than the capacity for self-transcendence. At the point where that possibility comes into view we realize that there is nothing to preserve, for it has surpassed the need. How can the giving that gives itself away be contained? It proclaims the right to go without rights, to renounce one's rights, which, the Franciscans discovered, are only legal rights. The right that cannot be lost is the only right that counts, but then it has ceased to count for it is inalienable. Even when it is taken away it has not been lost, for then it is preserved most of all. That is the inexhaustible mystery that the language of rights haltingly serves to delineate. Transcendence, it appears, cannot become present but is always recognized in its movement beyond anything present. Rights that seem to name something specific turn out to name the willingness to withdraw from the specific. Whatever content is assigned to a right, the logic of rights is the readiness to overturn it. We may still possess rights that register particular claims, but once we trace the source of that assertion we discover it lies in our capacity to surrender the claim. Only those who are always more than they claim can be assigned the status of claimants. They are not in the claims but have transcended them. That is why they must be treated with inextinguishable reverence and awe. By possessing rights that cannot be alienated, they are recognized as guardians of transcendence. In the end there is no point at which they have reached the limits of what is owed to them. The debt can never be amortized. Instead, it continually grows in response to the need of the recipient. But this is also why the distribution of entitlements to goods and services must not be framed in the language of rights. It is the nature of rights that they cannot be limited, while all entitlements operate within the finite sphere of everything in this world. To receive a benefit, the capacity to provide it must exist, while rights aim at securing the inexhaustible value of each person. Entitlements belong to this world, while rights mark our trajectory beyond it. They can be brought into balance only by doing all that we can to save the other while knowing we cannot save him. Mother Teresa's ministry privileged each one over any scheme to address all. The person outshines the aggregate. Rights mark the boundary of transcendence when we admit that one, the one in need, outweighs the needs of the whole.[41] Each is entitled to more than we can give because that is what it means to live within the recognition of inexhaustibility. Rights bring the imperative of transcendence into view.

Neither the source of rights nor their implementation can draw on a finite scale of measurement. There may be a kind of vertigo in the whole enterprise. In the end we cannot even eliminate the right to yield our rights, thereby demonstrating their superfluous character for those who are capable of stepping beyond them. Every finite attempt to capture the conditionality of rights is defeated by their unconditional dynamic. They are enjoyed by those who do not need them, and that is the principal basis of their acknowledgment.[42] Readiness to relinquish them is the unsurpassable rationale for their profession. What has already been surrendered cannot be taken away, and in that realization we glimpse their transcendent finality. That is why they are inexhaustible and universal. They cannot be contained in finite specifications for as soon as a limit is proposed it must immediately be set aside. This is why death with dignity is so utterly incoherent. The dignity we might assume to be in accord with a person's wishes are no sooner mooted than we can think of many circumstances in which dignity may be served by going beyond dignity. Throwing oneself on a grenade in order to save one's comrades hardly exemplifies an elevated demise. Yet becoming mincemeat may in that circumstance demonstrate the highest nobility. Dying in public on a cross contradicts any notion of what is fitting for a human being.[43] Yet Christians have come to regard it as the consummate expression of love. Nothing can deprive us of rights and dignity, it turns out, once we have submitted to the sacrifice to which we have been called. Redemption as the flower of suffering is the definitive victory that cannot be taken away. In it we see that the regime of rights and dignity ultimately guards what is impervious to loss. Neither natural nor human, rights betoken what transcends them.

In a world without reference to the transcendent the notion of rights is testament to the impossibility of its elimination. Rights are a mode of faith in what we can no longer comprehend but which, for all that, remains as faith. The invisible source of authority that has no acknowledgment in our world is nevertheless powerfully present through its absence. Nowhere is this more evident than in the tenacity with which we hold onto the one indisputable instance of transcendence. Rights language, guarding limitless dignity, reverberates with unmistakable overtones of the sacred. That may sit uneasily with the prevailing paradigm of finitude and may not even be well perceived there, but it is undeniable that this remains for us the language that pronounces the inexhaustible. All that exceeds the secular has nevertheless found a place within it. This may seem strange, even suggesting that the sacred has slipped unnoticed into a realm incompatible with it. But then we realize that transcendence and immanence are correlative and only await acknowledgment of their mutuality. There is nothing illegitimate about an opening to transcendence within the finite or with the finite as pointing to what is beyond it. In many respects that is their appropriate disclosure. It is only their confusion that is problematic. From the side of the immanent pole the challenge may be greatest because, by definition, it is incapable of depicting what transcends it.[44] The finite must regard everything under the lens of the finite. Yet it is not irrevocably closed to the infinite, for it contains the infinite unknowingly within itself. Its very self-understanding as finite requires it. The other, even the other whom it cannot comprehend, is already borne within. The confusion and uncertainty that attach to the language of rights exemplifies that pattern. Its conceptual relationship is only navigated with difficulty, often at the cost of open contradiction, and yet we are pulled inexorably in the direction of the transcendence that finitude conceals. The bigger question is surely whether the divinity toward which it points is properly presented.

Is the invisible source of authority glimpsed as invisible? Is it glimpsed as the movement of faith? The entire meditation issuing from Grotius testifies not only that it is, but that it is only within faith that the invisible is apprehended. The secular world that scrupulously avoids representation of the transcendent has made it possible for the transcendent to appear as transcendent. Existing nowhere within space and time, the transcendent exists solely within itself. In acknowledging its incapability of containing the transcendent, the secular world has allowed the transcendent to be displayed as transcendent. When we ask where this occurs we must respond that it is nowhere but within the hearts of those who perceive it without perceiving. The inwardness of the person is the locus of transcendence, for inwardness is transcendence as such. Faith, the faith that prevails even when it is lost, that holds onto God when there is no God, is the medium of that relationship. What is invisible cannot be concealed. In inwardness it endures for, as faith, it has already resolved to go beyond the visible. Contrary to a conventional misconception, this does not arise from a will to believe or a leap of faith. Neither is possible without the faith from which it arises. Before there is a resolution there is first the faith that draws it. We must believe in a leap of faith before we leap. This is why the search for the historical Jesus and evidence for the existence of God is beside the point. Neither is a project on which we would embark if we did not seek the God we already knew before we began.[45] As the horizon of seeking, faith precedes the whole. It is a search for the transcendence that already marks it. Without faith we would not be able to arrive at faith. Only one who transcends can encounter the transcendent. That is why the inviolability of the inner person is so crucial in a secular world. Through the regime of rights and dignity it proclaims faith as the sanctuary it will not invade. In that way even a secular world retains its hold on faith. It has kept faith in faith. Even if it is not capable of understanding that which it reveres, it nevertheless intuits the indispensability of what it holds within itself.

A secular state cannot, in other words, be atheistic. The invisible source of authority on which it depends cannot be concealed, even if such concealment could guard against its own undoing. The absence of God does not mean the disappearance of God. It may just as easily be read, I have insisted, as a readiness to perceive how God prevails as God. That which the secular world cannot contain is thus contained within itself, along with the world. By its self-conception the secular world is open to what is beyond it. Nowhere is that openness more deeply affirmed than in the reverence it accords to the one place within which the transcendent publicly shines. It affirms faith, even when it does not possess it, by according primacy to the inwardness that is faith. In the regime of rights a secular world acknowledges the foundation it cannot possess and thereby possesses it in the only way that it can be possessed. Rights are beyond deprivation for we cannot be deprived of what cannot be taken away. As the singular moment of transcendence, rights are the point at which a secular world transcends itself and, for a moment, ceases to be secular. Thus it is not just in its self-conception that the secular world exceeds itself. It is also and, more significantly, brought to yield to infinity in the reverence it accords to the rights and dignity of every person. By acknowledging the transcendent as transcendent, it has conceded its own limits. That is the invisible source of authority accessed through the faith in faith that continues to prevail. As with Marx and the great secular messiahs, it discovers that it cannot reject what it presupposes at every turn. The revolt against God could only take place by continually naming God. Marx had thought that a Communist society would not need to recall its origination in that highest assertion of human independence. Atheism, he remarked, would become impossible in practice for the question of God would become obsolete. Little did he suspect the folds of irony unfolded within this expectation.

A secular world is a world that cannot suppress its awareness of God. The awareness is disclosed in the ever deeper layers of conviction hidden within it. Even forgetting God is not an option, for then it would cease to be secular and run the risk of overstepping its own boundaries. Without God a secular world runs the perennial danger of claiming its own divinity. But it is when it must affirm the openness to divinity within each person, the unlimited capacity for self-transcendence each possesses, that it is compelled to submit to what exceeds its finite scale of measurement. Within a secular order every person is a shining beacon of transcendence. The inexhaustible respect for the rights and dignity of each is the point at which the secular submits to the invisible source of authority within it. Even if we grant that there is no God, the irrefragable submission to what is required would hold. That is its faith, the faith pronounced by Grotius at the very beginning of the secular world, before it even knew itself as secular. In the intervening years it has discovered that it has become even more incapable of renouncing what it yet cannot pronounce. It may not be able to say "God," but it cannot avoid his silent appeal. By not saying, it may have said more and better than can be said. That is its mystery, the mystery that pervades a world in which God is invisible. The one thing it cannot say is that God is no more, for by excluding God it denies the transcendence that marks its own existence. Nowhere is this more evident than in the impossibility of renouncing rights as the boundary that defines the meaning and limits of a secular world. Such a world is not just separated from God, but dedicated to the preservation of the unfathomability within which alone God can be acknowledged. Persons who transcend a secular scale of significance attest to the capacity of a secular world to transcend itself. By acknowledging the inexhaustible rights of its members, the state too participates in what is beyond it. Atheism *is* impossible within its practice.

NOTES

Chapter 1

1. Aleksandr Solzhenitsyn, "Templeton Lecture" (1983), in *The Solzhenitsyn Reader: New and Essential Writings, 1947–2005*, ed. Edward E. Ericson Jr. and Daniel J. Mahoney (Wilmington, DE: Intercollegiate Studies Institute, 2006), 577.

2. One thinks of the biting critique of the Spanish conquests by Bartolomé de Las Casas, *A Short Account of the Destruction of the Indies* (1542), or Francisco de Vitoria's invalidation of the legitimacy of Spanish rule in *On the American Indians* (1532), or the remarkably sympathetic treatment of the American colonists in the writings of Edmund Burke, as well as his prosecution of Warren Hastings for his mistreatment of the people of India. On the latter, see Richard Bourke, *Empire and Revolution: The Political Life of Edmund Burke* (Princeton, NJ: Princeton University Press, 2015).

3. "Live Not By Lies!," is the classic admonition Solzhenitsyn released just before his forced exile in 1974. *Solzhenitsyn Reader*, 556–60.

4. Joshua Mitchell, *American Awakening: Identity Politics and Other Afflictions of Our Time* (New York: Encounter, 2020), places contemporary turmoil within an intriguing theological framework.

5. Franz Jägerstätter may have been a rarity in voting against the Anschluss of Austria and Germany, although the awareness of the consequences were widespread. See *Franz Jägerstätter: Letters and Writings from Prison*, ed. Erna Putz (Maryknoll, NY: Orbis Books, 2009), which became the basis for the celebrated Terrence Malick film, *A Hidden Life* (2019).

6. Augustine, *City of God*, bk. IV, ch. 4.

7. "We could not match conviction with conviction, we had no ideas with which we could meet or oppose the ideas opposed to us. Was our society, which had always been so assured of its superiority and rectitude, so confident of its unexamined premises, assembled around anything more permanent than a congeries of banks, insurance companies and industries, and had it any beliefs more essential than a belief in compound interest and the maintenance of dividends?" T. S. Eliot, *The Idea of a Christian Society* (New York: Harcourt Brace, 1940), 65.

8. For that reason I think Samuel Moyn's excellent historical overview is incorrectly titled, *The Last Utopia: Human Rights in History* (Cambridge, MA: Belknap Press, 2012).

9. "At bottom, man has lost faith in his own value when no infinitely valuable whole works through him." Friedrich Nietzsche, *The Will to Power*, trans. Walter Kaufmann and R. J. Hollingdale, ed. Walter Kaufmann (New York: Vintage, 1968), 12.

10. "Is not our life on earth a long, unbroken period of trial?" Augustine, *Confessions*, trans. R. S. Sloane-Coffin (Harmondsworth: Penguin, 1962), bk. X, ch. 28.

11. David Walsh, *The Third Millennium: Reflections on Faith and Reason* (Washington, DC: Georgetown University Press, 1999), ch. 1, "The Christian Enlargement of Reason."

12. It is the loss of that perspective that occasioned Edmund Husserl to pour forth his famous lecture on the crisis of the European sciences. "Since the intuitively given surrounding world, this merely subjective realm, is forgotten in scientific investigation, the working subject is himself forgotten: the scientist does not become a subject of investigation. (Accordingly, from this standpoint, the rationality of the exact sciences is of a piece with the rationality of the Egyptian pyramids.)" Edmund Husserl, *The Crisis of the European Sciences and Transcendental Phenomenology*, trans. David Carr (Evanston, IL: Northwestern University Press, 1970), 295.

13. Charles Cochrane, *Christianity and Classical Culture* (Indianapolis: Liberty Fund, 2003; orig. pub. 1940).

14. Karl Jaspers, *The Origin and Goal of History,* trans. Michael Bullock (New York: Routledge, 2021; orig. pub. 1949).

15. St. Thomas Aquinas affirms Christ as the head of all men. *Summa Theologiae*, pt. III, Q.8, a.3. Commenting on this, Eric Voegelin observes, "In practice this means that one has to recognize, and make intelligible, the presence of Christ in a Babylonian hymn, or a Taoist speculation, or a Platonic dialogue, just as much as in a Gospel." *Collected Works*, vol. 12: *Published Essays 1966–1985*, ed. Ellis Sandoz (Baton Rouge: Louisiana State University Press, 1990), 294.

16. The inexpressibly delicate relationship of the soul with God, Kierkegaard explains, is like the case of a king who falls in love with a humble maiden and therefore must conceal who he is lest he overwhelm her. God takes on the suffering of love, its inner contradiction, for "not to disclose itself is the death of love; to disclose itself is the death of the beloved." Johannes Climacus, in *Philosophical*

Fragments, or a Fragment of Philosophy, ed. and trans. Howard V. Hong and Edna H. Hong (Princeton, NJ: Princeton University Press, 1985), 30.

17. Roger Scruton, *The Face of God* (London: Bloomsbury, 2012).

18. Denys Turner, *The Darkness of God: Negativity in Christian Mysticism* (Cambridge: Cambridge University Press, 1995); *Mother Teresa: Come Be My Light: The Private Writings of the Saint of Calcutta*, ed. Brian Kolodiejchuk (New York: Image, 2009). See also St. John of the Cross, *The Dark Night of the Soul* (1577).

19. Nietzsche, *The Will to Power*, 7.

20. Benedict XVI made the same point with great concision when he addressed the Collège des Bernardins in Paris in 2008. "The monks," he said, "did not set out to create a Christian culture: they sought God." I am indebted to Camelia Lelesan for this reference.

21. Friedrich Nietzsche, *Thus Spoke Zarathustra*, trans. Walter Kaufmann (New York: Penguin, 1978), 260.

22. Aleksander Solzhenitsyn, *Gulag Archipelago*, trans. Thomas Whitney (New York: Harper, 1975), 2:618; Victor Frankl, *Man's Search for Meaning*, trans. Ilse Lasch (New York: Washington Square, 1963), 124.

23. Liu Xiaobo, *No Enemies, No Hatred: Selected Essays and Poems*, ed. Perry Link, Tienchi Martin-Liao, and Liu Xia (Cambridge, MA: Belknap Press, 2013). See also Etty Hillesum, *An Interrupted Life: The Diaries 1941–43 and Letters from Westerbork*, trans. Arnold J. Pomerans (New York: Holt, 1996).

24. It is of course widely acknowledged that Bonhoeffer was on his way to that deeper vision as he meditated in the dialogue of his last letters and connected it all back to Grotius. "And we cannot be honest unless we recognize that we have to live in the *etsi deus non daretur*. And this is just what we do recognize—before God! God himself compels us to recognize it. So our coming of age leads us to a true recognition of our situation before God. God would have us know that we must live as men who manage our lives without him. The God who is with us is the God who forsakes us (Mark 15:34)." Dietrich Bonhoeffer, Letter from Tagel Prison, July 16, 1944, in *Letters and Papers from Prison*, ed. Eberhard Bethge (New York: Macmillan, 1953), 360. This was the culmination of a path that had become clear in 1937 with *The Cost of Discipleship*, trans. R. H. Fuller (New York: Touchstone, 1995).

25. "But why does this final evaluation matter so much to me? After all, at that point I shouldn't care. But I do care because I'm convinced that my existence—like everything that has ever happened—has ruffled the surface of Being, and that after my little ripple, however marginal, insignificant, and ephemeral it may have been, Being is and always will be different from what it was before. All my life I have simply believed that what is once done can never be undone and that, in fact, everything remains forever. In short, Being has a memory." Václav Havel, *To the Castle and Back: A Memoir*, trans. Paul Wilson (New York: Knopf, 2006), 329–30.

26. Blaise Pascal, *Pensées*, S94/ L60, trans. Rogier Ariew (Indianapolis: Hackett, 2005), 20. The Montaigne reference is to *Essays* II, ch. 12. For this

reading of Pascal and Montaigne see Jacques Derrida, *Acts of Religion*, ed. Gil Anidjar (New York: Routledge, 2002), 57.

27. See Jeremy Geddert, *Hugo Grotius and the Modern Theology of Freedom* (New York: Routledge, 2017).

28. Richard Kearney, *Anatheism: Returning to God after God* (New York: Columbia University Press, 2011); Joseph Cardinal Ratzinger and Jürgen Habermas, *Dialectics of Secularization: Reason and Revelation*, trans. Brian McNeil (San Francisco: Ignatius, 2006).

29. Fyodor Dostoevsky, *The Brothers Karamazov*, trans. Constance Garnett (New York: Modern Library, 1950), bk.7, ch. 4, 437.

30. Hans Joas, *The Power of the Sacred: An Alternative to the Narrative of Disenchantment*, trans. Alex Skinner (Oxford: Oxford University Press, 2021).

31. Hans Joas, *The Sacredness of the Person: A New Genealogy of Human Rights*, trans. Alex Skinner (Washington DC: Georgetown University Press, 2013). For a more philosophic take on the same development, see David Walsh, *The Priority of the Person* (Notre Dame, IN: University of Notre Dame Press, 2020), especially ch. 1, "The Priority of the Person as the Modern Differentiation."

32. John Milbank, *Theology and Social Theory: Beyond Secular Reason* (Oxford: Blackwell, 1990).

33. William Desmond, *God and the Between* (Oxford: Wiley-Blackwell, 2008).

34. Jean-Luc Marion, *A Brief Apology for a Catholic Moment*, trans. Stephen Lewis (Chicago: University of Chicago Press, 2021); Pierre Manent, *Beyond Radical Secularism: How France and the Christian West Should Respond to the Islamic Challenge*, trans. Ralph Hancock (South Bend, IN: St. Augustine's Press, 2016).

Chapter 2

1. For a very illuminating reflection on the difficulty we have making sense of the two realities we inhabit, see Thomas Nagel, *Mind and Cosmos: Why the Materialist Neo-Darwinian Conception of Nature Is Almost Certainly False* (New York: Oxford University Press, 2012). Or see the title of Tom Stoppard's play, *The Hard Problem* (London: Faber & Faber, 2015), that alludes to the same issue.

2. Jürgen Habermas, *An Awareness of What Is Missing: Faith and Reason in a Post-Secular Age*, trans. Ciaran Cronin (Cambridge: Polity, 2010).

3. The term was one he introduced in his famous conversation with Joseph Ratzinger, *The Dialectics of Secularization: On Reason and Religion*, trans. Brian McNeil (San Francisco: Ignatius, 2006). Its significance surely lies in its overturning of the premise on which Charles Taylor's large rumination, *A Secular Age* (Cambridge, MA: Harvard University Press, 2007), was based on the eve of its appearance. At the very least it raises the central question as to whether the secular age can understand itself within its own terms.

4. The tomb of Lenin, the embalmment of Mao, and the outpouring of emotion on the death of Kim Il-sung are just the most obvious cases in a long line of brutality.

5. The situation is perfectly captured in Jacques Derrida's exercise in mourning at the departure of the spirit of Marx that coincided with the collapse of Communism in 1991: *Specters of Marx: The State of the Debt, the Work of Mourning, and the New International*, trans. Peggy Kamuf (London: Routledge, 1994). Something parallel is glimpsed by Ivan Karamazov as he recounts the reaction of the Grand Inquisitor to the Christ whose return is distinctly unwelcome. That ironic return comes full circle in the dissidents whose readiness for self-sacrifice is the definitive defeat of a mundane power. Liu, *No Enemies, No Hatred*.

6. We recall that the original meaning of *secularization* was to take what was previously in service to the church to make it available for civil use. That core meaning endures in the term even as its context is forgotten. See Stephen A. McKnight, *Sacralizing the Secular: The Renaissance Origins of Modernity* (Baton Rouge: Louisiana State University Press, 1989), esp. ch. 1, "Secularizing and Sacralizing Patterns in Modernity."

7. The notion of reoccupation has been particularly exposed by the great effort of Hans Blumenberg to mount a defense of the modern age as legitimate within its own terms. *The Legitimacy of the Modern Age*, trans. Robert Wallace (Cambridge, MA: MIT Press, 1985).

8. This famous remark appears in the context of Marx's renunciation, not only of the idea of God, but even of the question of God in the "Economic and Philosophic Manuscripts," in *The Marx-Engels Reader*, ed. Robert Tucker (New York: Norton, 1978), 92.

9. See the fascinating discussion of this in relation to the twin understandings of nature in Aristotle as that which is formed and that which forms and, therefore, eludes identification. Eric Voegelin, "What Is Nature?," in *Anamnesis: On the Theory of History and Consciousness*, trans. M. J. Hanak and Gerhart Niemeyer, ed. David Walsh (Columbia: University of Missouri Press, 2002).

10. See the famous study by Marcel Mauss, *The Gift*, trans. Jane Guyer (1925; Chicago: Hau, 2016).

11. The case of Maximillian Kolbe, who volunteered his own life for a man whom he did not know during a selection process at Auschwitz, is a particularly striking example. Elaine Murray Stone, *Maximilian Kolbe: Saint of Auschwitz* (New York: Paulist, 1997).

12. This notion is well captured in John McNerney, *Wealth of Persons: Economics with a Human Face* (Eugene, OR: Cascade, 2016).

13. "It is not from the benevolence of the butcher, the brewer, or the baker, that we expect our dinner, but from their regard to their own interest. We address ourselves, not to their humanity but to their self-love, and never talk to them of our own necessities but of their advantages . . . and by directing that industry in such a manner as its produce may be of the greatest value, he intends only his own gain, and he is in this, as in many other cases, led by an invisible hand to promote an end which was no part of his intention." Adam Smith, *The Wealth of Nations*, vol. 1, bk. 1, ch. 2; and bk. 4, ch. 2.

14. The relationship becomes transparent in what Hegel calls "a system of needs." G. W. F. Hegel, *Philosophy of Right*, Third Part, "Ethical Life."

15. Alasdair MacIntyre, "Poetry as Political Philosophy: Notes on Burke and Yeats," in *Ethics and Politics: Selected Essays* (Cambridge: Cambridge University Press, 2006), 2:163. I am indebted to Brad Lewis for this infamous quip.

16. Michael Short, *The Big Short: Inside the Doomsday Machine* (New York: Norton, 2010), vividly dramatized in the movie of the same title.

17. See Warren Buffet's "thank you" letter to Uncle Sam, *New York Times*, November 17, 2010.

18. Mary Hirschfeld, *Aquinas and the Market: Toward a Humane Economy* (Cambridge, MA: Harvard University Press, 2018).

19. This is evident in his location of the economy within Ethical Life and in the communitarian elements implicitly present within it. Hegel, *Philosophy of Right*.

20. See the analysis of "Bad Faith" in Jean Paul Sartre's *Being and Nothingness*.

21. This is why the slave becomes the engine for the forward movement of history. Hegel, *The Phenomenology of Spirit*, ch. IV, sec. A.

22. Responding to Thrasymachus's assertion that every art serves its own interest, Socrates insists that, on the contrary, each serves its respective subject matter and therefore cannot be rewarded through it. Compensation must come from outside its service in the form of payment. *Republic*, bk. I.

23. Andrew Pinsent, *The Second Person Perspective in Aquinas's Ethics: Virtues and Gifts* (New York: Routledge, 2012).

24. Michael Novak, *The Joy of Sports: End Zones, Bases, Baskets, Balls, and the Consecration of the American Spirit* (Lanham, MD: Madison, 1994).

25. "All my life," Václav Havel reflects, "I have simply believed that what is once done can never be undone and that, in fact, everything remains forever. In short, Being has a memory." Havel, *To the Castle and Back*, 330.

26. The subject who accepts the Categorical Imperative has thus received this mandate. "Act only on that maxim through which you can at the same time will that it should become a universal law." Immanuel Kant, *Groundwork of the Metaphysics of Morals*, trans. Mary Gregor (Cambridge: Cambridge University Press, 1997), ch. 2, 402 in marginal citation.

27. John Stuart Mill, *On Liberty*, in *On Liberty and Other Essays*, ed. John Gray (New York: Oxford University Press, 1991).

28. See the difference between the consequential defense of liberty in ch. 2 and the strictly moral one in ch. 3 of *On Liberty*. It is well known that Mill's own account of Utilitarianism represents a defeat for the central principle of utility as overriding morality.

29. An insight that is at the center of David Brooks, *The Second Mountain: The Quest for a Moral Life* (New York: Random House, 2020).

30. The phrase originates with Alexis de Tocqueville who used it in reference to the associational life he found in America. "Feelings and opinions are recruited, the heart is enlarged, and the human mind is developed only by the reciprocal influence of men upon one another." *Democracy in America*, vol. 2, bk. 2, ch. 5.

31. Marx's great analysis of alienation begins with the product as a power over against the worker who becomes poorer the more he produces. "Economic and Philosophic Manuscripts," 74. Its counterpart is the call of John Paul II not to

abolish private property but to place priority on the worker rather than the work. *Laborem Excercens* (1981).

32. "The 'freedom' inherent in such a state is the condition of being released from every care in the world save one; namely the care not to be idle in fulfilling one's role in the enterprise, not to inhibit or prejudice that complete mobilization of resources which constitutes such a state.... The member of such a state enjoys the composure of the conscript assured of his dinner. His 'freedom' is warm, compensated servility." Michael Oakeshott, *On Human Conduct* (Oxford: Clarendon, 1975), 317.

33. Jean-Luc Marion, *Being Given: Toward a Phenomenology of Givenness*, trans. Jeffrey Kosky (Stanford: Stanford University Press, 2002); Benedict XVI, *Caritas in Veritate* (2009).

34. *Marx-Engels Reader, Manifesto of the Communist Party*, 491.

35. *Marx-Engels Reader*, 54.

36. The title of Václav Havel's most famous essay encapsulates the reason that all totalitarians tremble before witnesses that refuse to be silent. "The Power of the Powerless," in *Open Letters: Selected Writings 1965–1990*, ed. Paul Wilson (New York: Vintage, 1991).

37. "God is spirit, and those who worship Him must worship in spirit and truth." John 4:24.

38. Eric Voegelin, "Immortality: Experience and Symbol," in *Collected Works*, vol. 12: *Published Essays, 1966–1985*.

39. Nagel, *Mind and Cosmos*.

Chapter 3

1. Pushing against the spirit of separation from which a secular world has emerged, we find the clarion call of "integralism" that would either include the world or renounce it. See P. Edmund Waldstein, OCist., and Peter Kwasniewski, eds., *Integralism and the Common Good: Selected Essays from The Josias*, vol. 1. (Brooklyn: Angelico, 2021); Rod Dreher, *The Benedict Option* (New York: Sentinel, 2017).

2. Pope Francis's meeting with Sheikh Ahmed al-Tayeb in 2016 was one such grand gesture.

3. The term originates with Plato in the *Symposium*, but it has been embraced by Eric Voegelin and more recently become a linchpin in the reflections of William Desmond.

4. Voegelin has done more than most in suggesting that the cosmos could furnish many analogies for the divine but itself remained beyond an analogical grasp. "Reality can be experienced either as the whole in which it is transparent for the presence of the divine ground, or as the manifold of existent things in tension toward the non-existent ground." *Collected Works*, vol. 17: *The Ecumenic Age*, ed. Michael Franz (Columbia: University of Missouri Press, 2000), 78.

5. Plato, *Republic* 509b: "and Goodness is not the same thing as being, but even beyond being, surpassing it in dignity and power."

6. "The philosopher must not condemn—for the tension between faith and reason, their conspiracy and conflict in time, is a mystery. Whether the traditionalist believer who professes truth in doctrinal form is not perhaps farther removed from truth than the intellectual objector who denies it because of its doctrinal form, he does not know. God alone knows who is nearer to the end that is the beginning." Voegelin, "Immortality: Experience and Symbol," 65.

7. James Emery White, *The Rise of the Nones* (Grand Rapids, MI: Baker, 2014).

8. Cicero, *On the Nature of the Gods*. See the discussion in Voegelin, *The Ecumenic Age*, Introduction.

9. Psalm 14:1.

10. This was the great source of Luther's insight and appeal. Gerhard Ebeling, *Luther: An Introduction to His Thought*, trans. R. A. Wilson (Philadelphia: Fortress, 1970).

11. "When Moses can hear the voice appoint the servant of Yahweh, he has grown spiritually into the servant of Yahweh. The command could be rejected only by a man who could never hear; the man who can hear cannot reject, because he has ontologically entered the will of God, as the will of God has entered him." Eric Voegelin, *Collected Works*, vol. 14: *Israel and Revelation*, ed. Maurice Hogan (Columbia: University of Missouri Press, 2001), 458.

12. See St. Thomas on the name of God. *Summa Theologiae*, I, Q. 13, a.11.

13. Yet as Jacques Derrida reminds us, the poison of writing is at the same time a remedy within this dialectical relationship. See "Plato's Pharmacy," in *Dissemination*, trans. Barbara Johnson (Chicago: University of Chicago Press, 1982).

14. Friedrich Nietzsche, *Untimely Meditations*, trans. R. J. Hollingdale (Cambridge: Cambridge University Press, 1997).

15. Sartre, *Being and Nothingness*, pt. 4, ch. 2.

16. John Milbank, *Beyond Secular Order* (Oxford: Wiley, 2013).

17. "The Freedom of a Christian," in *Martin Luther: Selections from His Writings*, ed. John Dillenberger (New York: Anchor, 2021), 42–85.

18. Emanuel Levinas quotes Descartes's Third Meditation, including its Augustinian resonances, to the effect that "my perception of the infinite, that is God, is in some way prior to my perception of the finite that is myself." "Here," Levinas declares, "bearing witness is the exception to the rule of being: in it the Infinite is revealed without appearing, without *showing* itself as Infinite." *God, Death, and Time*, trans. Bettina Bergo (Stanford: Stanford University Press, 2000), 197; original emphasis.

19. Joseph Ratzinger, *Eschatology: Death and Eternal Life*, trans. Michael Waldstein (Washington, DC: Catholic University of America Press, 1988).

20. Matthew Arnold, "Dover Beach."

21. On the new convergence in various forms of spiritual and political power, see Katherine Kelaidis, *Holy Russia? Holy War? Why the Russian Church Is Backing Putin against Ukraine* (London: SPCK, 2023); and the less lethal invocation of P. Edmund Waldstein, OCist., ed., *Integralism and the Common Good*, vol. 2: *The Two Powers* (Brooklyn: Angelico Press, 2022).

22. The hold of cosmological faith is however powerfully present even within our secular world, as Mircea Eliade explains in *The Sacred and the Profane* (New York: Harcourt Brace, 1987).

23. This was the problem that so fascinated Max Weber as he penned his classic, *The Protestant Ethic and the Spirit of Capitalism* (1904).

24. This is surely why even exemplary studies often leave us with a sense of something incomplete. See Brad Gregory, *The Unintended Reformation: How a Religious Revolution Secularized Society* (Cambridge, MA: Belknap Press, 2015).

25. Few have reached the penetration of Voegelin's insight into the way a civilization can advance and decline at the same time. "The more fervently all human energies are thrown into the great enterprise of salvation through world immanent action, the farther the human beings who engage in this enterprise move away from the life of the spirit. And since the life of the spirit is the source of order in man and society, the very success of a Gnostic civilization is the cause of its decline." Eric Voegelin, *The New Science of Politics* (Chicago: University of Chicago Press, 1952), 131.

26. The long medieval struggle over the temporal power of the church deflected it from its spiritual mission so profoundly that it provoked a continuing demand for reform of the church from within. The Reformation was only the tipping point of that centuries-old struggle. See, for example, Giles of Rome, *On Ecclesiastical Power* (1301), as opposed to the Norman Anonymous, *The Consecration of Bishops and Kings* (ca. 1100). Oliver O'Donovan and Joan Lockwood O'Donovan, eds., *From Irenaeus to Grotius: A Sourcebook in Christian Political Thought* (Grand Rapids, MI: Eeerdmans, 1999).

27. Benedict XVI in *Spe Salvi* (2007) reflects on the need to place a limit on temporal existence in order for it to be bearable and quotes Ambrose on death as a remedy. "Perhaps many people reject the faith today simply because they do not find the prospect of eternal life attractive. What they desire is not eternal life at all, but this present life, for which faith in eternal life seems something of an impediment. To continue living for ever—endlessly—appears more like a curse than a gift. Death, admittedly, one would wish to postpone for as long as possible. But to live always, without end—this, all things considered, can only be monotonous and ultimately unbearable. This is precisely the point made, for example, by Saint Ambrose, one of the Church Fathers, in the funeral discourse for his deceased brother Satyrus: 'Death was not part of nature; it became part of nature. God did not decree death from the beginning; he prescribed it as a remedy. Human life, because of sin[,] . . . began to experience the burden of wretchedness in unremitting labor and unbearable sorrow. There had to be a limit to its evils; death had to restore what life had forfeited. Without the assistance of grace, immortality is more of a burden than a blessing.'"

28. This was why he called on believers to talk less and live their faith more. "If those glad tidings of your Bible were written in your faces you would not need to insist so obstinately on the authority of that book: your works, your actions ought continually to render the Bible superfluous, through you a new Bible ought to be continually in course of creation." Friedrich Nietzsche, *Human, All*

Too Human, trans. R. J. Hollingdale (Cambridge: Cambridge University Press, 1986), par. 98. Heidegger may be one of the few to recognize in Nietzsche the opposite of the conventional picture of him as an atheist. "What to common sense looks like 'atheism,' and has to look like it, is at bottom the very opposite." Martin Heidegger, *Nietzsche II: The Eternal Recurrence of the Same*, ed. and trans. David Krell (New York: Harper, 1984), par. 98.

29. Curiously, it was St. Thomas who crystallized the use of the term "metaphysics" as a separate science when he wrote his commentary on Aristotle's *meta ta physica* (lit., "after the *Physics*"). See the summary in Voegelin, *Anamnesis*.

30. For an overview, see Michael Rosen, *Dignity: Its History and Meaning* (Cambridge, MA: Harvard University Press, 2012).

31. A valiant refusal of that reconciliation is John Rist, *What Is a Person? Realities, Constructs and Illusions* (Cambridge: Cambridge University Press, 2020). My own preferred route is the displacement of the question: David Walsh, *Politics of the Person as the Politics of Being* (Notre Dame, IN: University of Notre Dame Press, 2016).

32. C. S. Lewis, *Till We Have Faces: A Myth Retold* (San Francisco: Harper, 2017).

33. Hans Urs von Balthasar, *Love Alone Is Credible*, trans. D. C. Schindler (San Francisco: Ignatius, 2004).

34. See John Stuart Mill, *Collected Works*, vol. 10: *Essays on Ethics, Religion, and Society*, ed. J. M. Robson (London: Routledge, 1969).

35. Balthasar, "The 'Beatitudes' and Human Rights," in *Explorations in Theology*, vol. 5: *Man Is Created*, trans. Adrian Walker (San Francisco: Ignatius Press, 2014), 442–59.

36. This was the message of the Elder Zossima's brother who, as he lay dying, declared we are already in paradise without seeing it. Fyodor Dostoevsky, *The Brothers Karamazov*, trans. Constance Garnett (New York: Modern Library, 1950), 343.

37. Albert Camus famously voiced the ideal of becoming "a saint without God." *The Plague*, trans. Stuart Gilbert (New York: Vintage, 1948), 230. Simone Weil would not even pray lest prayer itself were to become an obstacle between her soul and God. See *Waiting for God* (1951). But the original is surely the cry of Christ on the cross that echoed Psalm 22:1, "My God, my God, why has thou forsaken me?" Mark 15:34.

38. Karol Wojtyla meditates steadily on this in *A Sign of Contradiction* (Providence, RI: Cluny, 2021), a Lenten retreat he gave to Pope Paul VI and the Curia in 1976.

Chapter 4

1. Marx, "Economic and Philosophic Manuscripts of 1844," 92.

2. Most notably in his famous dictum, the final sentence of the *Tractatus Logico-Philosophicus* (1921), "Whereof one cannot speak, thereof one must be silent." But, of course, the statement has already said it without saying.

3. This was a topic of endless fascination for Voegelin, who understood that the identification of dream and reality meant that "the critical exploration of cause and effect in history is prohibited" and rational action replaced by "magic operations in the dream world." Voegelin, *New Science of Politics*, 170; and "The Eclipse of Reality" (1970), in *Collected Works*, vol. 28: *What Is History and Other Late Unpublished Writings*, ed. Thomas Hollweck and Paul Caringella (Columbia: University of Missouri Press, 1990).

4. Most poignantly voiced by Thomas Nagel, *Mind and Cosmos: Why the Materialist Neo-Darwinian Conception of Nature Is Almost Certainly False* (New York: Oxford University Press, 2012).

5. Benedict XVI famously asserted that the church had from the beginning placed itself on the side of reason, as in "The Regensburg Address" (2006). Previously John Paul II had given the most synthetic account of the interrelationship between faith and reason in the culminating encyclical of his pontificate, *Fides et Ratio* (1998).

6. Roger Scruton, *On Human Nature* (Princeton, NJ: Princeton University Press, 2017).

7. Nagel perceptively points out that the hardheaded secular position that the question of God is simply irrelevant to the kind of explanations we entertain is itself an evasion. "It requires that we leave the largest question unanswered—in fact, that we leave it unasked, because there is no such question. But there is: It is the question 'What am I doing here?' and it doesn't go away when science replaces a religious world view." Thomas Nagel, *Secular Philosophy and the Religious Temperament: Essays 2000–2008* (New York: Oxford University Press, 2009), 8.

8. "Every purely moral value system (that of Buddhism, for example) ends in nihilism." Nietzsche, *Will to Power*, par. 19 (1883–80).

9. This is one of the reasons for the growing willingness of scholars of the history of philosophy to acknowledge that God and the sacred cannot so conveniently be ejected from the modern world. See the remarkable collection of essays, *The Persistence of the Sacred in Modern Thought*, ed. Chris L. Firestone and Nathan A. Jacobs (Notre Dame, IN: University of Notre Dame Press, 2012).

10. David Walsh, *The Modern Philosophical Revolution: The Luminosity of Existence* (New York: Cambridge University Press, 2008), ch. 1.

11. Michael Polanyi, *Personal Knowledge: Towards a Post-Critical Philosophy* (Chicago: University of Chicago Press, 2015).

12. "This book is about a single problem: how to combine the perspective of a particular person inside the world with an objective view of that same world, the person and his viewpoint included." In this opening sentence Thomas Nagel at once formulates and resolves the problem. *The View from Nowhere* (New York: Oxford University Press, 1986), 3.

13. The term "secular" referred originally (1300) to clergy assigned to the world rather than those bound to a religious community. Later (1610) it would be applied to property taken from the church and thus "secularized." The origin is in the Latin *saeculum*, the present age, later a century. The one constant in these shifting meanings is the separation from a world that lies beyond this one. See https://www.etymonline.com/word/secularize?ref=etymonline_crossreference.

14. Stephen Carter, *The Culture of Disbelief: How American Law and Politics Trivialize Religious Devotion* (New York: Basic Books, 1993).

15. John Rawls, "The Idea of Public Reason Revisited," in *The Law of Peoples* (Cambridge, MA: Harvard University Press, 1999), 131–80.

16. Jacques Maritain, quoting St. Thomas, declares, "They alone in all the universe are willed for their own sake." *The Person and the Common Good*, trans. John J. Fitzgerald (Notre Dame, IN: University of Notre Dame Press, 1966), ch. 2, 17.

17. John Stuart Mill recognized that he lived in an age that was in transition toward a new form of belief that would replace the defunct form of Christianity. This was how he came to recommend, while rejecting its coercive aspects, Auguste Comte's Religion of Humanity, as having "superabundantly shown the possibility of giving to the service of humanity, even without the aid of belief in a Providence, both the psychical power and the social efficacy of a religion." *On Utilitarianism*, ch. 3.

18. John Rawls, "On My Religion," published with his senior thesis, *A Brief Inquiry into the Meaning of Sin and Faith*, ed. Thomas Nagel (Cambridge, MA: Harvard University Press, 1999).

19. David Walsh, *The Growth of the Liberal Soul* (Columbia: University of Missouri Press, 1997).

20. Ralph Waldo Emerson, *Emerson: Essays and Lectures* (New York: American Library, 1983); George Kateb, *The Inner Ocean: Individualism and Democratic Culture* (Ithaca, NY: Cornell University Press, 1992).

21. Walsh, *The Growth of the Liberal Soul*, ch. 1, "Crisis of Liberal Politics."

22. "These serious, excellent, upright, deeply sensitive people who are still Christians from the very heart: they owe it to themselves to try for once the experiment of living for some length of time without Christianity, they owe it to *their faith* in this way for once to sojourn 'in the wilderness'—if only to win for themselves the right to a voice on the question whether Christianity is necessary." Friedrich Nietzsche, *Daybreak: Thoughts on the Prejudices of Morality*, trans. R. J. Hollingdale (Cambridge: Cambridge University Press, 1982), par. 61; original emphasis.

23. Voegelin, "The Beginning and the Beyond," in *What Is History?*, ch. 5.

24. Peter Berger, *A Rumor of Angels* (New York: Doubleday, 1970).

25. Robert Bellah, *Religion in Human Evolution: From the Paleolithic to the Axial Age* (Cambridge, MA: Belknap Press, 2011), is a magisterial treatment that is only made possible by its displacement of the secular frame of reference. Like Brendan Purcell's *From Big Bang to Big Mystery* (Hyde Park, NY: New City, 2012), it shows how religion includes the observer.

26. The madness of the ideological drive for transformation could only be satisfied through the touch of divine transcendence. David Walsh, *After Ideology: Recovering the Spiritual Foundations of Freedom* (San Francisco: Harper, 1990).

27. The call is always directed to a particular person who receives it as the call of a person. See the chapter on Moses in Voegelin, *Israel and Revelation*.

28. Walsh, *Politics of the Person as the Politics of Being*.

29. G. W. F. Schelling worked hard to crystallize this realization that God can only be known personally, rejecting the path of God as an idea. "On the

contrary, just as I am not satisfied, in the case of individuals who are important to me, to know that they exist, but demand continuing proof of their existence, so here: we demand that the divinity draw even closer to the consciousness of mankind; we demand that it be an object of consciousness not merely in its effects but in itself." *Schellings Werke*, vol. 5, ed. Manfred Schröter (Munich: Beck, 1927–59), 753 / *Schellings Philosophy of Mythology and Revelation*, trans. Victor C. Hayes (Armidale: Australian Association for the Study of Religion), 198.

30. Voegelin's last essay was on the so-called ontological argument that he more properly titled, "Quod Deus Dicitur." *Published Essays, 1966–1985*, ch. 14.

31. This was the burden of Hans Blumenberg's widely admired reflection, *The Legitimacy of the Modern Age*, trans. Robert M. Wallace (Cambridge, MA: MIT Press, 1983).

32. Once perfection is reached the aspiration for it is redundant. This was the big insight of Alexandre Kojève's analysis of the idea of the end of history—no more historical development. Alexandre Kojève, *Introduction to the Reading of Hegel: Lectures on the "Phenomenology of Spirit,"* ed. Allan Bloom (Ithaca, NY: Cornell University Press, 1980). See the discussion in Barry Cooper, *The End of History: An Essay on Modern Hegelianism* (Toronto: University of Toronto Press, 1984).

33. It is the paradox of existence so powerfully evoked by Kierkegaard. "Only momentarily can a particular individual, existing, be in a unity of the infinite with the finite that transcends existing. This instant is the moment of passion." Søren Kierkegaard, *Philosophical Fragments*, trans. Edna H. Hong and Howard V. Hong (Princeton, NJ: Princeton University Press, 1985), 197.

34. Simone Weil, "Hesitations Concerning Baptism," in *Waiting for God*, trans. Emma Craufurd (New York: Capricorn, 1951), Letter I, 43–51.

Chapter 5

1. *ehyeh asher ehyeh*, I AM WHO I AM, has remained mysterious even as its core, I AM WITH YOU, has always been clear.

2. Barry Cooper, *Paleolithic Politics: The Human Community in Early Art* (Notre Dame, IN: University of Notre Dame Press, 2022).

3. For a recent example of the historiographic approach, see Richard Elliott Friedman, *The Exodus: How It Happened and Why It Matters* (New York: Harper, 2017). Voegelin, in contrast, makes the case for the impossibility of separating the historical events from their spiritual meaning, in his *Israel and Revelation*.

4. *Summa Theologiae*, I, Q. 29, a.3.

5. Søren Kierkegaard, *Fear and Trembling / Repetition*, ed. and trans. Howard V. Hong and Edna H. Hong (Princeton, NJ: Princeton University Press, 1983), 70.

6. This is surely the core of the misnamed "ontological argument," for St. Anselm rightly begins it in a prayer and St. Thomas revises it as a way to God already known before it begins. Even Kant never seems to be taken in by the straw man version he roundly castigates. That long meditation was among the last works on which Hegel was occupied before his death. G. W. F. Hegel, *Lectures*

on the Proofs of the Existence of God, trans. Peter Hodgson (Oxford: Oxford University Press, 2007).

7. A particularly striking formulation from Heidegger is that "a question is always bathed in a light that emanates from the question itself." *Nietzsche*, vol. 2: *The Eternal Recurrence of the Same*, ed. and trans. David Krell (New York: Harper, 1984), 187.

8. Stephen Hawking, *The Theory of Everything: The Origin and Fate of the Universe* (Beverly Hill, CA: New Millennium, 2003).

9. "in truth, there was only *one* Christian and he died on the cross." Friedrich Nietzsche, *The Anti-Christ: A Curse on Christianity* (Harmondsworth: Penguin, 1968), I, par. 39.

10. James St. Leger, *The "Etsiami Daremus" of Hugo Grotius: A Study in the Origins of International Law* (Rome: Angelicum, 1962).

11. Mother Teresa, *Come Be My Light: The Private Writings of the Saint of Calcutta*, ed. Brian Kolodiejchuk (New York: Doubleday, 2007).

12. Karol Wojtyla, *Faith According to St. John of the Cross*, trans. Jordan Aumann (Eugene, OR: Wipf and Stock, 2009); and *Teachings for an Unbelieving World: Newly Discovered Reflections on Paul's Sermon at the Areopagus* (Notre Dame, IN: Ave Maria Press, 2020).

13. The insistence by both Hobbes and Locke on the dependence of natural law on God as its source has been, perhaps for that very assertion, less reassuring than Grotius's confidence that it retains its full validity even without God. See the treatment of Hobbes and Locke in Walsh, *The Growth of the Liberal Soul*, chs. 4 and 5.

14. This seems to be the deepest thread in Taylor's account of "immanent transcendence," that life no longer needs an end beyond itself to support self-transcendence within it. "The Christian paradox drops away: death is no longer the source of life. But there is a new paradox: there seems to be a renewed affirmation of transcendence. But at the same time, this is denied, because this point has absolutely no anchorage in the nature of reality." Taylor, *Secular Age*, 726. Overlooked here is the insight that it is precisely this self-transcendence that has always indicated a life beyond life, even if it cannot be imagined as a mere extension of this one.

15. This is why even after the interlocuters have reached a definition of justice as a harmony of the parts in the city and the soul, in book 4 the conversation turns to the question of its actualization. It can only be, Socrates explains, when they have become convinced that justice is what is ultimately good. "It is also evident that, although many are content to do what seems just or honorable without really being so, and to possess a mere semblance of these qualities, when it comes to good things, no one is satisfied with possessing what only seems good: here all reject the appearance and demand the reality." *Republic*, Bk. 4, 505d–e.

16. The distinction is well explained in Jeremy Geddert, *Hugo Grotius and the Modern Theology of Freedom: Transcending Natural Rights* (New York: Routledge, 2017).

17. Immanuel Kant, *The Metaphysics of Morals*, trans. Mary Gregor (Cambridge: Cambridge University Press, 1991), 278.

18. The imperative of shining the light of day on war crimes and crimes against humanity surely derives from that source. Hannah Arendt's *Eichmann in Jerusalem* (New York: Penguin, 2006) remains a paradigmatic example.
19. Matthew 24:35.
20. In embracing the secular world foreseen in Grotius's "etsi Deus non daretur," Bonhoeffer affirms its Christian derivation. "Here is the decisive difference between Christianity and all religions. Man's religiosity makes him look in his distress to the power of God in the world: God is the *deus ex machina*. The Bible directs man to God's powerlessness and suffering; only the suffering God can help. To that extent we may say that the development towards the world's coming of age outlined above, which has done away with a false conception of God, opens up a way of seeing the God of the Bible, who wins power and space in the world by his weakness. This will probably be the starting point for our 'secular interpretation.'" Bonhoeffer, Letter from Tagel Prison, July 16, 1944, in *Letters and Papers from Prison*, 361.
21. A good example of the earlier secularizing view is Alessandro Passerin d'Entrèves, *Natural Law: An Introduction to Legal Philosophy* (London: Hutchinson, 1951), but it remains a staple in Richard Tuck, *Natural Rights Theories: Their Origin and Development* (Cambridge: Cambridge University Press, 1979). The deeper background is the one that Harold Berman derived from Gratian, who emphasized the inseparability of *lex* and *ius*. "Ius is the genus, lex is a species of it." Harold J. Berman, *Law and Revolution: The Formation of the Western Legal Tradition* (Cambridge, MA: Harvard University Press, 1983), 145.
22. Its seventeenth-century beginning is well chronicled in John Redwood, *Reason, Ridicule, and Religion: The Age of Enlightenment in England 1660–1750* (Cambridge, MA: Harvard University Press, 1976).
23. "We have no government armed with power," John Adams declared in his first year as vice president, "capable of contending with human passions unbridled by morality and religion. Our constitution was made only for a moral and religious people. It is wholly inadequate for the government of any other." Quoted in Stanley Hauerwas, *A Community of Character* (Notre Dame, IN: University of Notre Dame Press, 1981), 79.
24. John Locke, "A Letter Concerning Toleration," in *Political Writings of John Locke*, ed. David Wooten (New York: Mentor, 1993), 410.
25. It is evident that the "new natural law" thinkers retain the idea of natural law as a participation in the divine governance of all things. John Finnis, *Natural Law and Natural Rights* (Oxford: Oxford University Press, 1980).
26. This was always what characterized the classical *phusei dikaion*, right by nature, at least in the reading given it by Eric Voegelin. It remained a participation in preeminent reality. *Anamnesis*, ch. 6, "Right By Nature."
27. Immanuel Kant, *Critique of Practical Reason*, trans. Mary Gregor (Cambridge: Cambridge University Press, 1997).
28. The notion of an "ethical overload" is an interesting formulation for which we have Jürgen Habermas to thank. See his "Three Normative Models of Democracy," in *Democracy and Difference*, ed. Seyla Benhabib (Princeton, NJ: Princeton University Press, 1996).

29. Ratzinger and Habermas, *The Dialectics of Secularization*.

30. Jean Bodin, *Colloquium of the Seven About the Secrets of the Sublime: Heptaplomeres*, trans. Marion Kuntz (Princeton, NJ: Princeton University Press, 1975). It is notable that both Rawls and Voegelin cite this as the paradigm of tolerance.

31. Weil, *Waiting for God*.

32. Perhaps never more eloquently expressed than in Henri de Lubac's *Drama of Atheist Humanism*, trans. Edith M. Riley (New York: New American Library, 1950).

33. It is what makes all of the prison camp literature so compelling, for such witnesses have found faith on the other side of despair. See Liu Xiaobo, *No Enemies, No Hatred*.

34. Voegelin references the need for certainty as the fatal development within Christianity, but in many respects Grotius is a vivid counterexample. *New Science of Politics*, ch. 4.

35. Jeremy Geddert sketches that wider context within which the purely legal notion of justice in Grotius unfolds. *Hugo Grotius and the Modern Theology of Freedom*.

36. Louis Dupré, *Passage to Modernity* (New Haven, CT: Yale University Press, 1993); Michael Gillespie, *The Theological Origins of Modernity*.

37. This is surely what Heidegger meant in signaling that the death of God was no longer an event in history but *the* event of history. It first becomes articulate in his famous turn in the *Beiträge* where he insists that within "reservedness Da-sein attunes itself to the *stillness* of the passing of the last god." Martin Heidegger, *Contributions to Philosophy (From Enowning)*, trans. Parvis Emad and Kenneth Maly (Bloomington: Indiana University Press, 1999), par. 5; original emphasis.

38. Jean-Luc Marion has made this central to his notion of the Catholic moment. See his *Brief Apology for a Catholic Moment*, trans. Stephen Lewis (Chicago: University of Chicago Press, 2021).

39. For a visual representation, see the meditative effect of the large panels that form the Rothko Chapel in Houston.

40. Immanuel Kant, "Idea for a Universal History," Third Proposition, in *Political Writings*, trans. H. B. Nisbet (Cambridge: Cambridge University Press, 1991).

41. See John Stuart Mill, who asked himself one day if he would be happy if all that he was working for was to be suddenly realized and discovered that the answer would be a resounding, "No!" "The whole foundation on which my life was constructed fell down. . . . I seemed to have nothing left to live for." *Autobiography*, ed. John M. Robson (New York: Penguin, 1989), 112.

42. This may explain why Mill's religious writings are the writings of a believing nonbeliever. See, in particular, "The Utility of Religion."

43. See the opera by Leos Janacek, *The Macroupolis Case*, which concerns the amorous adventures of a woman who is five hundred years old.

44. Friedrich Nietzsche, *The Gay Science*, trans. Josefine Nauckhoff (Cambridge: Cambridge University Press, 2001).

45. Søren Kierkegaard, *The Concept of Irony, with Continual Reference to Socrates*, trans. Howard V. Hong and Edna H. Hong (Princeton, NJ: Princeton University Press, 192).

46. It is no accident that Hegel and Heidegger are embraced by Hans Urs von Balthasar as crucial interlocuters for his own theology. See Cyril O'Regan, *Anatomy of Misremembering: Von Balthasar's Response to Philosophical Modernity*, vol. 1: *Hegel* (New York: Herder, 2014).

Chapter 6

1. See the remark of Charles Darwin in which he reveals his innermost conviction "that the universe is not the result of blind chance. But then with me, the horrid doubt always arises whether the convictions of man's mind which has developed from the minds of the lower animals, are of any value or at all trustworthy. Would any one trust in the convictions of a monkey's mind, if there are any convictions in such a mind." Letter to W. Graham, July 3, 1881, in *The Life and Letters of Charles Darwin*, ed. Francis Darwin (New York: Basic Books, 1959).

2. Voegelin astutely points out the parallel between Descartes's *Meditations* and the *Cloud of Unknowing* in his "Letter to Alfred Schütz Concerning Edmund Husserl," in *Anamnesis*, 45–61.

3. "I have therefore found it necessary to deny *knowledge* in order to make room for *faith*." Immanuel Kant, *Critique of Pure Reason*, trans. Norman Kemp Smith (London: Macmillan, 1933), B, xxx; original emphasis. See the discussion of this famous statement in Walsh, *The Modern Philosophical Revolution*, 31.

4. In the introduction to his magisterial account of the modern revolutionary movement, James Billington speculated on the possibility that we might be approaching the moment when the "fire in the minds of men" is about to burn itself out. Even today when the embers have been inflamed with renewed passion, albeit in the form of fragments of ideology rather than the great intellectual systems of the past, we may consider with him whether "the end may be approaching of the political religion which saw in revolution the sunrise of a perfect society." "I am further disposed," he continues, "to wonder if this secular creed, which arose in Judaeo-Christian culture, might not ultimately prove to be only a stage in the continuing metamorphosis of older forms of faith and to speculate that the belief in secular revolution, which has legitimized so much authoritarianism in the twentieth century, might dialectically prefigure some rediscovery of religious evolution to revalidate democracy in the twenty first." James H. Billington, *Fire in the Minds of Men: Origins of the Revolutionary Faith* (New York: Basic Books, 1980), 14.

5. Ralph C. Wood, *Flannery O'Connor and the Christ Haunted South* (Grand Rapids, MI: Eerdmans, 2005).

6. Taylor, *A Secular Age*, 726.

7. John Paul II, *Fides et Ratio* (1998).

8. "Was it not here, in these prison cells, that the great truth dawned? The cell was constricted, but wasn't *freedom* even more constricted?" Aleksandr Solzhenitsyn, *The Gulag Archipelago*, trans. Thomas Whitney (New York: Harper, 1974), 1:614; original emphasis. See the discussion in Walsh, *After Ideology*, ch. 2, "Catharsis."

9. The hero of Solzhenitsyn's *First Circle*, Gleb Nerzhin, reflects on the turning point he had reached in resolving to place conscience above all else. "I had no idea what good and evil were, and whatever was allowed seemed fine to me. But the lower I sink into this inhumanly cruel world, the more I respond to those who, even in such a world, speak to my conscience." Aleksandr Solzhenitsyn, *First Circle*, trans. Thomas Whitney (New York: Bantam, 1968), 600.

10. Perhaps none more movingly than in Liu Xiaobo's final statement at his trial in 2009 which furnished the title to *No Enemies, No Hatred*, 321–26.

11. "Choruses from 'The Rock'" (1934).

12. Kant's version of this in his account of the categorical imperative. "Hence for us men it is wholly impossible to explain how and why the *universality of a maxim as a law*—and therefore morality—should interest us. This much only is certain: the law is not valid for us *because it interests us* (for this is heteronomy and makes practical reason depend on sensibility)." Immanuel Kant, *Groundwork of the Metaphysics of Morals*, trans. H. J. Paton (London: Hutchinson, 1948), 120/123; original emphasis.

13. Brad Gregory, *The Unintended Reformation: How a Religious Revolution Secularized Society* (Cambridge, MA: Belknap Press, 2015). Essentially the same argument had been made much earlier by Max Weber, *The Protestant Work Ethic and the "Spirit" of Capitalism* (1905).

14. It would be hard to surpass the classic warning of the abyss thereby opened than C. S. Lewis, *The Abolition of Man* (New York: Macmillan, 1947), but see also Carter Snead, *What It Means to Be Human: The Case for the Body in Public Bioethics* (Cambridge, MA: Harvard University Press, 2020).

15. Contra MacIntyre in *After Virtue* (1981), I am inclined toward the perspective of Kant that autonomy already points to an horizon of obligation, although the responsibility for actualizing it remains entirely ours. See also F. W. J. Schelling, *Philosophical Inquiries into the Nature of Human Freedom*, trans. James Gutmann (La Salle, IL: Open Court, 1936).

16. See the Vatican decree on religious liberty, *Dignitatis Humanae* (1965); Robert L. Wilken, *Liberty in the Things of God: The Christian Origins of Religious Liberty* (New Haven, CT: Yale University Press, 2021).

17. Dostoevsky, *The Brothers Karamazov*, 310.

18. Attributed to Ivan in *Brothers Karamazov*, 768.

19. "For only that is free which acts according to the laws of its own inner being and is not determined by anything else either within it or outside it." Schelling, *Human Freedom*, 62/384.

20. See Michael Rosen, *Dignity: Its History and Meaning* (Cambridge, MA: Harvard University Press, 2012), or George Kateb, *Human Dignity* (Cambridge, MA: Belknap Press, 2011), who struggle with the impossibility of conceptualizing

what underpins human dignity. My own alternative is "Dignity as an Eschatological Concept," in *Priority of the Person* (Notre Dame, IN: University of Notre Dame Press, 2020).

21. *Republic*, 508.

22. Timaeus and Critias and the Myth of Er who is restrained from drinking of the river of forgetfulness at the end of the *Republic*.

23. This is why St. Thomas's five ways do not constitute a proof of the existence of God but lead toward a God who cannot be included within the chain of causality they employ. It is why they conclude in each instance with "quod Deus dicitur," which is called God. In this sense he knew, as Nietzsche did, that God is not another being but the possibility of being.

24. This was the insight of Alexandre Kojève concerning the putative end of history that had been ascribed to Hegel. *Introduction to the Reading of Hegel*, trans. James H. Nichols (New York: Basic Books, 1969), 159–64. Of course, I no longer accept that Hegel has pronounced such a notion as the end of history.

25. *Nicomachean Ethics*, 1159a.

26. *The Story of My Life by Helen Keller* (1902), ch. 4. You can find the "water scene" in the famous movie from 1962, *The Miracle Worker*.

27. This is evident in the great five-volume study of the history of dogma by Jaroslav Pelikan but especially *The Christian Tradition: A History of the Development of Doctrine*, vol. 1: *The Emergence of the Catholic Tradition (100–600)* (Chicago: University of Chicago Press, 1975).

28. Voegelin, "Quod Deus Dicitur," in *Published Essays, 1966–1985*, 376–94.

29. See especially the judgment of the dead by those who are themselves dead in the conclusion of the *Gorgias*.

30. The famous "pure theory of law" advocated by Hans Kelsen seems to undergo that kind of modulation. One of the most perceptive comments on this is offered by Benedict XVI in his address to the German Reichstag. Benedict XVI, "The Listening Heart: Reflections on the Foundations of Law," Reichstag, Berlin, September 22, 2011, https://w2.vatican.va/content/benedict-xvi/en/speeches/2011/september/documents/hf_ben-xvi_spe_20110922_reichstag-berlin.html.

31. Fascination with the "rise of the nones" for this reason seems driven by the interest in where they are headed. Ryan Burges, *The Nones: Where They Came From, Who They Are, and Where They Are Going* (Minneapolis: Fortress, 2021).

32. Walt Whitman, "Toward the Unknown Region," memorably set to music by that great spiritual agnostic, Ralph Vaughan Williams.

33. Despite the titles, it is not clear that the authors entirely dismiss the notion of inalienable rights. Mary Ann Glendon, *Rights Talk: The Impoverishment of Political Discourse* (New York: Free Press, 1991); Jeremy Waldron, ed., *Nonsense upon Stilts: Bentham, Burke and Marx on the Rights of Man* (New York: Methuen, 1987).

34. See Jacques Maritain's introduction to UNESCO, *Human Rights: Comments and Interpretations* (New York: Columbia University Press, 1949).

35. "If we stand up for our dignity, we live nobly, no matter how much we may risk or suffer." Liu Xiaobo, *No Enemies, No Hatred*, 129.

36. The memory of the Tiananmen Square massacre functioned as a powerful witness to Liu. See Liu, "Listen Carefully to the Voices of the Tiananmen Mothers," in *No Enemies, No Hatred*, 3–12.

37. "Only my spirit and my conscience remain precious and important to me ... [while] our torturers have been punished most horribly of all: they are turning into swine, they are departing downward from humanity." Solzhenitsyn, *The Gulag Archipelago*, 1:130; 2:613.

38. The rebel, Camus explains, is one who affirms "there is a limit beyond which you shall not go.... Why rebel if there is not something permanent in oneself worth preserving?" *The Rebel*, trans. Anthony Bower (New York: Vintage, 1956), 16.

39. Brian Tierney, *The Idea of Natural Right* (Atlanta: Scholars Press, 1997), pt. 2: "Ockham and the Franciscans."

40. The prisoner, Bobynin, voices this insight when he tells the minister of state security, Abakumov, he could "pass it along to anyone at the top who still doesn't know that you are strong only as long as you don't deprive people of *everything*. For a person you've taken *everything* from is no long in your power. He's free all over again." Solzhenitsyn, *The First Circle*, 96; original emphasis.

41. Hans Urs von Balthasar, "The 'Beatitudes' and Human Rights," in *Explorations in Theology V: Man Is Created* (San Francisco: Ignatius Press, 2014), 442–59. I am grateful to John McNerney for calling my attention to this remarkable parallel. John Paul II confirmed that the Declaration of Universal Human Rights "remains one of the highest expressions of the human conscience in our times." John Paul II, Address to the General Assembly of the United Nations, New York, October 5, 1995, for the celebration of the fiftiethh anniversary of its founding.

42. See Mark Twain's observation that it is "by the goodness of God we have those three unspeakably precious things: freedom of speech, freedom of conscience, and the prudence never to practice either of them." *Following the Equator* (1897), ch. 20; Elizabeth Knowles, ed., *Oxford Dictionary of Quotations* (Oxford: Oxford University Press, 1999), 786.

43. Robert Spaemann, *Love and the Dignity of Human Life* ((Grand Rapids, MI: Eerdmans, 2012), 31.

44. The exception is when the material becomes the vehicle for the immaterial. This is the very meaning of sacramentality. I am indebted to James Greenaway for the excellent discussion of this in *A Philosophy of Belonging* (Notre Dame, IN: University of Notre Dame Press, 2023).

45. Something similar applies to the familiar search for the historical Jesus. See Jacob Neusner, "Who Needs 'The Historical Jesus'? An Essay Review," *Bulletin for Biblical Research* 4, no. 1 (1994): 113 ff.

INDEX

A
atheism
  as anti-theism, 74
  impossible in practice, 77, 94, 150, 155n8
  surmounted before opening, 110
  unhinging equilibrium, 75

B
Bodin, Jean
  Heptaplomeres, 112, 166n30
Bonhoeffer, Dietrich, on divine condescension, 15

C
Christ
  pivot of freedom, 132
  promise of transfiguration, 61
  as revelation of God and world, 60
  suffering love, 132

D
Darwin, Charles, "horrid doubt," 124
de Lubac, Henri, on supernatural, 24

Descartes, René, knowledge of infinite, 9
dissidents as heroic witnesses, 5
  "What Men Live By," 6
Dostoevsky, Fyodor
  icon of Christ, 136
  Inquisitor under judgement, 133
  legend of Grand Inquisitor, 106

F
faith
  alone carrying us toward God, 62
  being primordial, 125
  cannot be lost, 128
  without faith, 30
  with hope and love, 127
  living solely by faith, 55
  before meaning, 139
  rejuvenations of, 125
  surviving doubt, 124
freedom
  awakening self-recognition, 129
  bound to moral order, 131
  and C. S. Lewis, 130
  depending on limits, 133

freedom (*cont.*)
    over freedom, 130
    has been redeemed, 135
    as life of God, 136
    living by faith, 126, 128
    must be free, 137
    redeemed, 136
    of religion as first, 81
    transcendence significance of, 132
    from unconditional love, 133

G
God
    absence as disclosure, 23
    absence as presence, 12, 99, 104
    approaching us through himself, 14
    beyond all knowing, 92, 100
    beyond being, 117, 138
    in breaking of bread, 13
    can be found only within himself, 81, 90
    as condition of possibility, 103
    consummation of natural law, 21
    invisibility of, 11, 19
    known in transcendence, 21, 54, 76
    no intermediary but, 10, 14
    preeminently a person, 100
    question at edge of consciousness, 6, 73
    saved from superficiality, 114
    secular as trace of, 60
    as separation from himself, 116
    setting aside, we reach God, 108
    in spirit and truth, 13, 142
    and taste for unchecked power, 8
    as three persons, 100
Grotius, Hugo
    as alternate modern path, 117
    bolder than Kant, 111
    contemplating abyss, 20
    daring of, 109
    defining secular paradigm, 20
    justice as beyond justice, 106
    loss of God restoring, 113
    misreading of, 110
    nonchalance of, 104
    and question of divine authorization, 8
    reverberations of Christ, 116
    seized upon by modern anxiety, 108
    upholding law of God without God, 105

H
Habermas, Jürgen
    conversation with Ratzinger, 112
    on post-secular age, 33, 126, 154n2
    reluctance of, 94

I
ideological style
    without ideology, 2, 4
    makeshift ideologies, 7
    no revolutionary apocalypse, 5
    pugnacious style, 7
    resisted by truth, 4
    violence concealed by lies, 3
Islam, and secular neutrality, 2

J
Joas, Hans, enchantment, 24
justice, as inextinguishable, 107

K
Kant, Immanuel
    knowing beyond bounds, 79
    not grasping what he had grasped, 78
    and transcendental, 75
Kierkegaard, Søren, great insight, 101

L
language of paradox, 121
    Christian paradox, 122
    death as way to life, 122
liberal democracies
    attesting to transcendent, 84
    versus autocracies, 5

brooking no restraints, 6
rights as hold on transcendence, 85
Locke, John
   freedom and faith, 131
   principal consideration for tolerance, 109
love
   discourse for atheists, 70
   God being, 71
   nothing higher, 71
   as Trinitarian, 69
   as unconditional, 69

M

Manent, Pierre, on Islam, 25
Marion, Jean-Luc, and Catholic transcendence, 25
Marx, Karl
   and anti-theism, 35
   meaning of alienation, 44
   and messianic, 74
   spiritual vision of, 46
metaphysics, not a realm, 66
Mill, John Stuart, on liberty, 42

N

Nagel, Thomas, on mind and cosmos, 50
natural law
   as arriving at God, 110
   mandate cannot fail, 113
   as transcendental, 111
Nietzsche, Friedrich,
   could not acknowledge miracle of morality, 113
   and madman, 120
   on uncanny, 14
nihilism
   overturning secular paradigm, 15
   "uncanniest of all guests," 14

P

Pascal, Blaise
   and Montaigne on "invisible source," 18, 153n26

shaking of foundations, 17
sideways glance of aphorism, 18
person, the
   can give self personally, 101
   core cannot be alienated, 144
   dignity and rights, 8
   freedom as mark, 136
   freedom in obligation, 44
   genesis from beyond being, 80
   outside good and evil, 42
   as immaterial, 32
   impervious to loss, 147
   known as persons, 31
   known beyond what is known, 79
   neither in soul nor mask, 67
   putting self into task, 39
   relation prior to self, 91
   rights as inexhaustible, 82
   sacramental significance, 33
   shaft of transcendence, 146
   touch of immortality, 49
Plato
   good beyond being, 117, 137
   and Grotius, 107
   myth and faith, 138
   Republic on justice in itself, 105

R

Rawls, John
   secular guarding transcendent, 83
   unspeakably precious core, 83
reason
   cannot be explained, 102
   demanding self-limitation, 78
   dependent on openness to mystery, 77
   deriving from revelation, 102
rectitude
   Aristotle mistaken, 38–39
   of markets, 38
religion
   Cicero on binding back, 54
   closure to transcendence, 57
   practical atheists, 53
   renewal of, 58

religion (*cont.*)
  secular incomprehension, 51
  transcendence eluding, 55
  world religions, 54
revelation
  already there before beginning, 87
  of God and world, 86
  of heart of God, 61
  not in history, 56
  not in monuments, 63
  as personal, 90
  rupture of transcendence, 89
  as structure of questioning, 88
  of transcendent, 56
  turning point of history, 102
  as what it has always been, 98
rights
  faith as sanctuary that will not be invaded, 149
  overtone of sacred, 148
  transcendence of secular, 149

S

scholarship, standing within truth of God, 27
science
  displaced by scientism, 76
  not included in science, 103
secular civilization
  admission of futility, 59
  affirmation of spiritual, 85
  beyond what is here, 118
  cannot be atheistic, 119
  cannot be explained, 87
  cannot be without God, 134
  cannot forget God, 150
  closer to what is missing, 26
  comprehension of itself, 60
  discerning uncanny, 93
  disclosing spirit, 46
  disclosing transcendent, 141
  impossibility of fulfillment, 138, 139
  and impossible burden of modernity, 10
  innerworldly transcendence, 64
  knowing God is beyond, 95, 114
  as liberated, 93
  movement of love, 119
  mystery of success, 111, 120
  needing self-limitation, 78
  no longer secular, 140
  not hostile to faith, 81
  not saying as a way of saying, 69, 93
  overturning secular, 124
  perspective of participants, 15
  political religions of, 33
  power of the powerless, 47
  preserving distance from God, 120
  religion of secularism, 82
  retaining faith, 126
  retired Pope, 15
  revering God as God, 12, 92
  reversal of secular values, 80
  rights as its faith, 143
  self-concealment of goodness, 141
  separation from divine order, 11
  sociological musings, 14
  spiritual resources, 9
  as transcendence, 22, 47, 48
  withdrawn from sacred, 34
Solzhenitsyn, Aleksandr
  and forgetting God, 1
  recovery of faith, 128
spirit
  can never be lost, 45
  disclosed by secular, 35
  as freedom, 43
  as gift, 36, 68
  inner coordination of, 37
  liberating from necessity, 40
  not caring about rewards, 41
  not measured by worldly success, 64
  pyramids not containing, 62
  transcending being, 34
symbols, of transcendence, 54

T
Taylor, Charles
    immanent transcendence, 126
    and sociological approach, 24
Tocqueville, Alexis de, absence of official endorsement of religion, 65, 131
tolerance, is reverence, 112

transcendence
    cannot be contained, 92
    as horizon, 99
    rights guard, 147

W
Wittgenstein, Ludwig, perspicuity of, 76

DAVID WALSH is professor of politics at the Catholic University of America. He is the author and editor of a number of books, including *The Priority of the Person* and *The Growth of the Liberal Soul*.

www.ingramcontent.com/pod-product-compliance
Lightning Source LLC
Chambersburg PA
CBHW050140240426
43673CB00043B/1737